THE **COMPLETE** **IDIOT'S** **GUIDE** TO

Quick and Easy Low-Carb Meals

A member of Penguin Group (USA) Inc.

For my family.

ALPHA BOOKS

Published by the Penguin Group

Penguin Group (USA) Inc., 375 Hudson Street, New York, New York 10014, U.S.A.

Penguin Group (Canada), 10 Alcorn Avenue, Toronto, Ontario, Canada M4V 3B2 (a division of Pearson Penguin Canada Inc.)

Penguin Books Ltd, 80 Strand, London WC2R 0RL, England

Penguin Ireland, 25 St Stephen's Green, Dublin 2, Ireland (a division of Penguin Books Ltd)

Penguin Group (Australia), 250 Camberwell Road, Camberwell, Victoria 3124, Australia (a division of Pearson Australia Group Pty Ltd)

Penguin Books India Pvt Ltd, 11 Community Centre, Panchsheel Park, New Delhi—110 017, India

Penguin Group (NZ), cnr Airborne and Rosedale Roads, Albany, Auckland 1310, New Zealand (a division of Pearson New Zealand Ltd)

Penguin Books (South Africa) (Pty) Ltd, 24 Sturdee Avenue, Rosebank, Johannesburg 2196, South Africa

Penguin Books Ltd, Registered Offices: 80 Strand, London WC2R 0RL, England

International Standard Book Number: 1-59257-313-4
Library of Congress Catalog Card Number: 2004113220

06 05 04   8 7 6 5 4 3 2 1

Interpretation of the printing code: The rightmost number of the first series of numbers is the year of the book's printing; the rightmost number of the second series of numbers is the number of the book's printing. For example, a printing code of 04-1 shows that the first printing occurred in 2004.

Printed in the United States of America

Note: This publication contains the opinions and ideas of its author. It is intended to provide helpful and informative material on the subject matter covered. It is sold with the understanding that the author and publisher are not engaged in rendering professional services in the book. If the reader requires personal assistance or advice, a competent professional should be consulted.

The author and publisher specifically disclaim any responsibility for any liability, loss, or risk, personal or otherwise, which is incurred as a consequence, directly or indirectly, of the use and application of any of the contents of this book.

Most Alpha books are available at special quantity discounts for bulk purchases for sales promotions, premiums, fundraising, or educational use. Special books, or book excerpts, can also be created to fit specific needs.

For details, write: Special Markets, Alpha Books, 375 Hudson Street, New York, NY 10014.

Publisher: *Marie Butler-Knight*
Product Manager: *Phil Kitchel*
Senior Managing Editor: *Jennifer Chisholm*
Senior Acquisitions Editor: *Renee Wilmeth*
Development Editor: *Christy Wagner*
Production Editor: *Megan Douglass*

Copy Editor: *Nancy Wagner*
Illustrator: *Chris Eliopoulos*
Cover/Book Designer: *Trina Wurst*
Indexer: *Brad Herriman*
Layout: *Becky Harmon*
Proofreading: *Donna Martin*

Contents at a Glance

Contents

What the recipe symbols mean:

- ● One-pot meal
- ■ Make-ahead

Appendixes

Foreword

Finally, there's a cookbook for me. *The Complete Idiot's Guide to Quick and Easy Low-Carb Meals* by Tod Dimmick was designed for busy people who aren't accomplished cooks but want to prepare tasty meals that fit into a low-carb lifestyle. It can be hard to admit to being a "complete idiot" in any capacity, but when it comes to the science of low-carb diets, I concede.

As I write this, I'm a good 20 pounds too heavy (like most Americans). My exercise routine consists of a weekly basketball game at the local Boys Club and taking the occasional long walk (usually to my local pizza parlor). I know I have to reduce the carbs in my diet, and this book has empowered me to do it.

I first met Tod Dimmick at Jasper White's Summer Shack in Cambridge, where I learned that Tod's latest project was going to be called *The Complete Idiot's Guide to Quick and Easy Low-Carb Meals*. I was intrigued, though I admit a bit skeptical.

As executive producer of the Boston-based *Phantom Gourmet* TV show, dining out in restaurants is the center of both my professional and personal life. The temptations can be overwhelming. Carbs seem almost unavoidable in the restaurant world, with bottomless breadbaskets, endless bottles of wine, and a taste of everyone else's dessert. Home is no respite from tantalizing treats, either; my wife, Alison, is quite the cook. One key point in our favor: We already knew that our bodies do not respond well when weighed down by bread, potatoes, and sweets.

As we started to put Tod's recipes to the test, we quickly realized how easy it can be to cook a complete, nutritious, and low-carb meal in minutes. But more important, we savored each and every bite of his easy-to-follow recipes, packed with tons of flavor and the freshest ingredients. When we understood how delicious reduced-carb meals can be, we didn't crave a bagel every morning and a bowl of ice cream at night.

The low-carb lifestyle isn't just another fad diet. Following Tod's recipes means I won't have to sacrifice taste for health. "Delicious and nutritious" does not have to be a zero-sum game. Deep down, I might still be a "complete idiot," but with Tod's guidance and a little extra exercise, at least I won't be an overweight idiot.

Daniel Andelman
executive producer
Phantom Gourmet

Dan Andelman is not the Phantom Gourmet, but he's the executive producer and host of the FEEDback Forum on this popular restaurant review and talk show. Dan is also the creator of PhantomGourmet.com, picked by *Yahoo! Internet Life* magazine as one of their favorite sites on the web.

Introduction

At one time or another, most of us have served and eaten a lot of foods loaded with flour and sugar. We eat fast food, instant foods, and prepared foods with a shelf life measured in years instead of days.

One reason for reliance on these "convenience" foods is the notion that a healthful, low-carb meal just takes too long to prepare. Get ready to learn just how fast and delicious such a meal can be!

And what about the taste of a home-prepared meal, with fresh ingredients? Well, there's no comparison.

This book focuses on the nuts and bolts of cooking low- and "good"-carb meals so you can keep to your chosen carb-focused diet—and love it every bite of the way. The goal of every dish in this book is to be tasty, low carb, and quick. To achieve this goal, each recipe follows some simple ground rules to make your life as easy (and healthful) as possible:

- **Use high-quality, low-carb ingredients.** Naturally low-carb ingredients such as fresh fruits, vegetables, nuts, meats, and seafood are delicious starting points. We get a head start with these tasty foods because they already have terrific flavor and texture. Our challenge is not to spend a long time with them, but to keep prep time down and let natural flavors do the work for us. If this sounds like an opportunity rather than a challenge, I agree with you.

- **Keep it simple.** Recipes in this book will use a small number of these high-quality ingredients, many used in fun and unusual combinations.

- **Call for accessible ingredients.** Most of the ingredients and seasonings in these recipes will be available at your local large grocery store.

- **Avoid processed foods.** Many highly processed foods are loaded with "bad" carbs, not to mention other preservatives and chemicals you'd probably rather not be eating. In this book, wherever possible, we'll use minimally processed, fresh ingredients.

- **Take advantage of quick cooking methods.** We'll be sautéing, simmering, broiling, pan-frying, grilling, and eating things raw.

- **Keep an eye on saturated fat.** This book is about low-carb meals, but that doesn't mean we'll ignore healthy eating advice. We'll avoid excessive amounts of saturated fat or provide low-fat options (as long as they are also low carb).

- **Control expense.** Eating and cooking low carb does not have to mean spending a lot of money.

◆ **Add in fun and flavor.** I live to eat, and I'm not interested in bland, uninspired food. Every recipe in this book is intended not only to be fast and low carb but also fun, delicious, and otherwise healthful. Without fun and flavor, what's the point?

How This Book Is Organized

The recipes in these pages cover everything from breakfast to snacks and from weeknight meals to carb-conscious entertaining. Some chapters are organized by specific topic (such as lunches or desserts), and others, in the important dinner theme, explore different ingredients in depth (such as seafood or red meat dishes).

Throughout, you'll find tips and suggestions to make quick, carb-conscious cooking a pleasure.

Part 1, "Tastes Great—Less Carbs!" is a low-carb cooking jump-start. We begin with a quick review of carbohydrates and low-carb ingredients for your fridge and your pantry. With these in hand, we'll serve up some classic (but carb-conscious) breakfasts, get cracking with egg dishes, and take a low-carb lunch break. We'll finish up this section by crunching through some low-carb snacks (a critical element of staying on track).

Part 2, "And for Dinner ...," slices into a wealth of savory, satisfying dinner recipes. We start with some of my favorite seafood recipes, then look at the incredible flexibility of poultry, pork, and other white meats. We'll grill (and otherwise prepare) a range of hearty red meat dishes, too. Then from many parts of the globe, we'll explore some of the huge range of shell bean and vegetarian recipes that help make carb-conscious cooking interesting and fun. And speaking of fun, we'll finish out the dinner section with a chapter on meals the kids will love but that will keep you on your diet, too.

Part 3, "Finish Out the Meal," picks up where the main course leaves off. We'll explore in depth one of my favorite topics—vegetables—first in vegetable side dishes, then in a selection of salads, from simple to hearty. Warning: Some of these salads can be meals by themselves. Then we'll spoon into soups and stews that can be made quickly and are rich and flavorful. Then we'll finish up with another favorite topic—desserts. We'll look at a number of quick, creamy, and chocolaty treats, as well as a selection of good-carb fruit-based desserts.

Need-to-Know Info

In each chapter, you'll find helpful hints in the form of small boxes with information related to the topic at hand. Here's what to look for:

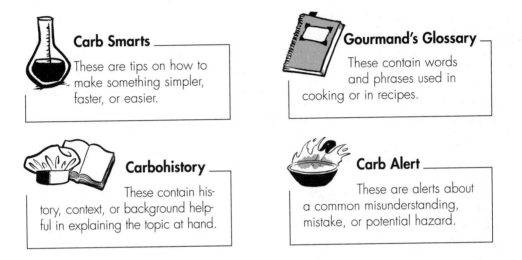

Carb Smarts

These are tips on how to make something simpler, faster, or easier.

Gourmand's Glossary

These contain words and phrases used in cooking or in recipes.

Carbohistory

These contain history, context, or background helpful in explaining the topic at hand.

Carb Alert

These are alerts about a common misunderstanding, mistake, or potential hazard.

Acknowledgments

This book was one of serendipity for me, a unique circumstance where my own interest in the whole low-carb topic coincides with the interests of many other people. As I worked on this project, I was astounded to learn how many people follow some version of a carb-conscious diet. I am grateful for the assistance of a number of these people in the creation of this work.

This book would not have been possible without the help of several test-kitchen veterans, including Jean Burke, Irene Carrick and Ann Marie Kott (New England), Anne and Derek Footer (West Coast), Judy Dorst (Northwest), and Marcia Friedkin (Gotham City). Thanks also to Freddie Dimmick (Mom), Dave Dimmick (Dad), Elaine Early (Mom-in-law), and many others for inspiration, recipe suggestions, and support.

I am indebted to Renee Wilmeth, senior acquisitions editor at Alpha Books, and to John Woods of CWL Publishing Enterprises, for their enthusiastic support of this project and invaluable guidance and feedback throughout.

Finally, thanks to my sons Spencer (9) and Kurt (6), who liked just about everything I did with chicken, but who weren't crazy about tofu. To my wife, Jen, whose belief makes everything possible, I love you.

And to Lexie the low-carb dog. She ate the tofu.

Special Thanks to the Technical Reviewer

The technical reviewer for *The Complete Idiot's Guide to Quick and Easy Low-Carb Meals* was Ellen Brown, a Providence, Rhode Island–based cookbook author, caterer, and food authority. The founding food editor of *USA Today*, she has written 10 cookbooks, including *The Complete Idiot's Guide to Slow Cooker Cooking*, *The Complete Idiot's Guide to Cooking with Mixes*, and *The Complete Idiot's Guide to Smoothies*. Her articles have appeared in more than two dozen publications, including *Bon Appétit*, the *Washington Post*, and the *Los Angeles Times*. *The Gourmet Gazelle Cookbook* won the IACP award in 1989, and she is a member of the prestigious "Who's Who of Cooking in America."

Trademarks

All terms mentioned in this book that are known to be or are suspected of being trademarks or service marks have been appropriately capitalized. Alpha Books and Penguin Group (USA) Inc. cannot attest to the accuracy of this information. Use of a term in this book should not be regarded as affecting the validity of any trademark or service mark.

Part 1

Tastes Great— Less Carbs!

Part 1 gets us started with fast, low-carb cooking. Chapter 1 begins with guidelines on how to make carb-conscious cooking part of your busy life, including a brief explanation of carbs and how to incorporate this knowledge into carb-conscious cuisine. This chapter also serves up essential off-the-shelf ingredients and the first of many tips for busy carb-conscious cooks. Then the fun begins with Chapter 2, a look at some breakfast classics, followed by an exploration of one of the world's oldest and best low-carb foods—eggs. We'll also check out some delicious carb-conscious lunches. While we're in this section, we'll also learn how to enjoy ourselves (and stay low carb) with snacks and appetizers.

Fast and Low

In This Chapter

- Making low-carb cooking fit into a busy life
- Carbohydrates 101
- The low-carb pantry
- Keeping the fun and flavor

All I ask of food is that it doesn't harm me.
—Michael Palin

In a simple sense, a *carb-conscious* diet helps us recover some balance. Centuries ago, our ancestors didn't even know they had this balance. But then, too, nothing was refined. The choices were simple: Most people consumed a diet rich in vegetables, fruits, nuts, whole grains, meats, and perhaps cheeses. People didn't have to think about eating low-carb foods—there wasn't a choice!

Modern industrialization has worked wonders, but the result is that our foods are loaded with refined flours and sugars (and other things) that we just can't handle. On a steady diet of these calorie-laden foods, our bodies react with all sorts of warning signs, of which weight gain is but one example. When we strip away some of these foods, many people see the opposite effect, from weight loss to overall better health.

The ingredients and recipes in this book are intended to help restore some of that balance to your diet.

When it comes to food, our busy lifestyles can be hazardous to our health. In the name of speed, it's tempting to rely on prepared meals, quick-cooking "instant" ingredients, and even fast food—all solutions that tend to be extremely high in carbohydrates (and other things we'd rather not eat). A diet of these foods has been associated with a huge range of health problems, from high cholesterol and diabetes to obesity. We might have chosen these foods because we thought that cooking a delicious, low-carb meal would be difficult and time-consuming, but *nothing could be further from the truth.*

From Atkins to the South Beach Diet, many of today's diets focus on carb counting and carb control. In this book, I do not prescribe a specific low-carb or "good"-carb diet. I simply provide a wide range of recipes, tips, and mealtime ideas that you can use to follow through with the diet you have chosen.

Gourmand's Glossary

Throughout this book, I refer to **carb-conscious** cooking. A carb-conscious cook loves good food and knows how to cook, but is also concerned with health and prepares a meal with an eye on carbohydrates. Carb-conscious cooking is a habit you want to have!

With smart ingredient choices, quick cooking methods, and a few preparation tricks, we'll have a low-carb meal on the table in no time. That's what this book is all about.

Carbohydrates: The Good, the Net, and the Bad

Carbohydrates are energy sources in our food and are found in several forms, including simple carbohydrates (as in table sugar), complex carbohydrates (whole wheat, vegetables, and fruits), and *fiber*. They are an essential part of any diet, along with fats, proteins, vitamins, minerals, and other nutrients.

Carbohistory

Most health experts do not advocate *eliminating* carbohydrates, as doing so can be very bad for your health. Carbohydrates are not inherently evil, and some are essential sources of energy. The emphasis of many diets today is on controlling the *quality* of the carbohydrates we eat, as well as, of course, the quantity. Replacing refined "bad" carbs in our diet with "good" carbs is a critical place to start. (More on the health benefits of good carbs later.)

But why do we have the different kinds of carbs? What are the *glycemic index* and the *glycemic load*, and what do you have to know about them to eat a healthful, low-carb diet? Read on:

Gourmand's Glossary

Minimally processed foods, including whole grains, nuts, fruits, and vegetables, are sources of both complex carbohydrates and **fiber** (or "roughage"), a carb that is not digested. Because fiber is included in the total carbohydrate listing on nutrition labels, it is subtracted from the total carb count for the purpose of a low-carb diet. Fiber is considered to be important to general health, and specifically related to cholesterol reduction.

♦ **Net carbohydrates.** Net carbs are the carbs you should count when you are following a carb-conscious diet. They are carbohydrates your body actually digests. *Fiber* is the one carbohydrate that is not digested, so a simple way to figure out the net carbs is to subtract fiber from the total carb count found on food labels. In other words, if a serving of a food contains 10 g total carb and 4 g fiber, the net carb count is 6. We also refer to net carbs as *nutritive carbs*.

♦ **Simple carbohydrates.** These carbs are found in highly processed foods made with white flour and sugar, such as white bread, pasta, white rice, bagels, and all kinds of sweets, from donuts and muffins to cake and candy. These carbs cause a spike in blood sugar, which, if constantly experienced, can be a factor in a host of health issues, from high blood pressure and diabetes to, of course, weight gain. One common characteristic of these foods is also the immediate sense of fullness, followed quickly by a "crash" as the spike disappears, as well as more food craving.

Gourmand's Glossary

In many books on low-carb diets and cooking, you'll find reference to the glycemic index and the glycemic load. The **glycemic index** is a way of describing how fast a given food raises blood sugar levels. The higher the number, the faster these levels spike after eating that food. Refined flours tend to be highest on this index, followed by sugars (and foods made with them). The **glycemic load** is the blood sugar spike you'd experience after consuming a single serving of a particular food.

◆ **Complex, or "good" carbohydrates.** Foods that contain complex carbohydrates release their energy (again in the form of blood sugar) much more gradually. There's no "spike" or the resulting crash. In this book, I refer to complex carbs as "good" carbs. Whole grains and foods with complex carbohydrates that break down slowly have a low glycemic index. Good carbs also bring nutrients, minerals, and vitamins essential to good health.

The foods called for in the recipes in this book are mostly low on the glycemic index and are intended to have a low glycemic load relative to many high carbohydrate foods.

Alternatives to White Bread, Flours, and Sugars

As the wise say, "everything in moderation." If you minimize your consumption of simple carbs, you're on your way. For that reason, in these pages we almost completely avoid sugar and white flour.

But won't that be difficult? Not necessarily. Many of us are accustomed to a lot of breads, chips, and baked goods in our diet. This cultural habit threatens to be an oncoming carbohydrate freight train that could derail our low-carb express. The good news is that bakers, food companies, and grocery stores also see this dinner-time pile-up and are offering more and more healthful, low-carb options.

Carb Smarts

Set a goal to minimize your intake of refined flour and sugar. That's easier said than done, I know. But do reduce your consumption of these not-so-good-for-you foods, and you'll be halfway there. However, eating well is just part of a healthy lifestyle. Another critical element is regular exercise.

Baked Goods and Starches

Low-carb and good-carb possibilities include the following:

◆ Brown rice

◆ Low-carb and whole-wheat soft tortillas

◆ Low-carb breads

◆ Low-carb pasta

◆ Low-carb tortilla chips

◆ Whole-wheat hot dog and hamburger buns

◆ Whole-wheat pasta

I've tried as many of these as I could find, and I'm happy to report that the chips are mostly pretty good. I've found some low-carb breads I didn't like at all, but others were quite tasty. This is a time of flux in the low-carb marketplace, and the offerings will continue to get better.

When you eat carbohydrates, choose good-carb foods: whole-grain over white bread, whole-wheat pasta over white, whole-grain (brown) rice over white. Yes, they taste a bit different, but give them a chance. I bet you'll find that the reason good-carb foods taste different is because they *have taste* rather than bland white foods, in which the nutrition has been removed (and sometimes sugar added).

Good-carb foods have more flavor and are more satisfying to eat. And I, for one, feel better because I'm eating food I know is good for me.

> **Carb Alert**
>
> Pay close attention to the ingredients in whole-grain breads. Look for a bread made with 100 percent whole wheat or 100 percent whole grain. Many breads seem to imply "healthful," with labels such as "multi-grain," "hearty," "wheat," etc., but the labels don't always actually mean much.

> **Carb Smarts**
>
> When you are serving dishes with pasta and rice, even the whole-grain "good"-carb versions, plan your meal so these are not the sole focus. In other words, don't serve a big plate of pasta, even whole-wheat pasta, and call it a meal. Instead, serve your pasta or rice as a side dish, with a vegetable and, say, a chicken breast. Do this and you immediately lower your reliance on carbs.

Low-Carb Flours and Baking Mixes

An increasing number of specifically low-carb baking mixes are available in grocery stores. These tend to be more expensive than conventional flour and taste quite a bit different (and so will be an acquired taste). Experiment with these low-carb baking mixes or low–net-carb flours such as soy flour to determine what you like.

Because of the time involved, we won't be doing a lot of baking in this book, with the exception of some quick breakfasts and desserts. For these, it's a good idea to carefully pick what you'll use to bake.

> **Carb Smarts**
>
> If you're not crazy about the flavor of low-carb baking mixes, blend them half and half with 100 percent whole-wheat flour. This raises the total carb count, but whole-wheat flour is considered a source of good carbs.

Artificial Sweeteners

The baking section of your grocery store has a large and growing selection of artificial sweeteners. Some have been around for years, and others, such as Splenda, are relatively new. In the case of desserts, I suggest using "spoon-for-spoon" sweeteners (sweeteners where 1 tablespoon is used to replace 1 tablespoon sugar).

Most artificial sweeteners are allowed in a low-carb diet, with the caveat advice to consume them in moderation. Some health experts voice concern over the potential health hazards of some sweeteners, particularly when consumed in high quantities. With the exception of desserts, I do not use artificial sweeteners in most of the recipes in this book.

Read Nutrition Labels!

If you've never much paid attention to nutrition labels, now is the time to start. Pick up any foodstuff and look at the ingredient list. You'll see that ingredients are listed in the order of the percentage that ingredient is of the total, with the highest percentage listed first. A breakfast cereal with sugar as the first or second ingredient, for example, has a lot more sugar than another with sugar (or another sweetener) fifth on the list. But be careful. If two sweeteners, say honey and brown sugar, are third and fourth on the list, the sweeteners together have a higher percentage. You'd be better off finding an alternative.

When reading labels, don't just look for sugar. Other suspects that have a similar effect (from a glycemic point of view) include corn syrup, high fructose corn syrup, honey, brown sugar, molasses, maple syrup, evaporated cane juice, and more.

Be careful of fat-free foods, too. To compensate, many of these foods are loaded with sugar.

Carb Alert _____

For many foods, taste and health appeal are in inverse relation to shelf life. If a food has enough preservatives in it to stay "fresh" on the shelf for 6 months, watch out! Better read those ingredients carefully. Some health experts, for example, are concerned about the use of hydrogenated and partially hydrogenated oils in many foods. On the other hand, some ingredients might sound alarming, such as ascorbic acid. That's something you want to consume—it's vitamin C!

Hit the Ground Running: Low-Carb Ingredients and Pantry Items

With many foods and ingredients on the "no-no" list, what's left for you to eat? In this section, you'll find a grocery list of the ingredients used for most of the recipes in this book. If you have most of these on hand, you'll be able to hit the ground running.

These foods are organized primarily by method of storage (fresh items in the fridge or on the counter for quick use with longer storage items in the pantry).

Fresh ingredients lend themselves to quick preparation. Natural ingredients are, well, a natural for not only quick cooking, but also healthful, low-carb cooking.

You'll find a detailed nutritional breakdown on these items and more in Appendix C.

Fresh Vegetables and Fruits

Some fruits, such as bananas and pineapples, and vegetables, such as corn and potatoes, are naturally high in carbs. These foods are not forbidden, but enjoy them in moderation as part of a carb-conscious diet. Because there are so many other delicious alternatives, I have not used these fruits or vegetables in this book.

Instead, the following vegetables and fruits get star billing in my recipes:

Vegetables

- ◆ Asparagus
- ◆ Broccoli
- ◆ Celery
- ◆ Cucumbers
- ◆ Green beans
- ◆ Lettuce
- ◆ Mushrooms
- ◆ Onions
- ◆ Peppers
- ◆ Spinach
- ◆ Tomatoes
- ◆ Zucchini squash

Carb Smarts

Onions have relatively more carbs (as a stand-alone vegetable) but are a terrific source of flavor when used in small amounts, and I call for them in many savory recipes. Similarly, tomatoes have more carbs than, say, asparagus, but they also bring indispensable flavor and nutrition. You'll find tomatoes, in moderation, in many recipes as well.

Fruits

- Apples, fresh
- Apricots, dried
- Blueberries
- Grapefruit
- Lemons and lemon juice
- Limes and lime juice
- Pears, fresh
- Raspberries, fresh
- Strawberries, fresh

Frozen berries are a convenient option to keep in mind. Watch out for canned fruits, however, as many are packed with sugar.

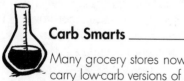

Carb Smarts _____

Any cook enjoys adding flavor, and the low-carb cook is no exception. Here are some of my favorites:

- Parmesan cheese adds rich, nutty flavor with only a small amount.
- Freshly squeezed lemon or lime juice is delicious on all kinds of dishes.
- Fresh herbs are a fragrant, irresistible tool for any cook.

The Fridge Is Your Friend

Here are some of the main ingredients you'll pull from the refrigerator for recipes in this book. I'm not listing juice, milk, beer, etc.; you probably already have those.

Carb Smarts _____

Many grocery stores now carry low-carb versions of dressing, ketchup, and barbecue sauce, as well as other condiments. Keep those on hand in place of the sugared stuff.

Condiments

- Chopped garlic
- Dijon mustard
- Mayonnaise
- Lemon juice and lime juice
- Low-carb barbecue sauce
- Low-carb ketchup
- Low-carb salad dressings

Dairy

- Butter or Smart Balance–type spreads
- Cheeses
- Eggs
- Cream
- Sour cream or light sour cream (both are low carb)

Meats and Seafood

- Beef (ground or steak—your favorite lean cut)
- Chicken and other poultry (especially boneless, skinless breasts for quick cooking)
- Pork (tenderloin, chops, ground pork)
- Seafood (all kinds)

Carb Alert

Enjoy butter and cream in small quantities. The flavor is terrific, but both are very high in saturated fat. Where possible, substitute olive oil for butter in cooking and a Smart Balance–type spread for other uses. I do not recommend standard margarine. Many brands are made with hydrogenated oils, which have been associated with many potential health problems.

And for the Seasonings ...

This dried seasonings shortlist will give the busy cook a jump-start:

- Apple pie spice
- Black pepper
- Chili powder
- Cinnamon, ground
- Crushed red pepper
- Cumin, ground
- Dill
- Italian seasoning
- Onion flakes
- Oregano
- Rosemary
- Sage

Carb Smarts

If you've got the choice, use fresh herbs. They bring a "green," juicy garden flavor that enhances any dish. Of course, the cook in a hurry will likely need to make good use of dried herbs (I do most of the time). When using dried herbs, keep in mind that they lose their flavor over time. Replace them after 4 to 6 months.

Nuts to You!

Nuts are one of the world's best low-carb foods, plus they're high in monounsaturated (good) fats, protein, and come ready to eat. Because many nuts are perfect snacks, you'll find detailed nutty information in Chapter 5. Some of my favorites are the following:

◆ Almonds

◆ Cashews

◆ Macadamia nuts

◆ Peanuts

◆ Pecans

◆ Pine nuts

◆ Pistachios

◆ Walnuts

In the Cabinet

Call it a cabinet, a shelf, or a pantry, the place where my nonrefrigerated foods live is one of my favorite places in the kitchen. Here are the building blocks for most meals, plus one or two surprises. Sometimes I'm there looking for something specific. Probably once a week I end up here, looking for ideas—the inspiration for dinner.

Carb Smarts

I'm not the most organized person in the world, so I use categories similar to those listed here actually printed on the shelves in my pantry (I'm not kidding). You know what they say, "A place for everything, and everything in its place." I try to keep in mind where things go, and it usually works.

Canned Vegetables and Grains

◆ Black beans

◆ Cannellini beans

◆ Chick peas

◆ Chopped garlic (refrigerate after opening)

◆ Diced tomatoes

◆ Green chilies

◆ Kidney beans

◆ Refried beans

◆ Sauerkraut

◆ Sliced mushrooms

◆ Tomato sauce

◆ Water chestnuts

Oils and Liquids

- Balsamic vinegar
- Canola oil
- Extra-virgin olive oil
- Hot red pepper sauce
- Red wine vinegar
- Soy sauce
- Teriyaki sauce (to be used in moderation, this will have sugar)
- Worcestershire sauce

Pasta and Starches

- Brown rice
- Soy flour
- Whole-grain oatmeal
- Whole-wheat flour
- Whole-wheat pasta

Canned Soups

- Beef broth
- Chicken broth
- Vegetable broth

Canned Meats and Seafood

- Chunk ham
- Chunk white chicken in water
- Chunk white tuna in water
- Salmon

Carb Smarts

Surprised to find mayonnaise on the "Condiments" list? Use the real thing we used to think was bad for us, not the fat-free stuff (which has more carbohydrates, plus other ingredients you might want to avoid). Of course, moderation is still the key. Watch out, however, for other condiments, such as ketchup and relish, which often have lots of added sugar.

Carb Smarts

Canned meats and seafood offer a range of instant, convenient ingredients for the busy, carb-conscious cook. In addition to the "usual suspects" I've listed, you could also stock your pantry with canned turkey, shrimp, or crab, for example. And you don't have to tell anyone these tasty morsels came from a can.

I'll Drink to That: Alcoholic Drinks and Carbohydrates

Alcoholic drinks contain carbohydrates, but some types have more than others. Mixers for drinks, for example, are often loaded with sugar. Here's how it breaks down.

	Serving Size	Total Carbohydrates
Beer	12 oz.	3.0 to 6.0
Light beer	12 oz.	7.5 to 13.0
Mixed drinks	8 oz.	1.2 to 6.0
Wine, red	6 oz.	.5 to 1.0
Wine, white	6 oz.	4.0 to 30+

The Case for the Low-Carb Lifestyle

Healthy cooking begins at home, where you can control your ingredients in a way that's impossible when you're not the cook.

The information and recipes in this book focus on minimizing carbohydrates, especially "bad" carb intake, but don't think you'll be sacrificing anything. Not only are the recipes in this book low-carb, but they're also packed with flavor and nutrition. Fat intake is reduced through careful selection of these ingredients, such as choosing lean cuts of meat and lots of vegetables. Fresh, wholesome ingredients make these dishes irresistible.

Low carb does not have to mean tasteless. These foods speak for themselves: fresh, crisp vegetables; naturally sweet fruits; juicy meats; seductively rich cheeses; herbs and spices that add zero carbs. These ingredients might be low on the glycemic index, but they're high on flavor!

Cooking yourself means less reliance on processed foods, prepared foods, and, of course, fast food. The food you and your family eat at home can be the foundation of a healthful life—in more ways than one.

The Least You Need to Know

♦ Minimize white flour and sugar in your diet, and you'll be making a terrific start.

♦ Familiarize yourself with the long list of healthy ingredients available for the carb-conscious cook. When you go shopping and when you prepare your meal, stick to those ingredients!

♦ Start by putting the ingredients in this chapter into your fridge and pantry, and you'll be ready to go!

♦ Don't think that cooking low carb or watching your carbs will mean sacrificing hearty, delicious meals. You'll find just the opposite as you look through the recipes in the following chapters.

Chapter 2

Start the Day Right: Breakfast the Low-Carb Way

In This Chapter

- ◆ Savory skillet stir-ups
- ◆ Outside-the-box quick breakfasts
- ◆ Good-carb breakfast favorites

Breakfast presents a conundrum for the carb-conscious *gourmand*. Many convenience-food breakfasts, from bagels to sweetened breakfast cereal, could top our daily carb allotment with just half a "normal" serving. As for donuts, let's not even go there. They contain enough fat, sugar, and refined flour to give your doctor a heart attack, not to mention you. And it seems we're always in a rush. If you're like me, during the week you're late getting out the door. Forget about spending 20 minutes making breakfast— 5 minutes is more like it.

This chapter focuses on ultra-quick low-carb and good-carb breakfasts, including some off-the-shelf solutions. Then, once the weekend finally rolls around, we relax a little with some good-carb versions of our favorites, like pancakes and French toast—dishes that take a few minutes longer but are still fast. A quick summary of each section follows.

For egg-specific recipes, take a look at Chapter 3.

> **Gourmand's Glossary**
>
> You're familiar with the term *gourmet:* a food connoisseur (read: know-it-all). A **gourmand,** on the other hand, is a person who loves good food—a lot. Count me in the latter category. My mission in this book is to show that carb-conscious meals can be a delight, even for the gourmand.

Quick Hot Breakfasts

Meats, vegetables, and whole grains offer nutritious low- and good-carb building blocks for delicious breakfasts. With one of these dishes under your belt, you'll have energy to face the day.

For Off the Shelf, Think Out of the Box

Let's face it, during the week, as much as we might like to cook something, we often have barely time to pour something into a bowl. The need for speed is a potential pitfall for the carb-conscious: It's all too easy to reach for something that's convenient but also kills your carb goals. However, it doesn't have to be this way, because an increasing number of foods are available that are both convenient and carb-smart, including a number of low-carb breakfast cereals. Keep one or two of these in your cabinet for a quick, low-carb breakfast.

Also keep in mind that these whole-grain foods are significant sources of "good" carbs and, thus, should be enjoyed with care for those on an extremely low-carb diet.

> **Carb Alert**
>
> As with all off-the-shelf foods, look carefully at the nutrition and serving size information on low-carb breakfast cereals. If the box lists the serving size as ½ cup but you usually eat 1 cup, you'll consume twice the carbs listed on the label.

The Weekend Is Here!

These hearty breakfast favorites, although quick, take a bit more time and are well-suited for the weekend. Low-carb bread will keep the total carb count to a minimum; 100 percent whole-wheat brings more "good" carbs to the table.

Broiled Bacon and Tomato Rafts

Prep time: 5 minutes • Cook time: 4 minutes • Serves: 2

Each serving has: 221 calories • 27 g protein • 27 g animal protein • < 1 g vegetable protein • 3 g carbohydrates • 1 g dietary fiber • 2 g net carbohydrates • 24 g fat • 6 g saturated fat • 58 mg cholesterol • 1,342 mg sodium • Exchanges: 1 high-fat meat, 3 lean meat, ½ vegetable

6 slices (about 8 oz.) ready-cooked lean Canadian back bacon (if the bacon you purchase is not already fully cooked, cook it first)

6 fresh tomato slices, each about ¼ -inch thick

8 fresh basil leaves or 1½ tsp. dried basil

¼ cup shredded mozzarella cheese

Salt and ground black pepper

Preheat the broiler; if your broiler has multiple settings, select the medium setting. Arrange bacon slices on a baking tray. Top each with 1 tomato slice and 1 basil leaf (or a pinch dried basil). Distribute cheese among tomatoes and broil on the next-to-highest rack for 4 minutes or until cheese is melted.

Distribute to plates, season with salt and pepper to taste, and serve.

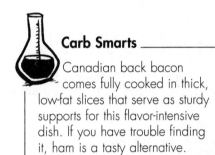

Carb Smarts

Canadian back bacon comes fully cooked in thick, low-fat slices that serve as sturdy supports for this flavor-intensive dish. If you have trouble finding it, ham is a tasty alternative.

Skillet Chicken Sausage and Veggies

Prep time: 5 minutes • Cook time: 8 minutes • Serves: 2

Each serving has: 441 calories • 20 g protein • 18 g animal protein • 2 g vegetable protein • 11 g carbohydrates • 2 g dietary fiber • 9 g net carbohydrates • 32 g fat • 9 g saturated fat • 141 mg cholesterol • 1,207 mg sodium • Exchanges: 3 medium-fat meat, 3 fat, 2 vegetable

2 TB. canola or olive oil

1 large green bell pepper, seeds and ribs removed, and diced into ½-inch pieces

½ lb. cooked chicken sausage links, sliced into ½-inch pieces

1 cup diced tomatoes in juice (canned or fresh)

Dash hot red pepper sauce

3 TB. shredded Parmesan cheese

Salt and ground black pepper

Heat oil in a small skillet over medium heat and cook bell pepper, stirring, for 3 minutes or until tender-crisp. Add sausage and cook, stirring, for 2 minutes or until sausage begins to brown. Add tomatoes and hot sauce and heat, stirring, for 3 minutes. Distribute to serving plates and season with Parmesan, salt, and pepper to taste.

Carb Smarts

The meat section of your grocery store is likely to have a selection of fully cooked sausages, including options made with chicken (and various other ingredients). Just verify that the package says "fully cooked"; otherwise they will need to be cooked!

Skillet Mushrooms and Bacon

Prep time: 4 minutes • Cook time: 14 minutes • Serves: 2

Each serving has: 546 calories • 41 g protein • 35 g animal protein • 6 g vegetable protein • 11 g carbohydrates • 6 g dietary fiber • 5 g net carbohydrates • 49 g fat • 15 g saturated fat • 107 mg cholesterol • 2,293 mg sodium • Exchanges: 4 high-fat meat, 1 vegetable, 2 fat

½ lb. thickly sliced bacon

3 scallions, roots and dark green parts removed, sliced into ⅛-inch pieces

1 (8-oz.) pkg. sliced white mushrooms

¼ cup sliced almonds

Salt and ground black pepper

Cook bacon in a large skillet over medium heat for 4 minutes per side or until crisp. Remove bacon to a paper-towel–lined plate, and drain most of the fat, leaving just enough to coat the bottom of the skillet. Add scallions and cook for 1 minute. Add mushrooms and almonds to the skillet and cook, stirring, for 5 minutes or until mushrooms soften. Distribute mushrooms to serving plates and crumble bacon over each serving. Season with salt and plenty of pepper.

Carb Alert _____

Although this book focuses on carb-conscious cooking, it's appropriate to keep an eye on dietary fat, especially saturated fat, of which bacon fat is an intensive source. To minimize saturated fat in this dish, pour off all the bacon fat and cook the mushrooms in something more benign, such as cooking oil.

Low-Carb Blueberry Cinnamon Oatmeal

Prep time: 3 minutes • Cook time: 5 to 10 minutes • Serves: 2

Each serving has: 168 calories • 6 g protein • 0 g animal protein • 6 g vegetable protein
• 38 g carbohydrates • 5 g dietary fiber • 32 g net carbohydrates • 0 g fat
• 0 g saturated fat • 0 g cholesterol • 10 mg sodium • Exchanges: 2 starch

2 cups old-fashioned oatmeal	Pinch ground cinnamon
½ tsp. salt	½ cup ripe blueberries, rinsed

Cook oatmeal per package instructions (the proportions of oats to liquid vary) and season with salt. (To cook: Stovetop is quick; microwave is even quicker.) Stir in cinnamon. Distribute to serving bowls and top with (or fold in) blueberries. I also like a splash of skim milk on my oatmeal.

Variations: If you like a bit more sweetness, a packet of artificial sweetener will do the job. Instead of blueberries, diced apple with cinnamon is a classic combination. Chopped peaches, strawberries, cherries, and raspberries are all terrific as well.

 Carbohistory

Oatmeal gets a lot of great press for being an extremely healthy food. When it comes to carbohydrates, many health experts believe that whole-grain, steel-cut oats, prepared with minimal processing, are the best choice. Bypass packages of oatmeal with ingredients other than "oats." You don't need 'em! Choose oatmeal comprised of whole rolled oats or, even better, steel-cut oats. To me, this oatmeal also has the best taste.

When it comes to cooking, you can prepare steel-cut oatmeal in less than 5 minutes in the microwave. It can also be prepared, with terrific creamy texture, by dumping the oatmeal, salt, and water into a slow cooker the night before, and setting the cooker to low. In the morning, you've got a terrific breakfast waiting. Preparation time required: about 2 minutes, and none of it in the morning when you're in a hurry.

Low-Carb Toasted Almond Wheat Cereal

Prep time: 3 minutes   •   Cook time: 8 minutes   •   Serves: 2

Each serving has: 272 calories   •   9 g protein   •   0 g animal protein   •   9 g vegetable protein   •   32 g carbohydrates   •   8 g dietary fiber   •   24 g net carbohydrates   •   9 g fat   •
< 1 g saturated fat   •   0 g cholesterol   •   10 mg sodium   •   Exchanges: 2 starch, 2 fat

2 cups wheat cereal   ¼ cup skim milk

⅓ cup sliced almonds, toasted or raw

Prepare cereal per package instructions (the proportions of wheat to liquid vary). (To cook:
Stovetop is quick; microwave is even quicker.) Mix in almonds and distribute to serving bowls.
Top with skim milk.

Carb Smarts

To toast nuts, simply spread them on a baking sheet and slide them under the
broiler on the top shelf. Toast for 1 minute, stir them around, and toast for another
minute or two, watching closely to prevent burning.

Raspberry Crunch Yogurt

Prep time: 3 minutes   •   Serves: 1

Each serving has: 249 calories   •   16 g protein   •   8 g animal protein   •   8 g vegetable protein   •   35 g carbohydrates   •   6 g fiber   •   29 g net carbohydrates   •   3 g fat   •   0 g saturated fat   •   0 g cholesterol   •   102 mg sodium   •   Exchanges: 1 milk, ½ fruit, ½ starch

1 (8-oz.) tub light raspberry yogurt   2 TB. wheat germ

¼] cup raspberries, fresh or frozen (and thawed)

Mix yogurt, raspberries, and wheat germ in a bowl and serve.

Carb Smarts

When carb-consciousness meets yogurt, we've got choices to make. Off-the-shelf yogurt in this country has a lot of sugar, and if you stick with it, you'll need to correspondingly reduce carbohydrate intake elsewhere. Then there is artificially sweetened "light" yogurt, the assumed choice here. And finally, you have another choice: plain yogurt (common on store shelves worldwide but less common here). I enjoy plain yogurt mixed with fruit, which adds the sweetness.

Blueberry-Vanilla Breakfast Yogurt

Prep time: 3 minutes • Serves: 1 person

Each serving has: 145 calories • 12 g protein • 12 g animal protein • 0 g vegetable protein • 22 g carbohydrates • 1 g fiber • 21 g net carbohydrates • 0 g fat • 0 g saturated fat • 5 mg cholesterol • 189 mg sodium • Exchanges: 1½ milk, ¼ fruit

1 (8-oz.) tub nonfat plain yogurt

¼ cup blueberries, fresh or frozen (and thawed)

¼ tsp. vanilla extract

1 pkg. artificial sweetener (optional)

Mix yogurt, blueberries, vanilla, and sweetener (if using) in a bowl, and serve.

Variation: Use other unsweetened berries, such as raspberries, blackberries, or strawberries.

Carbohistory

In the beginning of today's carb-conscious–eating era, fruit was regarded with suspicion, as a source of carbohydrates one should avoid. That perception has mostly changed, as our understanding has evolved to realize that carbs in fruit are much more healthy than those found in refined sugars and flours. Fresh fruits, such as blueberries, strawberries, and peaches, make terrific flavor contributions to any meal. Dried fruits are also delicious—*but* they also have more concentrated sugar than fresh fruit. Be sure to stick to ones that do not have added sugar.

Low-Carb French Toast with Fresh Strawberries

Prep time: 5 minutes • Cook time: 10 minutes • Serves: 4

Each serving has: 350 calories • 16 g protein • 6 g animal protein • 10 g vegetable protein • 33 g carbohydrates • 7 g fiber • 26 g net carbohydrates • 14 g fat • 3 g saturated fat • 162 mg cholesterol • 230 mg sodium • Exchanges: 2 starch, ½ medium-fat meat, 2 fat

2 TB. canola oil

3 large eggs

½ cup milk

8 slices low-carb or 100 percent whole-wheat bread

3 TB. wheat germ

1 pint fresh strawberries, rinsed, tops removed and cut into ¼-inch pieces

Heat oil in a large skillet over medium heat. Crack eggs into a large bowl, add milk, and whisk with a whisk or fork. Set the bowl next to the skillet. Dip a piece of bread into egg mixture and move it to the skillet. Sprinkle wheat germ over top of cooking toast and cook for about 2 minutes. Flip and cook for another couple minutes or until toast is nicely tanned. Serve topped with a spoonful of fresh strawberries.

Variation: Instead of strawberries, use "light" syrup, a sprinkling of sweetener, or simply enjoy the French toast with butter.

Low-Carb Pancakes

Prep time: 5 minutes • Cook time: 10 minutes • Serves: 4

Each serving has: 204 calories • 15½ g protein • 3½ g animal protein • 12 g vegetable protein • 10 g carbohydrates • 3 g fiber • 7 g net carbohydrates • 14 g fat • 3 g saturated fat • 53 mg cholesterol • 190 mg sodium • Exchanges: 1 lean meat, ½ medium-fat meat, ½ starch, 1½ fat

1 cup soy flour

1 tsp. baking soda

Pinch salt

½ cup unsweetened applesauce

2 large eggs

2 TB. canola oil

Mix soy flour, baking soda, and salt in a bowl. In another bowl, mix applesauce and eggs. Stir flour mixture into egg mixture until batter is mixed but still a little lumpy.

Heat oil in a large skillet over medium heat. Make 4 pancakes by spooning batter into the skillet, being sure pancakes stay separate. Cook until bubbles burst and stay open, then flip, cook for an additional minute, and serve or put in the oven on warm.

Variation: Use whole-wheat flour in place of the soy flour. This will add to the good-carb total.

Carb Smarts

When making French toast or pancakes, consider making a double batch. This might take an extra few minutes, but then you've got a breakfast just waiting for you in the fridge for Monday morning when there's no time to prepare anything.

Good-Carb Pancakes

Prep time: 5 minutes • Cook time: 10 minutes • Serves: 8 people

Each serving has: 407 calories • 24 g protein • 13 g animal protein • 11 g vegetable protein • 72 g carbohydrates • 11 g fiber • 61 g net carbohydrates • 11 g fat • 2 g saturated fat • 106 mg cholesterol • 841 mg sodium • Exchanges: 4 starch, 2 fat

3 cups whole-wheat flour	2 cups milk
½ tsp. salt	½ cup nonfat small curd cottage cheese
1½ tsp. baking soda	2 TB. canola oil
2 large eggs	

Carb Smarts

Cottage cheese is a secret weapon when it comes to pancakes. It adds a rich, creamy texture without adding much in the way of carbs.

Mix flour, salt, and baking soda in a large bowl. In a separate bowl, whisk eggs, milk, and cottage cheese. Stir egg mixture into flour until batter is mixed but still a little lumpy.

Heat oil in a large skillet over medium heat. Spoon batter into the skillet to make 3 or 4 pancakes, being sure pancakes stay separate. Cook until bubbles burst and stay open, then flip and cook for an additional minute; then serve or put into the oven on warm.

Serve with fresh fruit or "light" syrup.

Crustless Spinach and Bacon Quiches

Prep time: 3 minutes   •   Cook time: 15 minutes   •   Serves: 2

Each serving has: 240 calories   •   17 g protein   •   15 g animal protein   •   2 g vegetable protein   •   5 g carbohydrates   •   2 g fiber   •   3 g net carbohydrates   •   16 g fat   •   4 g saturated fat   •   318 mg cholesterol   •   536 mg sodium   •   Exchanges: 2 medium-fat meat, 2 fat, 1 vegetable

3 large eggs

½ cup frozen spinach, thawed and squeezed dry

¼ cup skim milk

3 TB. light sour cream

3 slices crisp, cooked bacon, crumbled, or ¼ cup bacon pieces

¼ tsp. salt

Pinch ground black pepper

Preheat the oven to 400°F. Grease 2 muffin pan cups if the cups are large or 4 if the cups are miniature-muffin size. In a bowl, mix eggs, spinach, milk, sour cream, bacon, salt, and pepper with a fork. Distribute egg mixture among the greased muffin cups and bake for 15 minutes or until eggs are firmly set (a fork or knife inserted into your "quiche" will emerge uncoated when eggs are cooked). Gently pry those little beauties out onto a plate and enjoy.

Variation: Cook and serve these breakfast delicacies in oven-safe ramekins.

The Least You Need to Know

- When it comes to the weekday breakfast, our definition of quick is pretty strict; 10 to 15 minutes max. On the weekend, we get a bit more relaxed, so 20 minutes might be okay.
- Oatmeal, low-carb cold cereal, yogurt, and fruit—with some special touches—are fast, healthy out-of-the-box options for a lightning-fast breakfast.
- Breakfasts can be delicious without being sweet (oatmeal with just fruit and milk), but if your sweet tooth prevails, consider using artificial sweeteners.
- Leftover pancakes and French toast offer delicious survival rations during the week when there's no time to cook.

Chapter 3

Magic Eggs

In This Chapter

- The perfect food?
- Omelets 101
- Scramble with a twist
- Variations on the egg theme

Alternately maligned and loved over the years, eggs have been part of breakfast since our ancestors first kept chickens. It is true that eggs bring saturated fat and cholesterol to the table. It's perhaps even more important, however, that these wonders of nature are packed with protein and nutrition and that the fat you'll find is a balance of saturated and unsaturated. An egg is a potent package that comes with almost no carbohydrates. And did I mention ease of preparation and unmatched flavor?

Omelets

Omelets are fast (3 to 4 minutes) and easy after a little practice. Give yourself the chance to try them a few times. If you end up with scrambled eggs the first time, they'll still be delicious.

The recipes in this section are for 1 (1 egg/serving) omelet. For 2 servings, a double omelet in a large skillet or omelet pan will work fine, or try 2 single-egg omelets in separate pans (that's impressive to watch).

Carb Smarts

Don't limit yourself to eggs for breakfast. A hearty omelet also makes the perfect lunch or dinner.

Scrambled Eggs

Sunny yellow scrambled eggs can be the definition of starting the day right. Plus, it's one of the easiest, most flexible dishes you can make.

Here are some of my favorite egg-based recipes. Simple, healthy, and full of rich egg flavor—makes me want to get up in the morning …

Italian Herb Omelet

Prep time: 3 minutes   •   Cook time: 3 minutes   •   Serves: 1

Each serving has: 312 calories   •   18 g protein   •   18 g animal protein   •   0 g vegetable protein   •   0 g carbohydrates   •   0 g dietary fiber   •   0 g net carbohydrates   •   27 g fat   •   7 g saturated fat   •   431 mg cholesterol   •   290 mg sodium   •   Exchanges: 2 medium-fat meat, 3 fat

1 TB. olive oil

2 large eggs

1 tsp. Italian seasoning

2 TB. shredded Parmesan cheese

Salt and ground black pepper

Heat oil in a small nonstick skillet over medium heat. Crack eggs into a bowl, add Italian seasoning, and whisk with a whisk or fork. Carefully pour egg mixture into the skillet and cook for 1 minute without stirring. Then, using a spatula that won't harm the skillet's nonstick surface, loosen eggs around the edges so omelet slides easily. When eggs are almost cooked through, sprinkle on Parmesan and, using the spatula, fold omelet over on itself. Lift the skillet over the serving plate and slide omelet out onto the plate. Serve, seasoning with salt and pepper to taste.

Carb Smarts

A good nonstick skillet is very helpful when it comes to cooking egg dishes, especially omelets. Without a nonstick skillet, you'll need to use a bit more oil. A wooden or nonstick spatula is also a good idea so you don't damage the skillet surface.

Chicken and Swiss Omelet

Prep time: 4 minutes • Cook time: 3 minutes • Serves: 1

Each serving has: 488 calories • 38 g protein • 37 g animal protein • 0 g vegetable protein • 0 g carbohydrates • 0 g dietary fiber • 0 g net carbohydrates • 37 g fat • 11 g saturated fat • 480 mg cholesterol • 506 mg sodium • Exchanges: 1 high-fat meat, 2 medium-fat meat, 3 lean meat, 3 fat

1 TB. olive oil	½ (6-oz.) can water-packed chunk white chicken meat, drained and broken into small pieces
2 large eggs	
Dash hot red pepper sauce (optional)	Salt and ground black pepper
¼ cup shredded Swiss cheese	

Heat oil in a small nonstick skillet over medium heat. Crack eggs into a bowl, add hot pepper sauce (if using), and beat with a whisk or fork. Carefully pour egg mixture into the skillet and cook for 1 minute without stirring. Then, using a spatula that won't harm the skillet's nonstick surface, loosen eggs around the edges so omelet slides easily. When eggs are almost cooked through, spread cheese and chicken meat over eggs and, using the spatula, fold omelet over on itself. Lift the skillet over the serving plate and slide omelet out onto the plate. Serve, seasoning with salt and pepper to taste.

Variations: Chopped leftover chicken is a natural in place of canned bird. Or you can substitute your favorite shredded cheese (the variation will change the nutritional profile, but cheese is also low carb).

Prosciutto Omelet

Prep time: 3 minutes   •   Cook time: 3 minutes   •   Serves: 1

Each serving has: 372 calories   •   21 g protein   •   21 g animal protein   •   0 g vegetable protein   •   0 g carbohydrates   •   0 g dietary fiber   •   0 g net carbohydrates   •   31 g fat   •   9 g saturated fat   •   441 mg cholesterol   •   765 mg sodium   •   Exchanges: 1 high-fat meat, 2 medium-fat meat, 3 fat

1 TB. olive oil	3 TB. chopped *prosciutto*
2 large eggs	Salt and ground black pepper
2 TB. shredded Parmesan cheese	

Heat oil in a small nonstick skillet over medium heat. Crack eggs into a bowl and beat with a whisk or fork. Carefully pour eggs into the skillet and cook for 1 minute without stirring. Then, using a spatula that won't harm the skillet's nonstick surface, loosen eggs around the edges so omelet slides easily. When eggs are almost cooked through, sprinkle on Parmesan and chopped prosciutto and, using the spatula, fold omelet over on itself. Lift the skillet over the serving plate and slide omelet out onto the plate. Serve, seasoning with salt and pepper to taste.

Gourmand's Glossary

Prosciutto, or dry, salt-cured ham, is salty, rich, and evocative of Italy. It is popular in many simple dishes where its unique flavor is allowed to shine. Although prosciutto-style ham is now produced worldwide, the original, from Parma, has unique flavor from the pigs' diet of whey and chestnuts.

Baby Shrimp Omelet

Prep time: 4 minutes • Cook time: 3 minutes • Serves: 1

Each serving has: 462 calories • 46 g protein • 46 g animal protein • 0 g vegetable protein • 0 g carbohydrates • 0 g dietary fiber • 0 g net carbohydrates • 29 g fat • 9 g saturated fat • 1,074 mg cholesterol • 386 mg sodium • Exchanges: 4 lean meat, 2½ medium-fat meat, 3 fat

1 TB. olive oil	1 (4-oz.) can tiny shrimp, drained
2 large eggs	2 TB. shredded Parmesan cheese
Dash hot red pepper sauce	Salt and ground black pepper

Heat oil in a small nonstick skillet over medium heat. Crack eggs into a bowl, add hot sauce, and beat with a whisk or fork. Pour egg mixture into the skillet and cook for 1 minute without stirring. Then, using a spatula that won't harm the skillet's nonstick surface, loosen eggs around the edges so omelet slides easily. When eggs are almost cooked through, spread tiny shrimp and Parmesan over eggs and, using the spatula, fold omelet over on itself. Lift the skillet over the serving plate and slide omelet out onto the plate. Serve, seasoning with salt and pepper to taste.

Variations: Crabmeat, available in cans the same size as shrimp, is a delicious substitution for shrimp (pick over crab meat to remove any remaining shell fragments).

Scrambled Eggs

Prep time: 3 minutes • Cook time: 4 minutes • Serves: 2

Each serving has: 281 calories • 16 g protein • 16 g animal protein • 0 g vegetable protein • 0 g carbohydrates • 0 g dietary fiber • 0 g net carbohydrates • 24 g fat • 5 g saturated fat • 424 mg cholesterol • 245 mg sodium • Exchanges: 2 medium-fat meat, 3 fat

2 TB. canola or olive oil	¼ cup skim milk
4 large eggs	Salt and ground black pepper

Heat oil in a small skillet over medium-low heat. Crack eggs into a bowl, add milk, and beat with a whisk or fork. Carefully pour egg mixture into the skillet and cook, stirring slowly to bring uncooked eggs in contact with the skillet, 3 to 4 minutes or to your desired consistency. Distribute to serving plates and season with salt and pepper to taste.

Variation: Add ⅓ cup shredded Swiss cheese (or your favorite) along with milk.

 Carb Alert

Avoid high heat when cooking eggs. The secret to creamy, luxuriant scrambled eggs is leisurely cooking over medium or medium-low heat, stirring all the while. You'll add a minute to cooking time (to a huge 4 minutes), but the flavor and texture is worth that "wait." As soon as your eggs reach the consistency you like, serve 'em up. The more eggs cook (or the higher the cooking temperature), the drier the eggs will get.

Southwest Scramble

Prep time: 3 minutes • Cook time: 5 minutes • Serves: 2

Each serving has: 291 calories • 16 g protein • 16 g animal protein • 0 g vegetable protein • 3 g carbohydrates • <1 g dietary fiber • 3 g net carbohydrates • 24 g fat • 5 g saturated fat • 424 mg cholesterol • 586 mg sodium • Exchanges: 2 medium-fat meat, 3 fat

2 TB. canola or olive oil

4 large eggs

¼ cup skim milk

⅓ cup no-sugar-added salsa (your favorite)

Salt and ground black pepper

Carb Smarts

Great omelet fillings are just as good in scrambled eggs. Almost all the usual suspects, including cheeses, meats, vegetables, and seasonings, are also perfect for carb-conscious cooking.

Heat oil in a small skillet over medium-low heat. Crack eggs into a bowl, add milk and salsa, and beat with a whisk or fork. Carefully pour egg mixture into the skillet and cook, stirring slowly to bring uncooked eggs in contact with the skillet, for 4 minutes or to your desired consistency. Distribute to serving plates and season with salt and pepper to taste.

Florentine Scramble

Prep time: 3 minutes   •   Cook time: 8 minutes   •   Serves: 2

Each serving has: 308 calories   •   19 g protein   •   18 g animal protein   •   1 g vegetable protein   •   1 g carbohydrates   •   < 1 g dietary fiber   •   0 g net carbohydrates   •   26 g fat   •   6 g saturated fat   •   429 mg cholesterol   •   370 mg sodium   •   Exchanges: 2 medium-fat meat, 3 fat

2 TB. canola or olive oil

2 cups fresh baby spinach leaves, rinsed and stemmed, or ⅓ cup frozen spinach (about ¼ [10-oz.] pkg.), thawed and squeezed dry

4 large eggs

¼ cup skim milk

3 TB. shredded Parmesan cheese

Salt and ground black pepper

Heat oil in a small skillet over medium heat and cook spinach, stirring, for 3 minutes or until spinach is cooked and, if using fresh, spinach has dramatically reduced in volume. Meanwhile, crack eggs into a bowl, add milk, and beat with a whisk or fork. Carefully pour egg mixture into the skillet with the spinach and cook, stirring slowly to bring uncooked eggs in contact with the skillet, for 4 minutes or to your desired consistency. Distribute to serving plates and season with Parmesan, salt, and pepper to taste.

Portobello Eggs

Prep time: 3 minutes • Cook time: 9 minutes • Serves: 2

Each serving has: 295 calories • 11 g protein • 7 g animal protein • 4 g vegetable protein • 6 g carbohydrates • 2 g dietary fiber • 4 g net carbohydrates • 26 g fat • 3 g saturated fat • 212 mg cholesterol • 235 mg sodium • Exchanges: 1 medium-fat meat, 1 vegetable, 3 fat

2 large (about 4 inches) bowl-shape portobello mushroom caps, stems removed, gills scraped out with a spoon, and wiped with a damp paper towel

3 TB. olive oil

⅓ tsp. Italian seasoning

2 large eggs

Salt and ground black pepper

Carb Smarts

If the stem side of the portobello cap is not sufficiently concave, the egg will slide off! Scoop out the gills so the egg will be held inside to cook. And if your mushroom caps are too rounded to sit well on the baking tray, use a sharp knife to cut a bit of the top off to give it a flat surface.

Preheat the broiler (if your broiler has multiple settings, select medium). Place mushroom caps on a baking tray, top side up, brush with 1 tablespoon oil, and broil on the next-to-highest rack for 3 minutes. Flip caps, drizzle each with half the remaining oil, sprinkle with a pinch of Italian seasoning, and broil for 3 minutes more. Slide the sizzling mushrooms out of the oven, crack 1 egg in each, slide back under the broiler, and broil for 3 minutes or until egg is cooked to your liking. Place each mushroom on a serving plate, season with salt and pepper to taste, and serve with a knife and fork.

Scottish Eggs

Prep time: 4 minutes • Cook time: 4 minutes • Serves: 2

Each serving has: 376 calories • 22 g protein • 19 g animal protein • 3 g vegetable protein • 10 g carbohydrates • 2 g fiber • 8 g net carbohydrates • 27 g fat • 5 g saturated fat • 230 mg cholesterol • 462 mg sodium • Exchanges: 2 medium-fat meat, 2 lean meat, 4 fat, 1 starch

2 TB. canola oil

2 slices low-carb or 100 percent whole-wheat bread

Butter or margarine

2 large eggs

4 oz. thinly sliced smoked salmon (available in grocery stores)

Ground black pepper

Heat oil in a medium skillet over medium heat. Toast and butter bread. When a drop of water "dances" on oil, the skillet is ready. Cook egg for about 1 minute or until egg white turns white about halfway to the surface. Carefully slide a spatula under egg and flip it in the skillet. Add ½ smoked salmon to the skillet to heat as egg finishes cooking. Cook egg for another minute. Place toast on a serving plate, slide salmon on top of toast, and place egg on salmon. Repeat with other egg, another piece of toast, and remaining salmon. Season with pepper to taste (you might not need salt, as salmon will be salty) and have breakfast in the Highlands.

Carbohistory

I met these Scottish Eggs in Scotland years ago, and I've loved them ever since. In the old country, they are served on what we would call a white flour biscuit. Whole-wheat toast helps us bring this delicious dish into the good-carb arena.

Over-Easy Egg Toast

Prep time: 4 minutes   •   Cook time: 4 minutes   •   Serves: 2 (scale as needed)

Each serving has: 310 calories   •   11 g protein   •   8 g animal protein   •   3 g vegetable protein   •   10 g carbohydrates   •   2 g fiber   •   8 g net carbohydrates   •   24 g fat   •   4 g saturated fat   •   217 mg cholesterol   •   145 mg sodium   •   Exchanges: 1 medium-fat meat, 1 starch, 4 fat

2 TB. canola oil	Butter or margarine
2 slices low-carb or 100 percent whole-wheat bread	2 large eggs
	Salt and ground black pepper

Carbohistory

This quick recipe had been perfected to an art at the Roaring Lion Bed and Breakfast in Waldoboro, Maine.

Heat oil in a large skillet over medium heat. Toast and butter bread and with a sharp knife (or even a large glass or cookie cutter) cut a round piece, about 3 inches in diameter in the center of toast. Remove the round piece but keep it.

Place toast in the heated skillet and crack 1 egg into each toast hole. Cook for 2 minutes per side or to your liking. Slide toast and egg onto a plate and replace round piece as a "lid" over egg. Season with salt and pepper to taste.

The Least You Need to Know

◆ Egg dishes are delicious, quick to prepare, and inherently low carb.

◆ With a little practice, you can make easy, elegant, tasty omelets.

◆ Vegetables, cooked meats, and cheeses are all delicious components of scrambled egg dishes.

◆ Whether on a mushroom, inside a piece of toast, or partnered with smoked salmon, eggs can make many low-carb, high-flavor meals.

Chapter 4

Low Carb at Lunch

In This Chapter

- Wrapping and rolling your way to a delicious lunch
- Making good use of your neighborhood deli
- Maximizing flavor with fresh vegetables
- Taking advantage of office lunch secrets
- Creating lunchtime dips, cooked meals, and more

Just because lunch is portable doesn't mean you have to resort to fast food. To prove this point, in this chapter, we'll look at wraps filled with tasty low-carb foods (some expected and some unexpected). We'll dig into hearty low-carb lunch salads. Ever dream of a hot lunch at work, but one that you make yourself? You'll find some here, along with extended appetizer dip-style lunches and, of course, a new, good-carb and low-carb approach to the lunchtime sandwich.

Then, for those times when you're eating in (or at least have access to a kitchen), we'll explore more hot, low-carb, and quick lunches. These delicious, carb-conscious dishes might just make lunch your favorite meal of the day.

That's a Wrap

When it comes to holding portable food together, you have some choices. In the low-carb corner, the options include the main ingredient itself, such as using sliced deli turkey as the wrapper; crisp leafy greens; or aluminum foil. In the good-carb corner, an increasing number of whole-grain and low-carb grain-based tortillas and breads are available to wrap it up.

The recipes in this chapter include examples of all these wrapping methods. They are, for the most part, interchangeable as you like.

More Carry-Out Cuisine

In many offices, the only source of heat is the microwave (generally used for popping popcorn and reheating leftovers). With a little imagination and quick prep, however, you can actually cook some tasty lunch dishes. I've included just two possibilities. An easy, healthy lunch at the office never tasted so good.

Good Carbs to Go

In the grocery store bakery, the carb-conscious cook has a growing number of options. Many of the large bakeries are cooking up low-carb breads, and I've seen low-carb tortillas (by the time you read this, there will almost certainly be more). And don't forget the original "good"-carb bread our ancestors ate: good old 100 percent whole wheat. All these options enable terrific good-carb lunches.

One caveat about bread, though: Watch out for labeling claims. Terms such as *multi-grain* sound good, but white flour is probably the first item on the ingredients list. Look instead for breads that indicate *100 percent whole wheat*.

Hot Lunches

If you've got access to a full kitchen at lunchtime, a world of opportunity awaits. We still keep things quick (have to get back to work), but we can extend our range beyond what we can carry in a plastic tub. Lunching near our own kitchen enables quick cooking, and thus these midday beauties.

Turkey, Arugula, and Almond Roll-Ups

Prep time: 8 minutes   •   Serves: 2

Each serving has: 417 calories   •   25 g protein   •   22 g animal protein   •   3 g vegetable protein   •   3 g carbohydrates   •   2 g dietary fiber   •   1 g net carbohydrates   •   22 g fat   •   7 g saturated fat   •   89 mg cholesterol   •   1,340 mg sodium   •   Exchanges: 4 very lean meat, ½ vegetable, 4 fat

½ lb. thickly sliced deli turkey (about 6 to 8 slices)

3 TB. mayonnaise

¼ cup sliced almonds

1 cup fresh arugula leaves, stemmed, washed, and dried (about 12 big leaves)

Salt and ground black pepper

Spread each turkey slice with mayonnaise and sprinkle with sliced almonds. Lay several arugula leaves over turkey, sprinkle salt and pepper to taste, and roll turkey over filling to form a bulky cylinder. Set rolls on a serving plate if you're serving right away. To take them with you, pack rolls in a sandwich bag or a small rectangular plastic container with a lid.

Variation: Toasted almonds add delicious flavor. Other fresh savory greens, such as watercress, can be used in place of the arugula.

Carb Smarts

When you're looking for convenient low-carb cuisine, take advantage of your friend, the deli. Turkey, chicken, and roast beef are all good candidates. Sliced ham and meat salads can also be terrific, but check for added sugar.

Roast Beef and Watercress Roll-Ups

Prep time: 8 minutes • Serves: 2

Each serving has: 231 calories • 31 g protein • 30 g animal protein • 1 g vegetable protein • 5 g carbohydrates • < 1 g dietary fiber • 5 g net carbohydrates • 12 g fat • 5 g saturated fat • 90 mg cholesterol • 128 mg sodium • Exchanges: 4 lean meat, 1 vegetable

½ lb. lean thickly sliced roast beef (about 6 to 8 slices)

2 TB. prepared horseradish

2 cups watercress leaves, stemmed, washed, and dried, about 8 sprigs

Salt and ground black pepper

Spread each roast beef slice with horseradish and arrange several watercress leaves so they will be rolled lengthwise. Sprinkle with salt and ground black pepper to taste. Roll roast beef over watercress to form a cylinder and bind with toothpicks if necessary. Serve immediately, or to take them with you, store in a rectangular plastic container with a lid.

Carb Smarts

Some wraps and roll-ups, such as those made with deli meats, don't need much help to hold together. Others, such as those where lettuce is the wrap, are best held together with a couple toothpicks and carried in a plastic container with a lid. A "wrap" I've used if I have them in the fridge are a couple extra-long scallion leaves. Another option (sort of the "maximum-hold styling gel" for your lunch) is to bind them in squares of aluminum foil.

Tuna Salad Wraps

Prep time: 8 minutes   •   Serves: 2

Each serving has: 245 calories   •   21 g protein   •   21 g animal protein   •   < 1 g vegetable protein   •   < 1 g carbohydrates   •   < 1 g dietary fiber   •   0 g net carbohydrates   •   14 g fat   •   3 g saturated fat   •   8 mg cholesterol   •   405 mg sodium   •   Exchanges: 3 very lean meat, 3 fat

1 (6-oz.) can chunk white tuna in water, drained	1 TB. Dijon-style mustard
1 celery stalk, trimmed, washed, and chopped into ¼-inch pieces	¼ tsp. dried dill
	Salt and ground black pepper
2 TB. mayonnaise	6 large romaine or iceberg lettuce leaves, washed and dried.

Scoop tuna into a bowl and break up any large chunks. Mix in celery, mayonnaise, mustard, dill, salt, and pepper. Distribute tuna salad among lettuce leaves, roll leaves lengthwise to form long cylinders, and pin with two or three toothpicks.

Carb Smarts

Crunchy lettuce leaves tend to break upon rolling. To solve this, lay them on a flat surface and crush them with the heel of your hand. Then they should roll (lengthwise) just fine.

Tuna is a top choice when it comes to carb-conscious food: great flavor, lots of protein, a good source of healthy fat, and affordable, too. That's not bad for a brown-bag lunch!

Ham 'n' Swiss Roll-Ups

Prep time: 8 minutes • Serves: 2

Each serving has: 380 calories • 42 g protein • 42 g animal protein • 0 g vegetable protein • 0 g carbohydrates • 0 g dietary fiber • 0 g net carbohydrates • 20 g fat • 11 g saturated fat • 143 mg cholesterol • 1,724 mg sodium • Exchanges: 4 very lean meat, 2 high-fat meat

½ lb. thickly sliced deli ham (about 6 to 8 slices)	2 TB. Dijon-style mustard 1 cup (½ [8-oz.] bag) shredded Swiss cheese

Spread each ham slice with mustard and sprinkle with cheese. Roll ham over cheese to form a cylinder. Serve immediately, or to take them with you, store in a sandwich bag or a small rectangular plastic container with a lid.

Variation: It's hard to resist heating these for 30 seconds in the microwave to melt the cheese before serving.

 Carbohistory

The challenge of transport (of wraps and roll-ups) can be addressed by picking up a big set of washable plastic containers. They're reusable, convenient, and will keep your lunch together beautifully. You'll also save on constantly buying and tossing baggies.

Smoked Salmon-Arugula Wraps

Prep time: 8 minutes • Serves: 2

Each serving has: 169 calories • 20 g protein • 17 g animal protein • 3 g vegetable protein • 4 g carbohydrates • 1 g dietary fiber • 3 g net carbohydrates • 5 g fat • 2 g saturated fat • 20 mg cholesterol • 980 mg sodium • Exchanges: 3 very lean meat, ½ fat

6 oz. thinly sliced smoked salmon (about 6 to 8 slices)

6 large romaine or iceberg lettuce leaves, washed and crushed flat to facilitate rolling

2 TB. light cream cheese, softened

2 TB. capers, drained

1 TB. fresh lemon juice

¼ tsp. dried dill

Ground black pepper

1 cup fresh arugula, stemmed, washed, and dried (about 12 big leaves)

Lay salmon slices on lettuce leaves. Spread cream cheese on salmon and distribute capers. Drizzle with lemon juice and sprinkle with dill. Sprinkle with black pepper. Lay a few arugula leaves on each, arranged so they will be rolled lengthwise. Roll lettuce leaves to form long cylinders around the filling and pin with two or three toothpicks.

Tex-Mex Microwave Lunch Scramble

Prep time: 5 minutes • Cook time: 3 minutes • Serves: 1

Each serving has: 190 calories • 14 g protein • 14 g animal protein • 0 g vegetable protein • 1 g carbohydrates • < 1 g dietary fiber • 0 g net carbohydrates • 13 g fat • 4 g saturated fat • 232 mg cholesterol • 264 mg sodium • Exchanges: 1 medium-fat meat, 1 high-fat meat

1 large egg

3 TB. shredded Mexican-style cheese (or your favorite)

3 TB. sugar-free salsa

2 TB. milk

Salt and ground black pepper

Before you leave for work, mix egg, cheese, salsa, milk, salt, and pepper in a microwave-safe plastic container with a tight-fitting lid. Store the container in the fridge or a cooler pack until lunchtime. When you're ready to eat, crack the lid and cook on high for 1 minute, stir, and cook for another minute or until done.

Microwave Spinach and White Bean Stew

Prep time: 3 minutes • Cook time: 4 minutes • Serves: 1

Each serving has: 275 calories • 18 g protein • 4 g animal protein • 14 g vegetable protein • 34 g carbohydrates • 11 g dietary fiber • 23 g net carbohydrates • 3½ g fat • 2 g saturated fat • 7 mg cholesterol • 984 mg sodium • Exchanges: 1 very lean meat, ½ medium-fat meat, 1 starch, 1 vegetable

½ (10-oz.) pkg. frozen spinach (it might help to thaw it first before cutting that brick in half; don't worry about squeezing it dry)

1 (15-oz.) can chicken broth

⅔ cup (½ [15-oz.] can) cannellini beans, drained and rinsed

2 TB. shredded Parmesan cheese

Dash hot red pepper sauce

Pinch salt and ground black pepper

Before you leave for work, put frozen spinach, broth, beans, Parmesan cheese, hot pepper sauce, salt, and pepper into a microwave-safe plastic container with a tight-fitting lid. Store the container in the fridge or a cooler pack until lunchtime. When you're ready to eat, crack the lid and cook on high for 4 minutes, stirring once, or until heated to your preferred temperature. Stir again and devour.

Variation: If you want meat in your stew, add ½ cup chopped cooked chicken or ½ (6-ounce) can white chicken meat, drained.

Piquant Ham Salad in Iceberg Bowls

Prep time: 8 minutes   •   Serves: 2

Each serving has: 488 calories   •   25 g protein   •   22 g animal protein   •   3 g vegetable protein   •   6 g carbohydrates   •   2 g dietary fiber   •   4 g net carbohydrates   •   44 g fat   •   9 g saturated fat   •   45 mg cholesterol   •   1,378 mg sodium   •   Exchanges: 4 lean meat, ½ vegetable, 8 fat

½ lb. ham, chopped into ¼-inch pieces

1 celery stalk, trimmed, washed, and chopped into ¼-inch pieces

½ cup chopped fresh parsley

½ cup toasted pine nuts

2 TB. mayonnaise

2 TB. balsamic vinegar

Salt and ground black pepper

Dash hot red pepper sauce

1 small (about 5 inches across) head crisp iceberg lettuce, cut in half lengthwise and inner leaves removed to form 2 bowls (reserve removed lettuce for another use)

Scoop chopped ham into a bowl and mix in celery, parsley, pine nuts, mayonnaise, vinegar, salt, pepper, and hot pepper sauce. Divide salad between iceberg bowls and store in containers with tight-fitting lids in the fridge. Enjoy at lunchtime with a knife and fork.

Carb Smarts

Many grocery stores sell ham steaks, a convenient cut of cooked meat that can be quickly chopped for this salad. And in the same area, you might even find packages of ready-chopped ham.

Quick Homemade Hummus

Prep time: 8 minutes • Serves: 2

Each serving has: 536 calories • 15 g protein • 0 g animal protein • 15 g vegetable protein • 45 g carbohydrates • 12 g dietary fiber • 33 g net carbohydrates • 32 g fat • 4 g saturated fat • 0 mg cholesterol • 1,171 mg sodium • Exchanges: 2 very lean meat, 2 starch, 6 fat

1 (15-oz.) can chickpeas, drained and rinsed	1 tsp. salt
1 TB. chopped garlic	2 TB. olive oil
Juice of 1 lemon	¼ cup *tahini*

Gourmand's Glossary

Hummus is a thick Middle Eastern spread made of puréed chickpeas (also called garbanzo beans), lemon juice, olive oil, garlic, and often tahini. **Tahini** is sesame paste and is available in the international food section of many grocery stores.

Process chickpeas, garlic, lemon juice, salt, olive oil, and tahini in a food processor and blend until the texture is fine and creamy. If hummus is too thick, add more olive oil.

Variation: For a flavor shortcut, consider purchasing a jar of chopped or minced garlic (in the vegetable section of the grocery store). The flavor sacrifice is minimal, and you'll save a lot of time. Serve with cucumber sticks, baby carrots, and celery stalks, and you've got a tasty, easy-to-carry lunch.

Endive Stuffed with Piquant Tuna Salad

Prep time: 5 minutes • Serves: 4

Each serving has: 231 calories • 14 g protein • 10 g animal protein • 4 g vegetable protein • 12 g carbohydrates • 8 g dietary fiber • 4 g net carbohydrates • 13 g fat • 4 g saturated fat • 4 mg cholesterol • 324 mg sodium • Exchanges: 1½ very lean meat, 2 vegetable, 3 fat

1 (6-oz.) can chunk white tuna in water, drained

½ celery stalk, rinsed and chopped into ¼-inch pieces

¼ cup mayonnaise

1 TB. small capers, drained and rinsed

1 tsp. lemon juice

1 tsp. fresh dill or ¼ tsp. dried

Dash hot red pepper sauce

Pinch ground black pepper

2 heads *Belgian endive*

Parsley for garnish (optional)

In a bowl, mix tuna, celery, mayonnaise, capers, lemon juice, dill, hot pepper sauce, and pepper. Place the bowl on a serving platter. Break endive into component leaves and arrange large leaves around the bowl of tuna salad. Serve with a spreading knife or a spoon, placing a generous spoonful of tuna salad in each endive cup and garnishing with parsley (if using). To carry with you, place endive leaves in a separate container from tuna salad, store in the fridge, and combine at lunchtime.

Carb Smarts

To accelerate tuna salad dishes from 5 minutes to 30 seconds, pick up some deli tuna salad from the store (be sure there's no sugar added). Spoon tuna salad into endive cups and add a sprig of parsley.

Gourmand's Glossary

Belgian endive is a crisp, slightly astringent green that resembles a small bullet-shape head of romaine lettuce. Endives are popular vehicles for appetizers. The individual leaves can be broken off and used as crisp scoops for all kinds of fillings. Buy the largest endives you can. The big outside leaves are the most useful for stuffing. You can save the smaller core leaves to slice and use in a salad.

Smoked Ham and Sprout Sandwich

Prep time: 5 minutes   •   Serves: 1

Each serving has: 215 calories   •   17 g protein   •   12 g animal protein   •   5 g vegetable protein   •   16 g carbohydrates   •   5 g dietary fiber   •   11 g net carbohydrates   •   3 g fat   •   1 g saturated fat   •   24 mg cholesterol   •   1,100 mg sodium   •   Exchanges: 2 very lean meat, 1 starch, ½ vegetable

2 slices smoked deli ham	½ cup alfalfa sprouts, rinsed and dried
2 slices low-carb bread	Ground black pepper
2 tsp. prepared sugar-free mustard (your favorite)	

Arrange ham on one slice of bread. Spread ham with mustard, top with sprouts, and sprinkle with black pepper. Top with remaining slice of bread. Transport in a sandwich-size plastic container with a lid or a sandwich bag.

Variation: Use 100 percent whole-wheat bread in place of the low-carb bread. (But remember, this will increase the nominal carb count.)

 Carbohistory

What fillings, you ask, can be used to make a low-carb sandwich? More are on the list than off. Here are some of my favorites:

- Sliced cheddar, provolone, or Swiss cheese
- Fresh tomato slices
- Sliced lean deli meats (almost all kinds except those processed with sugar)
- Sliced mild onion
- Lettuce, arugula, watercress, and other greens
- All kinds of sprouted seeds
- Mayonnaise (not the fat-free kind; it has more carbs than the regular)
- Most mustards

Cheddar Chicken Wrap

Prep time: 5 minutes • Serves: 1

Each serving has: 540 calories • 37 g protein • 33 g animal protein • 4 g vegetable protein • 15 g carbohydrates • 8 g fiber • 7 g net carbohydrates • 39 g fat • 14 g saturated fat • 78 mg cholesterol • 1,540 mg sodium • Exchanges: 4 very-lean meat, 1 high-fat meat, ½ starch, 6 fat

1 large low-carb soft tortilla

¼ lb. sliced deli chicken or 1 cup thinly sliced cooked leftover chicken

2 TB. mayonnaise

¼ cup shredded cheddar cheese

Salt and ground black pepper

2 large romaine or iceberg lettuce leaves, rinsed, dried, and crushed flat to facilitate rolling

Spread tortilla with chicken, mayonnaise, cheese, salt and pepper to taste, and lettuce leaf. Tuck in the sides to enclose filling and roll tortilla, firmly but gently from one side. Cut in half on the diagonal. Store in a plastic container with a lid or a large plastic food storage bag.

Carb Alert

Just because a bread has fewer carbs does not mean it's good for you. Don't forget to check out the ingredients. Nutrition experts caution us to avoid hydrogenated oils and excess preservatives.

Vegetarian Wrap

Prep time: 5 minutes   •   Serves: 1

Each serving has: 630 calories   •   27 g protein   •   14 g animal protein   •   10 g vegetable protein   •   29 g carbohydrates   •   15 g fiber   •   14 g net carbohydrates   •   42 g fat   •   16 g saturated fat   •   60 mg cholesterol   •   782 mg sodium   •   Exchanges: 2 high-fat meat, 4 fat, 1½ vegetable, ½ starch

2 oz. fresh chevre (goat's milk cheese), softened

1 large low-carb soft tortilla

¼ cup sliced almonds (toasted in a 350°F oven for 5 minutes, if possible)

1½ cups bagged mixed-greens salad mix, chopped into ¼-inch pieces (if the pieces are not already small enough to use)

Salt and ground black pepper

2 TB. Italian or vinaigrette dressing

Spread softened chevre on tortilla, top with almonds and salad mix, and sprinkle with salt and pepper. Tuck in the sides to enclose filling and roll tortilla, firmly but gently from one side. Cut in half on the diagonal. Store in a plastic container with a lid or a large plastic food storage bag. Pour dressing into a small plastic container alongside and dress just before eating.

Gourmand's Glossary

Chevre, or fresh goat's milk cheese, is a typically creamy-salty soft cheese that looks like cream cheese but has a richer, slightly tangy flavor. Chevres vary in style from mild and creamy to aged, firm, and flavorful. Artisanal chevres are usually more expensive and sold in smaller quantities; these are often delicious by themselves. Other chevres produced in quantity are less expensive and often more appropriate for combining with fruit or herbs.

Open-Faced Tomato and Provolone Sandwiches

Prep time: 5 minutes • Cook time: 5 minutes • Serves: 2

Each serving has: 181 calories • 9 g protein • 7 g animal protein • 2 g vegetable protein • 9 g carbohydrates • 3 g fiber • 6 g net carbohydrates • 8 g fat • 5 g saturated fat • 5 mg cholesterol • 395 mg sodium • Exchanges: 1 high-fat meat, 1 starch, 1 vegetable

2 (½-inch thick) fresh tomato slices

2 slices low-carb bread

½ tsp. Italian seasoning

Salt and ground black pepper

2 slices provolone cheese

Preheat your broiler. Set 1 tomato slice on each slice of bread, sprinkle with Italian seasoning, salt, and pepper, and top with 1 slice of provolone. Broil on the highest rack for 4 minutes or until cheese is melted and bread edges are toasted.

Variation: Use 100 percent whole-wheat bread in place of the low-carb bread. (This will increase the nominal carb count, though.)

Smoked Salmon Salad

Prep time: 8 minutes • Serves: 2

Each serving has: 411 calories • 28 g protein • 21 g animal protein • 7 g vegetable protein • 7 g carbohydrates • 4 g fiber • 3 g net carbohydrates • 33 g fat • 4½ g saturated fat • 15 mg cholesterol • 1,013 mg sodium • Exchanges: 4 very lean meat, 5 fat, ½ vegetable

4 large romaine lettuce leaves, washed and dried

8 oz. smoked salmon, cut into ½-inch pieces

½ cup sliced almonds, toasted

2 TB. olive oil

2 TB. chopped chives

1 tsp. lemon juice

Pinch of ground black pepper

2 lemon wedges

Set out 1 romaine leaf on each of 2 serving plates. Chop remaining 2 romaine leaves and mix in a bowl with smoked salmon, almonds, olive oil, chives, lemon juice, and pepper. Divide salmon salad between the 2 intact romaine leaves on their plates and serve garnished with lemon wedges.

Variation: Other salmon variations will also work, even canned salmon.

Grilled Cheddar-Mushroom Sandwiches

Prep time: 5 minutes • Cook time: 5 minutes • Serves: 2

Each serving has: 432 calories • 19 g protein • 15 g animal protein • 4 g vegetable protein • 19 g carbohydrates • 11 g fiber • 8 g net carbohydrates • 26 g fat • 15 g saturated fat • 75 mg cholesterol • 643 mg sodium • Exchanges: 2 high-fat meat, 1½ fat, ½ starch, 1 vegetable

1 TB. butter or margarine	4 slices cheddar cheese
4 slices low-carb bread	⅔ cup sliced white mushrooms
½ tsp. Italian seasoning	

Heat a large skillet over medium heat. Spread butter on 1 side of each piece of bread and sprinkle butter with a pinch of Italian seasoning. Place 2 bread slices, butter side down, in the skillet. Lay 1 cheese slice on each piece of bread in the skillet, then follow with mushrooms and remaining cheese slices. Top with remaining bread, butter side up. Cook for 3 minutes or until cheddar begins to melt and bread is toasted. Carefully flip sandwich with a spatula, cook for 3 additional minutes, and serve.

Variations: To make a more impressive sandwich, use Brie or fresh mozzarella in place of the cheddar. You won't have to cook this one as long (3 to 4 minutes total), as Brie melts quite easily.

The mushrooms will still have a crunch. For softer texture, sauté mushrooms in 2 tablespoons olive oil over medium heat for 4 minutes, then add them to your sandwich.

Italian Turkey-Pecan Chef Salad

Prep time: 8 minutes   •   Serves: 2

Each serving has: 420 calories   •   26 g protein   •   22 g animal protein   •   4 g vegetable protein   •   20 g carbohydrates   •   8 g fiber   •   12 g net carbohydrates   •   28 g fat   •   7 g saturated fat   •   56 mg cholesterol   •   916 mg sodium   •   Exchanges: 3 very-lean meat, 1 medium-fat meat, 4 fat

¼ cup pecans, toasted or raw

1 (6-oz.) can turkey meat, drained

½ (16-oz.) bag salad mix, washed and spun dry

½ crisp apple, rinsed, cored and chopped

⅓ cup shredded mozzarella cheese

¼ cup Italian dressing (your sugar-free favorite)

In a bowl, mix pecans and turkey with a fork, mashing to break up any large turkey chunks. Toss with salad mix, apple, and mozzarella cheese and drizzle with the salad dressing.

Ham and Nut Lunch Salad

Prep time: 10 minutes • Serves: 2

Each serving has: 556 calories • 29 g protein • 17 g animal protein • 12 g vegetable protein • 23 g carbohydrates • 6 g fiber • 17 g net carbohydrates • 36 g fat • 9 g saturated fat • 62 mg cholesterol • 1,161 mg sodium • Exchanges: 3½ very lean meat, 1 high-fat meat, 4 fat, 1 fruit

1 cup ham (about ½ lb.), cut ½-inch cubes

2 celery stalks, washed and chopped into ½-inch pieces

1 cup seedless green grapes, rinsed and halved

½ cup toasted pine nuts or chopped pecans or walnuts

½ cup shredded Swiss cheese

3 TB. sugar-free Italian dressing (or your favorite)

In a serving bowl, mix ham, celery, grapes, nuts, and cheese. Drizzle with dressing, toss, and serve.

Carb Smarts

Ham (the kind prepared without sugar) is one of the most convenient low-carb foods around. Whether sliced ham from the deli, ham steaks, or a whole ham, you can prepare "the other white meat" in myriad ways.

Pesto Tuna Melts

Prep time: 5 minutes • Cook time: 5 minutes • Serves: 2

Each serving has: 815 calories • 41 g protein • 35 g animal protein • 6 g vegetable protein • 19 g carbohydrates • 11 g fiber • 8 g net carbohydrates • 56 g fat • 17 g saturated fat • 14 mg cholesterol • 1,134 mg sodium • Exchanges: 3 very lean meat, 2 high-fat meat, 5 fat, 1 starch

1 (6-oz.) can chunk white tuna in water, drained	2 TB. toasted *pine nuts*
3 TB. prepared pesto sauce	4 slices low-carb bread
2 TB. mayonnaise	4 slices sharp provolone or regular provolone cheese

Preheat the broiler. In a bowl, mix tuna, pesto sauce, mayonnaise, and pine nuts. Lay bread pieces on a baking sheet in a single layer and toast for 2 minutes or until just beginning to crisp. Remove tray from broiler and distribute tuna mixture evenly among slices. Top each slice with provolone and broil for 3 minutes or until cheese is melted.

Gourmand's Glossary

Pine nuts (also *pignoli* or *piñon*) are edible nuts grown on pine trees. They are rich, flavorful, and, yes, a bit pine-y. Pine nuts are a traditional component of pesto and are one of those irresistible flavor boosters that add interest to a dish. A bag of pine nuts in your pantry (or in your freezer, if you tend to use them slowly) will come in handy for many recipes in this book.

Skillet Broiled Roasted Red Pepper Frittata

Prep time: 10 minutes • Cook time: 10 minutes • Serves: 2

Each serving has: 655 calories • 42 g protein • 42 g animal protein • < 1 g vegetable protein • 3 g carbohydrates • 2 g fiber • 1 g net carbohydrates • 53 g fat • 28 g saturated fat • 330 mg cholesterol • 1,280 mg sodium • Exchanges: 4 high-fat meat, 2 medium-fat meat, 1 vegetable, 1½ fat

1 TB. olive oil	1 (8-oz.) pkg. shredded cheddar cheese
1 tsp. chopped garlic	½ cup shredded Parmesan cheese
2 large eggs	½ tsp. Italian seasoning
1 TB. *dried minced onion*	2 TB. chopped fresh chives
1 cup water-packed roasted red peppers (about ⅔ [12-oz.] jar), drained, patted dry on paper towels, and cut into ½-inch pieces	Salt and ground black pepper

Preheat the broiler. Heat oil in a small, oven-safe skillet over medium-low heat. Cook garlic in the skillet for 1 minute, stirring. Meanwhile, mix eggs, onion, red peppers, shredded cheeses, Italian seasoning, chives, salt, and pepper in a bowl. Pour egg mixture into the skillet and stir to incorporate garlic. Cook, without stirring, for 5 minutes or until frittata has solidified almost to the surface (test with a knife). Sprinkle Parmesan over top of frittata. Transfer the skillet to the next-to-highest shelf under the broiler and broil for 3 minutes or until frittata is set all the way through. Remove, cool for 5 minutes, and cut into slices.

Gourmand's Glossary

Minced onion is available in the spice section of your grocery store. This form of onion brings flavor without chopping, although give it time in contact with the moisture in a dish to allow the flavor to spread.

Variations: You can use many vegetables and meats in place of (or in addition to) the roasted red pepper. Mushrooms, spinach, chopped ham, prosciutto, cooked chicken, and halved cherry tomatoes come to mind.

The Least You Need to Know

- For quick, low-carb building blocks, head to your deli.
- Crisp vegetables pair beautifully with savory meats in wraps and sandwiches.
- With a microwave, a cooked lunch at the office is minutes away.
- Low-carb and whole-wheat bread and tortillas enable fast, tasty lunch dishes.

Chapter 5

Snack Attack!

In This Chapter

- Snacking your way to a healthful diet
- Nutritional analysis for nuts, fruits, cheeses, and vegetables
- Going nuts is good for you
- Picking your fruit-based snack options

Some people feel bad about their desire to snack, but that desire is natural. Our distant ancestors likely survived on foraging for little bits of food at a time. Of course, in today's society, eating every bit of food we come across (sort of "foraging in the kitchen/office") can get us into trouble. Our distant relatives didn't *also* have three full meals a day.

Although snacking is okay, the challenge is to snack, yet avoid the ultra–high-carb snacks we're surrounded by. All it takes is following some basic steps to avoid digging into that bag of chips:

- Identify low- and good-carb snacks (luckily, that's what this chapter is all about).
- Control portion size. If I have one pound of almonds with me, guess how much I'll end up eating. Instead, pack a reasonable snack in a container or zipper bag. Portion sizes vary according to the food.

Nuts are a very concentrated source of nutrition—a little goes a long way. Vegetables, on the other hand, are largely water, so you can eat a lot more of them to get to a similar nutritional place.

◆ Be sure you have good snacks on hand when you need them.

Go Nuts

Many nuts are terrific low-carb snacks. They have minimal net carbs, are high in fiber and protein, and because of the high fat content, are very satisfying so you might not feel the need to eat a huge amount. Plus, the fats are mostly considered "good" fats (unsaturated or low in saturated fats).

Food	Serving Size	Carbohydrate Count Total	Net
Almonds	1 oz. or ¼ cup	5	1
Cashews	1 oz. or ¼ cup	9	7
Macadamia nuts	1 oz. or ¼ cup	4	1
Peanuts	1 oz. or 3 TB.	5	3
Pecans	1 oz. or ⅓ cup	5	3
Pine nuts	1 oz. or ¼ cup	5	2
Pistachios	1 oz. or ¼ cup shelled or ½ cup with shells	9	6
Pumpkin seeds (Pepitas)	1 oz. or ¼ cup	5	4
Soybeans, roasted	1 oz. or ¼ cup	9	4
Sunflower seeds	1 oz. or 3 TB.	5	2
Walnuts, English	1 oz. or ¼ cup	4	2

 Carb Alert

With all snacks, but especially fruits and nuts, pay close attention to the suggested serving size when measuring out a snack. Otherwise, it's easy to exceed carb limits.

For nuts, 1 ounce equals 30 grams (another common unit of measure on nut packaging). With many nuts, 1 ounce is about ¼ cup.

Say Cheese!

Cheeses are one of my favorite snacks. Long off-limits to people concerned with fat consumption, cheeses are more acceptable—within reason—as a part of a carb-conscious diet because cheeses are terrific sources of protein and have virtually no carbohydrates.

Nevertheless, the "within reason" part refers to the high levels of saturated fat of some of these delicacies. The following cheese varieties are not only low in carbs but also low in fat. Many other cheeses such as blue, Brie, Gouda, and other favorites are also extremely low in carbs but are much higher in saturated fat.

Food	Serving Size	Carbohydrate Count	
		Total	*Net*
Mozzarella (part-skim)	1 oz.	>1	0
Cheddar (low-fat)	1 oz.	>1	0
Monterey Jack (low-fat)	1 oz.	1	1
Swiss (low-fat)	1 oz.	0	0
Cottage (fat-free)	½ cup	5	5
Feta	1 oz.	1	1
Fresh goat's milk	1 oz.	1	1

Vegetable Patch

Fresh vegetables have great texture and flavor and require minimum preparation to make a quick snack.

For serving fresh, raw vegetables as a snack, simply cut the veggies into sticks. Or just eat the whole veggie if you're talking about slender veggies like green beans. If you want some seasoning, start with a sprinkling of salt. For a bit more heft, try a low-carb dressing or even cream cheese.

 **Carb Alert**

Although most vegetables easily fall into the low-carb (or good-carb) category, some veggies, such as beets, corn, peas, and potatoes, fall into the high-carb category. Chances are, if it's starchy, it's high-carb.

The following chart lists some of my favorite low- and good-carb vegetable snacks.

Food	Serving Size	Carbohydrate Count Total	Net
Asparagus	100 g or 6 spears	5	3
Broccoli	150 g or ¼ bunch	8	3
Cabbage	120 g or 1½ cups	8	5
Carrots	80 g or 1 medium carrot	8	6
Celery	110 g or 2 stalks	5	3
Cucumbers	100 g or ½ (8-inch) cucumber	3	2
Cauliflower	100 g or ¼ bunch	5	3
Green beans	110 g or 1 cup	7	3
Lettuce	120 g or 2 cups	4	2
Mushrooms	100 g or 6 medium-size mushrooms	4	3
Radishes	100 g or 8 radishes	3	3
Summer squash	100 g or ½ (8-inch) squash	4	2
Sweet bell peppers	150 g or 1 pepper	7	5
Tomatoes	150 g or 1 tomato	7	6

Fruity Snacks

Fruits can be an important part of the carb-conscious diet. Many fruits are loaded with nutrition and fiber. They are also, of course, natural sources of sugar. For that reason, evaluate which fruit you choose for snacking and keep a close eye on quantity.

Carb Alert

Carefully read the label on dried fruits. Many fruits have added sugar, which moves that snack from "good" to "avoid."

Some fruits are much lower in net carbs (blueberries and other berries), and others are much higher in carbohydrates (like bananas!). This doesn't mean never have fruits, but it does mean you should consume carefully in the context of a carb-conscious diet. Tropical fruits such as mango and banana fall into the relatively high-carb category. Raisins, because of their super-high natural sugar, are not on the suggested list, either.

Food	Serving Size	Carbohydrate Count	
		Total	*Net*
Apples, dried	40 g or about 4 pieces	10	8
Apples, fresh	1 (154 g)	22	17
Applesauce, unsweetened	½ cup	14	13
Apricots, dried	40 g or 5 pieces	22	19
Blueberries	140 g or 1 cup	18	14
Cherries, dried	40 g or about 8	19	18
Cherries, fresh	140 g or 1 cup	22	19
Grapefruit	154 g or ½ grapefruit	16	14
Grapes	138 g or 1½ cups	24	23
Nectarines, dried	40 g or 3 pieces	25	22
Nectarines, fresh	140 g or 1 nectarine	16	14
Olives	15 g or 5 olives	0	0
Oranges	154 g or 1 orange	21	18
Peaches, dried	40 g or 3 pieces	25	22
Peaches, fresh	98 g or 1 peach	10	8
Pears, fresh	166 g or 1 pear	25	21
Prunes, dried	40 g or 4 pieces	26	24
Raspberries	140 g or ¾ cup	29	27
Strawberries, fresh	147 g or 8 medium-size fruit	12	8

To make dried fruit portion control easier, I've used a serving size of 40 grams, a common denominator on dried fruit packaging. The actual number of pieces of fruit will vary according to size; for example, for peaches, 40 grams = 3 pieces; for apricots, 5 pieces.

For more fruity recipes, see Chapter 17.

Favorite Snack Recipes

With all these raw ingredients, the possibilities for delicious, low-carb snacks are almost limitless. Here are just a few of my favorites.

Marinated Olives

Prep time: 2 minutes • Serves: 1

Each serving has: 264 calories • 1 g protein • 0 g animal protein • 1 g vegetable protein • 4 g carbohydrates • 4 g dietary fiber • 0 g net carbohydrates • 32 g fat • 3 g saturated fat • 0 mg cholesterol • 1,758 mg sodium • Exchanges: 6 fat

¼ lb. pitted kalamata olives

1 TB. extra-virgin olive oil

Pinch Italian seasoning

Put olives into a plastic container with a lid, drizzle with olive oil, and sprinkle with Italian seasoning. When it comes time to open that container, you've got a savory snack (with no charge for the visions of Mediterranean countryside that come with the olives). If your olives have pits, a small container for them is not a bad idea.

Variations: Use another variety of olive, such as Nicoise, Mission, Spanish, or a mixture.

 Carbohistory

Olives are a natural low-carb fruit (yes, they're a fruit), and indeed, one of the oldest foods in recorded history. The flavors, distinct for each variety, evoke their regions of origin. Part of the olive's sharp flavor derives from curing, a process that usually includes salt. Black olives are ripe, green olives are unripe fruit. The degree of ripeness will affect flavor and texture, and everyone has his preference.

Tsatsiki (Greek Cucumber Dip)

Prep time: 8 minutes   •   Serves: 2

Each serving has: 130 calories   •   6 g protein   •   6 g animal protein   •   < 1 g vegetable protein   •   10 g carbohydrates   •   1 g dietary fiber   •   9 g net carbohydrates   •   7½ g fat   •   1 g saturated fat   •   3 mg cholesterol   •   622 mg sodium   •   Exchanges: ½ milk, ½ vegetable, 1½ fat

1 cup plain yogurt

1 cucumber, ½ peeled and finely chopped and ½ cut into sticks

1 TB. chopped garlic

1 TB. olive oil

2 tsp. lemon juice

½ tsp. ground black pepper

½ tsp. salt

1 cup crisp raw snow pea pods, stemmed, rinsed, and cut into pieces

1 large celery stalk, rinsed, trimmed, and cut into sticks

In a small container with a lid, mix yogurt, cucumber, garlic, olive oil, lemon juice, pepper, and salt. Place cut pea pods and celery in a larger container. To serve, scoop up tsatsiki with vegetables.

Fresh Jicama Sticks

Prep time: 5 minutes   •   Serves: 4

Each serving has: 46 calories   •   1 g protein   •   0 g animal protein   •   1 g vegetable protein   •   11 g carbohydrates   •   6 g dietary fiber   •   5 g net carbohydrates   •   0 g fat   •   0 g saturated fat   •   0 mg cholesterol   •   0 mg sodium   •   Exchanges: 2 vegetable

1 lb. *jicama*, peeled and sliced into ½ × ½ × 4-inch sticks

Juice of 1 lime

Dash hot red pepper sauce (optional)

Place jicama sticks in a container with a tightly fitting lid and toss with lime juice and hot sauce (if using).

Gourmand's Glossary

Jicama is a juicy, crunchy, sweet, Central American vegetable that is eaten both raw and cooked. It is available in many large grocery stores as well as from specialty vendors.

Grape Tomatoes with Feta and Oil

Prep time: 4 minutes   •   Serves: 2

Each serving has: 207 calories   •   5 g protein   4 g animal protein   •   1 g vegetable protein   •   5 g carbohydrates   •   1 g dietary fiber   •   4 g net carbohydrates   •   21 g fat   •   4 g saturated fat   •   48 mg cholesterol   •   603 mg sodium   •   Exchanges: ½ medium-fat meat, 1 vegetable, 3 fat

1⅓ cup grape tomatoes, each cut in half

2 TB. olive oil

6 TB. crumbled feta cheese

½ tsp. Italian seasoning

Pinch salt and ground black pepper

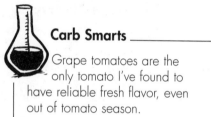

Carb Smarts

Grape tomatoes are the only tomato I've found to have reliable fresh flavor, even out of tomato season.

Place tomato halves in a container with a lid. Drizzle olive oil over, then sprinkle on cheese, Italian seasoning, salt, and pepper, and toss to coat. Later, by the time you get to your snack (say, a couple hours), herbs will have infused tomatoes and feta with delicious flavor.

Variation: Use your favorite Italian or vinaigrette dressing in place of olive oil, salt, and Italian seasoning.

Quick Tapenade

Prep time: 8 minutes   •   Serves: 6

Each serving has: 132 calories   •   1 g protein   •   0 g animal protein   •   1 g vegetable protein   •   4 g carbohydrates   •   2½ g dietary fiber   •   2 g net carbohydrates   •   14 g fat   •   3 g saturated fat   •   0 mg cholesterol   •   383 mg sodium

1 cup pitted kalamata olives

1 cup pitted green olives

¼ cup olive oil

2 scallions, cut into 1-inch segments

1 tsp. chopped garlic

1 tsp. fresh lemon juice

Dash hot pepper sauce

Pinch black pepper

In a food processor, coarsely process kalamata olives, green olives, olive oil, scallions, garlic, lemon juice, hot pepper sauce, and black pepper. Scrape mixture into a bowl (with a lid if it will be transported). Scoop with celery, carrot, and endive as dippers.

Spiced Almonds

Prep time: 5 minutes • Cook time: 8 minutes • Serves: 4 to 6

Each serving has: 275 calories • 10 g protein • 0 g animal protein • 10 g vegetable protein • 9 g carbohydrates • 5 g dietary fiber • 3 g net carbohydrates • 24 g fat • 2 g saturated fat • 0 g cholesterol • 133 mg sodium • Exchanges: 4 fat, 1 high-fat meat

8 oz. (about 2 cups) lightly salted almonds

Canola oil cooking spray

1 TB. *garam masala* or curry powder

Preheat the broiler. Spread almonds out on a baking sheet and spray with cooking spray. Evenly sprinkle nuts with garam masala and broil for 5 to 8 minutes on the next-to-highest rack, stirring frequently, until nuts are toasted. Store in the container or a bag.

Variation: This is also terrific with cashews, peanuts, walnuts, or other nuts.

Gourmand's Glossary

Garam masala is an Indian seasoning mix, rich with cinnamon, pepper, nutmeg, cardamom, and other spices.

Low-Carb Trail Mix

Prep time: 4 minutes • Serves: 4

Each serving has: 251 calories • 6 g protein • 0 g animal protein • 6 g vegetable protein • 27 g carbohydrates • 5 g dietary fiber • 22 g net carbohydrates • 14 g fat • 4 g saturated fat • 0 mg cholesterol • 181 mg sodium • Exchanges: 1½ fruit, 3 fat

⅔ cup (3 oz.) lightly salted peanuts or mixed nuts

⅓ cup dried apricots, cut into ¼-inch pieces

¼ cup bittersweet chocolate chips

Mix peanuts, apricot pieces, and chocolate chips. This will keep in a sealed container for several days. Children love this on road trips.

Variation: Use carob, other nuts, and dried fruits.

Celery and Almond Sauce

Prep time: 5 minutes   •   Serves: 4

Each serving has: 221 calories   •   9 g protein   •   0 g animal protein   •   9 g vegetable protein   •   8 g carbohydrates   •   4 g dietary fiber   •   4 g net carbohydrates   •   18 g fat   •   3 g saturated fat   •   0 mg cholesterol   •   342 mg sodium   •   Exchanges: 1 high-fat meat, 1 vegetable, 1 fat

½ cup natural-style (without sugar) "crunchy" almond or peanut butter

1½ tsp. soy sauce

1½ tsp. sesame oil

Salt to taste (optional)

4 large celery stalks rinsed, trimmed, and cut crosswise into 4 (5 × 1½-inch) sticks

Thoroughly mix nut butter, soy sauce, sesame oil, and salt, if desired, in a small bowl. Spread onto celery sticks and store in the fridge for a couple days in separate small containers with tightly fitting lids.

 Carb Alert _____

Look carefully at peanut butter ingredients. "Natural" peanut butter, found in your grocery store, will list the ingredients as "Peanuts and salt." That's it. Others contain sweeteners, hydrogenated oils, and other not-so-good stuff. In my opinion, the natural-style peanut butter is not only better for you, but it also just plain tastes better.

Marinated Mushrooms

Prep time: 4 minutes   •   Serves: 2

Each serving has: 47 calories   •   4 g protein   •   0 g animal protein   •   4 g vegetable protein   •   5 g carbohydrates   •   1 g dietary fiber   •   4 g net carbohydrates   •   2 g fat   •   0 g saturated fat   •   0 mg cholesterol   •   410 mg sodium   •   Exchanges: 1 vegetable, ½ fat

1 (8-oz.) pkg. sliced white mushrooms   3 TB. Italian dressing (your favorite)

Toss mushrooms with dressing in a sealed container and eat them with a fork.

Mushrooms freshly tossed with this marinade have a pleasant hearty bite. The longer they marinate, the softer and more flavorful they become.

Carb Smarts

Meaty, satisfying mushrooms are another near-perfect low-carb food. Sliced white mushrooms save time, but if you've got an extra minute, slice whole mushrooms yourself for better texture. You can also easily make your own marinade by mixing 1 tablespoon olive oil, 1 teaspoon balsamic or wine vinegar, 1 pinch salt, and ½ teaspoon Italian seasoning, then tossing it into the mushrooms. Additional chopped garlic and other minced vegetables add to the fun.

Gingered Apple and Yogurt

Prep time: 4 minutes • Serves: 2

Each serving has: 130 calories • 6½ g protein • 6½ g animal protein • < 1 g vegetable protein • 23 g carbohydrates • 2 g dietary fiber • 21 g net carbohydrates • 2 g fat • < 1 g saturated fat • 7 mg cholesterol • 87 mg sodium • Exchanges: 1 fruit, ½ low-fat milk

1 fresh, crisp apple such as Fuji or Granny Smith, peeled, cored, and chopped into ¼-inch pieces

1 cup plain yogurt

1 tsp. fresh ginger root, peeled and grated

2 pkg. artificial sweetener (optional)

Mix apple, yogurt, ginger, and sweetener (if using) in a bowl and serve.

Carb Smarts _____

You can find fresh ginger root in the vegetable section of many grocery stores. Its fresh, sweet flavor is unmistakable and very different from the powdered dry stuff in the dry seasonings section. Buy a root, peel it, and keep it in a freezer bag in your freezer. When you need it, simply grate it frozen, and stick the rest back in the freezer for next time.

Frozen Berry Shake

Prep time: 4 minutes • Serves: 2

Each serving has: 115 calories • 6½ g protein • 6½ g animal protein • < 1 g vegetable protein • 18 g carbohydrates • 2 g dietary fiber • 16 g net carbohydrates • 2½ g fat • 1 g saturated fat • 7 mg cholesterol • 86 mg sodium • Exchanges: ½ fruit, ½ low-fat milk

1 cup plain yogurt

1 cup frozen mixed berries

⅓ cup water

2 pkg. artificial sweetener (optional)

Carb Smarts

This delicious shake can pass as dessert, lunch, breakfast, or a snack, depending on the time of day (and the size of your masterpiece).

Put yogurt, berries, water, and sweetener (if using) into a blender and pulse to a creamy consistency. Add a little more water if necessary to facilitate blending. Serve on the veranda with a view of the grounds.

Variations: This shake is delicious made with frozen raspberries, blueberries, and strawberries. If you've got fresh fruit, so much the better! Your shake won't be as cold, but it will be just as irresistible.

The Least You Need to Know

◆ Fresh vegetables require a minimum of prep but bring a wealth of flavor and texture.

◆ For a naturally nutritious, low-carb snack, "go nuts."

◆ Pay close attention to the nutrition label. Serving size is important, as well as other noncarb ingredients.

◆ Cheese is one of the easiest (and oldest) low-carb snacks.

◆ Fruit snacks bring fresh flavors, nutrition, and a hint of sweetness to snack time.

◆ With a bit of knowledge and preparation, quick and tasty low-carb snacks are not only possible, they're easy.

Chapter 6

Low-Carb Appetizers

In This Chapter

◆ Delectable seafood appetizers

◆ Low-carb dips you'll want to meet

◆ Small bites with big flavor

At many social events, the carb-conscious guest is walking in a carbohydrate minefield. Most chips, toasts, and crackers are made with white flour, not to mention hydrogenated oils and other things increasingly identified as potentially harmful.

Don't lose heart! In this chapter, we'll explore a surprisingly wide range of delicious, low-carb appetizers that are better for you and still delicious.

Some of the tasty vegetable snacks and dips from the last few chapters are also great appetizers!

Seafood Appetizers

Seafood appetizers are appealing for a number of reasons. One big part of their appeal is that many of them are (at least to those of us used to salsa and chips) unusual and even elegant. Seafood starters can be incredibly quick and bring fun, unusual flavors to any event.

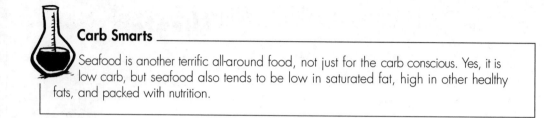

Carb Smarts _____

Seafood is another terrific all-around food, not just for the carb conscious. Yes, it is low carb, but seafood also tends to be low in saturated fat, high in other healthy fats, and packed with nutrition.

Take a Dip

The dip recipes in this chapter are easy, packed with flavor, and just a little bit unusual.

Oh, and for our purposes in this book, a _dip_ is an appetizer fluid enough to be scooped up with a chip or other vehicle. A _spread_ is thicker, better served with a knife for spreading.

Small Bite, Big Flavor

I'll also give you recipes for fast, yet elegant appetizers that take advantage of simple combinations of ingredients. Each brings great flavor, and when they're assembled, they're even better.

For much more on appetizers, check out my book, _The Complete Idiot's Guide to 5-Minute Appetizers_.

Shrimp "Bouquet" with White Cocktail Sauce

Prep time: 15 minutes   •   Serves: 6

Each serving has: 115 calories   •   9 g protein   •   8 g animal protein   •   1 g vegetable protein   •   3 g carbohydrates   •   1 g fiber   •   2 g net carbohydrates   •   10 g fat   •   2 g saturated fat   •   79 mg cholesterol   •   145 mg sodium   •   Exchanges: 1 very-lean meat, ½ vegetable, 2 fat

¼ cup (2 oz.) sour cream

¼ cup mayonnaise

2 TB. prepared horseradish

1 TB. lemon juice

1 tsp. dried dill

Pinch black pepper

Bamboo skewers (about 20)

1 large red bell pepper, cut in half, seeds and ribs removed, and cut into slivers about ¼ × 2 inches

1 large yellow bell pepper, cut in half, seeds and ribs removed, and cut into slivers about ¼ × 2 inches

½ lb. (31 to 40 count) cooked shrimp, tail off

In a bowl, blend sour cream, mayonnaise, horseradish, lemon juice, dill, and black pepper. Onto each skewer, slide a red pepper sliver about 1 inch down from the point, a yellow pepper sliver over that at right angles, forming a cross, and finally stick a shrimp on top, curling into the air. Repeat with other skewers. Arrange these "flowers" in a vase and serve with the sauce for dipping alongside. Stick a real flower in the middle for a grin.

Variation: For a 5-minute appetizer rather than a 15-minute one, omit peppers and just spear shrimp on the ends of skewers.

Carb Smarts

"Medium" shrimp (31 to 40 count) are the perfect size for an appetizer bite. The count refers to the number of shrimp in 1 pound, so 31 count means there are 31 in 1 pound.

Shrimp and Jicama Bites

Prep time: 5 minutes • Serves: 6

Each serving has: 135 calories • 26 g protein • 25 g animal protein • 1 g vegetable protein • 5 g carbohydrates • 3 g fiber • 2 g net carbohydrates • 1½ g fat • ½ g saturated fat • 220 mg cholesterol • 225 mg sodium • Exchanges: 4 very-lean meat, 1 vegetable

8 oz. jicama (about 2 cups), peeled and cut into ¾-inch pieces

½ lb. (31 to 40 count or about 18) cooked shrimp, tail off

1 TB. lime juice

2 TB. fresh chives, chopped

Ground black pepper

Place jicama and shrimp into a mixing bowl, drizzle with lime juice, and toss to coat. With toothpicks, spear first a shrimp and then a piece of jicama and arrange bites on a serving plate. Sprinkle with chives and a sprinkling of black pepper and serve.

Variation: If you can't find jicama, try substituting an equivalent amount of sliced water chestnuts.

Bacon-Wrapped Scallops

Prep time: 10 minutes • Cook time: 4 minutes • Serves: 6

Each serving has: 292 calories • 21 g protein • 21 g animal protein • 0 g vegetable protein • 0 g carbohydrates • 0 g fiber • 0 g net carbohydrates • 20 g fat • 6 g saturated fat • 64 mg cholesterol • 1,047 mg sodium • Exchanges: 1½ very-lean meat, 1½ high-fat meat, 1 fat

½ lb. fresh bay scallops, rinsed and patted dry on paper towels, or ½ lb. fresh sea scallops, cut into quarters

½ lb. bacon, slices cut in quarters (resulting in 1×2-inch pieces)

Toothpicks, soaked in water to minimize chance of burning

Preheat the broiler. Wrap each scallop in a piece of bacon and hold in place with a toothpick. Place bacon-wrapped scallops on a baking tray and broil on the second-from-highest rack for 2 minutes per side or until bacon is crisp and scallops are cooked. Remove to a serving tray and pass with napkins to catch any drips.

Clam Dip

Prep time: 5 minutes   •   Serves: 6

Each serving has: 205 calories   •   15 g protein   •   14 g animal protein   •   1 g vegetable protein   •   4 g carbohydrates   •   2 g fiber   •   2 g net carbohydrates   •   14 g fat   •   7 g saturated fat   •   43 mg cholesterol   •   393 mg sodium   •   Exchanges: 1 very-lean meat, 1 high-fat meat, 1 vegetable, 1 fat

1 (6.5-oz.) can chopped clams, drained, juice reserved

1 cup sour cream

½ pkg. (4 oz.) cream cheese, softened

1 tsp. lemon juice

1 TB. minced onion

1 tsp. Worcestershire sauce

1 sprig parsley

1 lb. celery sticks

In a food processor fitted with a steel blade, process clams, sour cream, cream cheese, lemon juice, onion, and Worcestershire sauce to a creamy consistency. If necessary, add some of the reserved clam juice to loosen up the dip. With a rubber spatula, scrape dip into a serving bowl and garnish with sprig of parsley. Serve with celery sticks (or low-carb tortilla chips, which will increase the good-carb count).

If you think about it ahead of time, put this dip together and let it chill for an hour (or even all day) in the fridge. The flavors will blend.

Salmon Spread with Roasted Red Peppers

Prep time: 5 minutes   •   Serves: 6

Each serving has: 219 calories   •   9 g protein   •   9 g animal protein   •   < 1 g vegetable protein   •   1 g carbohydrates   •   < 1 g fiber   •   0 g net carbohydrates   •   20 g fat   •   5 g saturated fat   •   3 mg cholesterol   •   264 mg sodium   •   Exchanges: 1 very-lean meat, ½ high-fat meat, 3 fat

1 (6-oz.) can pink salmon, drained, skin and bones discarded, if necessary

1 (8-oz.) pkg. cream cheese, softened

½ cup (about 4 oz.) roasted red peppers, rinsed and patted dry on paper towels

¼ cup minced fresh chives

2 TB. olive oil

1 tsp. lemon juice

Additional chives for garnish (optional)

4 *Belgian endive* heads, broken into leaves

In a food processor fitted with a steel blade, process salmon, cream cheese, red peppers, chives, olive oil, and lemon juice to a creamy consistency. With a rubber spatula, scrape spread into a serving bowl and garnish with chives (if using). Place spread in the center of a plate or platter. Arrange endive leaves around the bowl, all pointing outward to create a flower pattern. Serve with a knife to spread.

Variation: Whole-wheat crackers are delicious with this spread. (This raises the good-carb count, though.)

Smoked Salmon–Asparagus Wraps

Prep time: 5 minutes   •   Serves: 4

Each serving has: 44 calories   •   7 g protein   •   6 g animal protein   •   1 g vegetable protein   •   2 g carbohydrates   •   1 g fiber   •   1 g net carbohydrates   •   1 g fat   •   < 1 g saturated fat   •   6 mg cholesterol   •   278 mg sodium   •   Exchanges: 1 very-lean meat, ½ vegetable

1 (4-oz.) pkg. thinly sliced smoked salmon (available in grocery stores), cut into 2 × 3-inch pieces

½ lb. thin (about ⅓ inch across) asparagus spears, bottom half removed for another use, top 3 inches *blanched* for 1 minute

2 TB. lemon juice

Salt to taste (might not be necessary, as smoked salmon is often salty)

1½ tsp. fresh dill or ½ tsp. dried

Lemon "twists" as garnish

Wrap 1 strip smoked salmon around 1 asparagus spear and secure with a toothpick. Arrange spears on a serving plate, drizzle with fresh lemon juice, and sprinkle with salt and dill. Garnish with lemon twists and serve.

Gourmand's Glossary

To **blanch** something is to quickly submerge it in boiling water and then just as quickly douse it (or submerge it) in cool water. Blanching many vegetables enhances color and flavor.

A **lemon "twist"** is an attractive way to garnish an appetizer or other dish. Cut a thin, about ⅛-inch–thick cross-section slice of a lemon. Then take that slice and cut from the center out to the edge of the slice on one side. Pick up the piece of lemon and pull apart the two cut ends in opposite directions.

Warm Artichoke Dip

Prep time: 5 minutes • Cook time: 2 minutes • Serves: 6

Each serving has: 334 calories • 11 g protein • 6 g animal protein • 5 g vegetable protein • 11 g carbohydrates • 10 g fiber • 1 g net carbohydrates • 24 g fat • 12 g saturated fat • 27 mg cholesterol • 349 mg sodium • Exchanges: 1 high-fat meat, 2 vegetable, 3½ fat

1 (14-oz.) can artichoke hearts or pieces, broken into 1-inch pieces	2 scallions, roots and dark green leaves removed, minced
½ cup mayonnaise	Dash hot red pepper sauce
½ cup sour cream or light sour cream	4 Belgian endive heads, broken into leaves
1 cup (½ [8-oz.] pkg.) shredded Swiss cheese	

In a microwave-safe bowl, mix together artichoke, mayonnaise, sour cream, cheese, scallions, and hot pepper sauce. Microwave on high for 2 minutes or until dip begins to bubble and cheese is melted. Stir and serve with endive leaves (or vegetable sticks or low-carb tortilla chips, though tortillas will increase the good-carb count).

 Carbohistory

Chips and dip are one of those ever-present institutions at parties. For those focusing on fat consumption, the dip has always been the problem. For the carb-conscious party guest, the dip is usually fine, but now the chips are suspect. Those crispy dip vehicles quickly add up the carbs. A partial solution is at hand, however. An increasing number of low-carb tortilla and other chips are coming onto the market. The best news is that they taste pretty good. The caution, still, is to watch the number you eat. These chips are low carb, not no carb. The suggested serving is often 1 ounce, or about 15 chips.

Piquant Tuna Dip

Prep time: 5 minutes   •   Serves: 6

Each serving has: 282 calories   •   20 g protein   •   8 g animal protein   •   12 g vegetable protein   •   9 g carbohydrates   •   4 g fiber   •   5 g net carbohydrates   •   20 g fat   •   4 g saturated fat   •   21 mg cholesterol   •   438 mg sodium   •   Exchanges: 1 very-lean meat, ½ starch, 4 fat

1 (6-oz.) can chunk white tuna packed in water, drained

½ cup light sour cream

¼ cup mayonnaise

2 scallions, roots and dark green parts removed, cut into ½-inch pieces

1 TB. lemon juice

½ (1.25-oz.) packet chili seasoning mix

Additional thinly sliced scallions for garnish (optional)

½ (6-oz.) bag low-carb tortilla chips (about 15 chips per person)

In a food processor fitted with a steel blade, process tuna, sour cream, mayonnaise, scallions, lemon juice, and chili seasoning mix until almost smooth. With a rubber spatula, scrape dip into a serving bowl and, if possible, chill for several hours. Garnish with scallion slices (if using) and serve with low-carb tortilla chips.

Variation: Use Belgian endive leaves in place of tortilla chips to lower the carb count.

Quick Tuna Dip

Prep time: 5 minutes • Serves: 6

Each serving has: 177 calories • 12 g protein • 8 g animal protein • 4 g vegetable protein • 13 g carbohydrates • 10 g fiber • 3 g net carbohydrates • 9 g fat • 5 g saturated fat • 29 mg cholesterol • 460 mg sodium • Exchanges: 1 very-lean meat, 1 vegetable, 2 fat

1 (6-oz.) can white tuna packed in water, drained	1 TB. lemon juice (fresh, if possible)
1 cup sour cream	Pinch ground black pepper
1 (.53-oz.) pkg. vegetable soup mix	4 Belgian endive heads, broken into leaves

Using a fork, mix together tuna, sour cream, vegetable soup mix, lemon juice, and pepper in a serving bowl, breaking up any large tuna chunks. Chill for 1 hour or so to allow the flavors to blend. Serve with Belgian endive leaves as dippers.

Variation: Use canned salmon, skin and bones removed if necessary, in place of tuna.

Carb Smarts

Chilling soup-mix recipes gives those dried ingredients time to absorb moisture and time for the flavors to spread. If you need that flavor in a hurry, though, accelerate the process by putting the soup mix in a microwave-safe bowl, stirring in 2 tablespoons water, and heating for 15 seconds. Then mix the soup mix into the dip. The heat and moisture will help the flavors spread.

Quick Spinach Dip

Prep time: 5 minutes • Serves: 6

Each serving has: 193 calories • 12 g protein • 6 g animal protein • 6 g vegetable protein • 15 g carbohydrates • 12 g fiber • 3 g net carbohydrates • 8 g fat • 6 g saturated fat • 23 mg cholesterol • 355 mg sodium • Exchanges: 1 very-lean meat, ½ medium-fat meat, 1 vegetable, 2 fat

1 (10-oz.) pkg. frozen chopped spinach, thawed and squeezed dry

1 cup sour cream

½ cup fat-free small curd cottage cheese

½ cup shredded Parmesan cheese

½ tsp. garlic salt

Dash hot red pepper sauce

4 Belgian endive heads, broken into leaves

Thoroughly mix spinach, sour cream, cottage cheese, Parmesan cheese, salt, and hot pepper sauce in a serving bowl. Serve with Belgian endive leaves for a low-carb appetizer.

Variation: For a slightly higher-carb appetizer, serve with low-carb tortilla chips.

 Carb Alert

To my taste, fat-free cottage cheese is a good alternative to regular cottage cheese. Light cream cheese, light sour cream, and light mayonnaise are also good options. The taste (and texture), however, are so different in the *fat-free* versions of cream cheese, sour cream, or mayonnaise that I do not recommend them.

Garden Salsa

Prep time: 5 minutes • Serves: 6

Each serving has: 170 calories • 12 g protein • 0 g animal protein • 12 g vegetable protein • 13 g carbohydrates • 5 g fiber • 8 g net carbohydrates • 8 g fat • 1 g saturated fat • 0 g cholesterol • 629 mg sodium • Exchanges: 1½ vegetable, ½ starch, 2 fat

2 large (about 8 oz.) fresh tomatoes, rinsed, cored, seeded, and chopped into ¼-inch pieces

½ cup sweet onion, such as Vidalia, peeled and chopped into ¼-inch pieces

1 (4.5-oz.) can chopped green chilies, drained

¼ cup chopped fresh cilantro

2 TB. lime juice

2 TB. red wine vinegar

1 tsp. kosher salt

1½ tsp. fresh oregano or ½ tsp. dried

¼ tsp. hot red pepper sauce

½ (6-oz.) bag low-carb tortilla chips (about 15 chips per person)

Carb Smarts

When tomatoes are in season, use fresh tomatoes in this salsa for delicious flavor. I've adapted this classic from Marion Cunningham's *Fanny Farmer Cookbook*.

In a serving bowl, combine tomatoes, onion, chilies, cilantro, lime juice, vinegar, salt, oregano, and hot pepper sauce. Serve with low-carb chips or as a topping on other Mexican-style dishes.

Fresh salsa is best eaten soon after it's made, but it will survive in the fridge for a day or two.

Guacamole

Prep time: 5 minutes • Serves: 6

Each serving has: 311 calories • 14 g protein • 1 g animal protein • 13 g vegetable protein • 15 g carbohydrates • 8 g fiber • 7 g net carbohydrates • 23 g fat • 6 g saturated fat • 13 mg cholesterol • 401 mg sodium • Exchanges: ½ vegetable, ½ starch, 5 fat

2 ripe avocados

¾ cup sour cream

1 small fresh tomato, rinsed, cored, seeded, and chopped into ¼-inch pieces

3 TB. lemon juice

1 tsp. chopped garlic

½ tsp. salt

¼ tsp. hot red pepper sauce

½ (6-oz.) bag low-carb tortilla chips (about 15 chips per person)

Cut avocados in half lengthwise and discard pits. Scoop out flesh into a bowl and add sour cream, tomato, lemon juice, garlic, salt, and hot pepper sauce. Mix with a fork to a chunky consistency. Serve with low-carb tortilla chips.

White Bean Dip

Prep time: 5 minutes • Serves: 8

Each serving has: 150 calories • 7 g protein • 1 g animal protein • 6 g vegetable protein • 18 g carbohydrates • 10 g fiber • 8 g net carbohydrates • 6½ g fat • 4 g saturated fat • 13 mg cholesterol • 410 mg sodium • Exchanges: ½ starch, 1 vegetable, 1½ fat

1 (15-oz.) can cannellini (white kidney) beans, drained and rinsed

1 cup sour cream or light sour cream

1 small fresh tomato, rinsed, cored, seeded, and quartered

½ (4.5-oz.) can chopped green chilies, drained

3 TB. olive oil

1½ TB. chopped garlic

1 tsp. Italian seasoning

½ tsp. salt

4 Belgian endive heads, broken into leaves

In a food processor fitted with a steel blade, process beans, sour cream, tomato, chilies, olive oil, garlic, Italian seasoning, and salt until smooth. With a rubber spatula, scrape dip into a serving bowl and chill for 1 hour to allow the flavors to blend. Serve surrounded by endive leaves.

Olive Spread

Prep time: 5 minutes • Serves: 6

Each serving has: 216 calories • 6 g protein • 2 g animal protein • 4 g vegetable protein • 14 g carbohydrates • 11 g fiber • 3 g net carbohydrates • 17 g fat • 3 g saturated fat • 2 mg cholesterol • 242 mg sodium • Exchanges: 1 vegetable, ½ medium-fat meat, 3 fat

1 (6-oz.) can pitted ripe black olives, drained	¼ cup chopped fresh parsley
¼ cup chopped walnuts or pine nuts (toasted if possible)	1 TB. chopped garlic
	½ tsp. salt
¼ cup shredded Parmesan cheese	¼ tsp. ground black pepper
¼ cup olive oil	4 Belgian endive heads, broken into leaves

In a food processor fitted with a steel blade, process olives, walnuts, Parmesan cheese, olive oil, parsley, garlic, salt, and pepper just enough to pulverize olives but leaving plenty of texture. With a rubber spatula, scrape spread into a serving bowl and serve surrounded by endive leaves (and surrounded by images in your mind of the Tuscan countryside).

Ricotta Dip with Sun-Dried Tomatoes

Prep time: 5 minutes • Serves: 6

Each serving has: 134 calories • 7 g protein • 5 g animal protein • 2 g vegetable protein • 8 g carbohydrates • 2 g fiber • 6 g net carbohydrates • 10 g fat • 3 g saturated fat • 13 mg cholesterol • 159 mg sodium • Exchanges: 1 medium-fat meat, 1½ vegetable, 2 fat

1 cup (8 oz.) part-skim milk ricotta cheese	1 TB. chopped chives for garnish (optional)
½ cup oil-packed sun-dried tomatoes, drained, with 2 TB. oil reserved	2 large carrots, scraped, quartered lengthwise, and cut in half to form 4-inch sticks
¼ tsp. garlic salt	2 small cucumbers, scraped, quartered lengthwise, and cut in half to form 4-inch sticks
Dash hot red pepper sauce	

In a food processor fitted with a steel blade, process ricotta, tomatoes and oil, garlic salt, and hot sauce until almost smooth but with visible tomato pieces remaining. With a rubber spatula, scrape dip into a serving bowl, sprinkle with chives (if using), and serve surrounded by carrot and cucumber sticks.

Prosciutto-Artichoke Bites

Prep time: 5 minutes • Cook time: 3 minutes • Serves: 6

Each serving has: 73 calories • 4 g protein • 2 g animal protein • 2 g vegetable protein • 8 g carbohydrates • 4 g fiber • 4 g net carbohydrates • 4 g fat • 1 g saturated fat • 3 mg cholesterol • 397 mg sodium • Exchanges: ⅓ medium-fat meat, 1 vegetable, ½ fat

1 (14-oz.) can artichoke bottoms (about 6 bottoms), drained

⅓ cup diced prosciutto

⅓ cup shredded Parmesan cheese

1 TB. olive oil

½ tsp. dried oregano

Preheat the broiler. Arrange artichoke bottoms on a baking tray, concave side up, and distribute diced prosciutto among artichoke bottoms, spreading prosciutto to cover bottoms. Distribute Parmesan cheese over prosciutto. Drizzle each artichoke with olive oil and dust with a pinch of oregano. Broil on the high rack for 3 minutes or until cheese begins to melt and oil bubbles.

For a sit-down appetizer, serve one bottom on a plate with a knife and fork. For a stand-up appetizer, cut each bottom into quarters and serve on a platter with toothpicks.

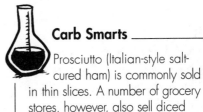

Carb Smarts

Prosciutto (Italian-style salt-cured ham) is commonly sold in thin slices. A number of grocery stores, however, also sell diced prosciutto, which is often less expensive than the sliced version.

Endive-Chevre Bites

Prep time: 5 minutes • Serves: 6

Each serving has: 174 calories • 10 g protein • 6 g animal protein • 4 g vegetable protein • 10 g carbohydrates • 8 g fiber • 2 g net carbohydrates • 11 g fat • 6 g saturated fat • 22 mg cholesterol • 229 mg sodium • Exchanges: 1 high-fat meat, 1 vegetable, ½ fat

6 oz. fresh *chevre*, softened

3 TB. toasted pine nuts

1 TB. lemon juice

½ tsp. Italian seasoning

¼ tsp. ground black pepper

3 Belgian endives, broken into leaves

5 to 6 lemon slices

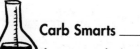

Carb Smarts

If you can't find toasted pine nuts in your grocery store, simply spread raw pine nuts on a baking tray in a single layer and broil for 2 to 3 minutes or until just beginning to tan.

Mix chevre, pine nuts, lemon juice, Italian seasoning, and pepper in a bowl and, if possible, chill for 1 hour to let flavors spread. Place about 1 teaspoon herbed chevre on the thick end of each large Belgian endive leaf and arrange leaves in concentric circles, filling side in, on a large platter. Sprinkle with more black pepper, place 1 lemon slice in the center of the platter and others around the perimeter, and serve.

Quick Low-Carb Bruschetta

Prep time: 5 minutes   •   Cook time: 4-5 minutes   •   Serves: 6

Each serving has: 136 calories   •   2 g protein   •   1 g animal protein   •   2 g vegetable protein   •   15 g carbohydrates   •   7 g fiber   •   8 g net carbohydrates   •   8 g fat   •   1½ g saturated fat   •   2 mg cholesterol   •   96 mg sodium   •   Exchanges: ½ starch, ½ vegetable, 2 fat

6 slices low-carb bread	1 tsp. dried oregano
3 TB. olive oil	¼ cup shredded Parmesan cheese
1 TB. chopped garlic	Ground black pepper
½ cup roasted red peppers, cut into 1-inch pieces	Kosher salt

Preheat the broiler. Cut each slice of bread on the diagonal, resulting in 4 triangles per slice. In a small bowl, mix olive oil and garlic. Arrange bread triangles on a baking tray and brush each triangle with garlicky olive oil. Broil for 2 minutes on the high rack or until bread begins to tan and crisp. Remove tray from broiler and top each triangle with a piece of red pepper, a pinch oregano, and a sprinkling of Parmesan cheese. Broil for 2 minutes or until cheese begins to melt. Remove to a platter, sprinkle with pepper and salt, and serve.

Variation: Use ½ cup mozzarella in place of the ¼ cup Parmesan for a more pizzalike dish. Use whole-wheat bread in place of the low-carb bread, although this will increase the good-carb count.

Broiled Mushroom Caps with Fresh Mozzarella

Prep time: 5 minutes • Cook time: 5 minutes • Serves: 6

Each serving has: 76 calories • 6 g protein • 5 g animal protein • 1 g vegetable protein • 2 g carbohydrates • 1 g fiber • 1 g net carbohydrates • 6 g fat • 2 g saturated fat • 12 mg cholesterol • 303 mg sodium • Exchanges: ½ medium-fat meat, ½ vegetable, ½ fat

1 (8-oz.) pkg. small white mushrooms, stems removed and wiped with damp paper towels

3 TB. olive oil

1 cup fresh small mozzarella balls (about 4 oz.), each ball cut in half, or larger balls cut into ½-inch pieces

½ tsp. Italian seasoning

½ tsp. salt

¼ tsp. ground black pepper

Preheat the broiler. Arrange mushroom caps, cap up, on a baking tray, brush caps with some oil (about 1 tablespoon), and broil for 2 minutes on the high rack. Remove the tray from the broiler and flip caps. Insert ½ mozzarella ball into each mushroom cap cavity. Drizzle mushrooms with remaining oil and sprinkle with Italian seasoning, salt, and pepper. Broil for 3 minutes or until filling is beginning to bubble. Arrange stuffed mushrooms on a platter and serve.

The Least You Need to Know

♦ Most seafoods make fast, delicious low-carb appetizers.

♦ Vegetables make terrific low-carb dippers for dips and spreads.

♦ Hot appetizers can be fast and easy if you stick to the right methods (such as broiling and using the microwave).

♦ Take full advantage of elegant matches for fast, tasty, low-carb appetizers (such as artichokes and prosciutto or mushrooms and mozzarella).

Part **2**

And for Dinner ...

Part 2 gets us to the dinner table with savory, fun, and sometimes even elegant carb-conscious meals. We start in Chapter 7 with a tempting array of seafood recipes. In Chapter 8, we learn that poultry and pork are not only versatile and delicious foods, but are also quick-cooking low-carb resources for the busy cook. In Chapter 9, we sink our teeth into rich, satisfying (and still low-carb!) red-meat–based recipes. Chapters 10 and 11 take us on a whirlwind good-carb tour with beans, a truly magical food, and vegetarian cuisine—both important elements of healthy diets across the globe. Finally, not to forget kids at the table, we'll have some fun in Chapter 12 with tasty recipes that appeal to kids when you need to feed the family but want to stick to your carb-conscious diet.

Chapter 7

Fish Food

In This Chapter

- ◆ Seafood as part of a healthy diet
- ◆ Ten-minute seafood entrées
- ◆ Good-for-you fish dishes
- ◆ Shellfish recipes

For the carb-conscious cook in a hurry, seafood is about as close to the perfect food as you can get. It is increasingly recognized as a tremendous source of healthy fats and protein and, for our purposes, very few carbohydrates.

And it's hard to beat the appeal of fresh seafood's delicate flavor. Those flavors vanish with too much heat, so the smart cook is "limited" to quick cooking. But that's perfect! The quick methods I use in this book, such as broiling, poaching, sautéing, grilling, and even microwave cooking, are just what we want. Heavy seasoning also smothers those delicate flavors. In this chapter, you'll see that a light touch is a hallmark of the quick (but skilled) cook!

Fish

This section explores some of the wide range of low-carb fish dishes that can be prepared in short order. From lightning fast to slightly more elegant (but still quick), some of my favorite fish-based recipes are in this chapter.

Carb Alert _____

Fresh fish is one situation where you *want* dinner to stare back at you. Fresh fish will have clear, glassy eyes. Less-fresh fish will have cloudy eyes. Buy the freshest seafood you can find, with a faint, pleasant briny smell. (Avoid anything that "smells fishy"!)

Nifty Shellfish

Shellfish, with their delicate flavor, quick-cooking characteristics, and nutrition, are perfect starting points for the carb-conscious cook in a hurry. I'll give you some favorite shellfish recipes in this chapter.

Carbohistory _____

Increased demand for seafood has resulted in the depletion of some wild fish and increased farming (with some reports of chemical contamination). When shopping for fresh fish, find a vendor you trust, seek out varieties with supplies that are stable, and, if purchasing farmed fish, do some homework to reassure yourself that the source has tested their product.

As of this writing, recommended seafood include the following:

- Catfish (farmed)
- Caviar (farmed)
- Clams (farmed)
- Crab, Dungeness, snow (Canada), or stone
- Halibut, Pacific
- Lobster, spiny/rock (United States, Australia)
- Mussels (farmed)
- Oysters (farmed)
- Salmon (canned or wild-caught)
- Sardines
- Shrimp/prawns (trap-caught)
- Striped bass (farmed)
- Sturgeon (farmed)
- Tilapia (farmed)
- Trout, rainbow (farmed)
- Tuna, albacore/yellowfin/bigeye (troll/pole-caught)

(Source: Seafood Watch, www.montereybayaquarium.com/cr/seafoodwatch.asp)

Microwave Wine-Poached Salmon

Prep time: 4 minutes • Cook time: 5 minutes • Serves: 4

Each serving has: 312 calories • 34 g protein • 34 g animal protein • 0 g vegetable protein • 0 g carbohydrates • 0 g dietary fiber • 0 g net carbohydrates • 26 g fat • 5 g saturated fat • 98 mg cholesterol • 102 mg sodium • Exchanges: 5 lean meat, 2 fat

1½ lb. salmon fillets (number of fillets will vary depending upon the size of fish)

2 TB. olive oil

2 TB. white wine

1 TB. lemon juice

1½ tsp. chopped fresh oregano or ½ tsp. dried

Ground black pepper and salt

Lemon wedges to garnish

Thoroughly rinse fillets in cold water, pat dry with paper towels, and place into a microwaveable casserole dish with a lid. Pour olive oil, wine, and lemon juice over fish and turn to coat. Sprinkle salmon with oregano, pepper, and salt. Cover and cook on high for 4 to 6 minutes or until done, turning once or twice if your microwave does not have a turntable (times vary depending on microwave power). Serve with lemon wedges.

Variations: Replace white wine, lemon juice, oregano, and black pepper with 2 tablespoons teriyaki sauce. Or if you're a sauce fan like me, make a quick sauce out of wine cooking liquid (after removing cooked salmon) by stirring in 2 or 3 tablespoons light sour cream. Drizzle that nectar over salmon.

Carb Alert

Fish "leather" might be a new idea for shoes, but that appeal doesn't apply to dinner. Watch fish carefully in the microwave to avoid tough, overcooked fish. Remove fish from the microwave when the flesh is just barely white (or light salmon, in the case of salmon).

Broiled Haddock with Mozzarella

Prep time: 5 minutes   •   Cook time: 6 minutes   •   Serves: 4

Each serving has: 260 calories   •   39 g protein   •   39 g animal protein   •   0 g vegetable protein   •   0 g carbohydrates   •   0 g dietary fiber   •   0 g net carbohydrates   •   13 g fat   •   4 g saturated fat   •   115 mg cholesterol   •   2,916 mg sodium   •   Exchanges: 5 very-lean meat, 1 high-fat meat, 1½ fat

1½ lb. haddock or other whitefish fillets (number of fillets will vary depending upon the size of fish)	½ tsp. ground cumin
	½ tsp. ground black pepper
	Pinch salt
2 TB. lemon juice	1 cup (4 oz.) shredded part-skim milk mozzarella cheese
2 TB. olive oil	
1½ tsp. chopped fresh oregano or ½ tsp. dried	Lemon wedges as garnish

Preheat the broiler. Thoroughly rinse fillets in cold water and pat dry with paper towels. Place fillets into an oven-proof baking dish, skin side down, in a single layer. Mix lemon juice, oil, and oregano and drizzle over haddock. Turn to coat both sides, but return to skin side down. Sprinkle fillet with cumin, black pepper, and salt and broil on the next-to-highest rack for 5 minutes or until flesh has just barely turned opaque. Drizzle fish with any remaining liquid from the dish, sprinkle with mozzarella, and broil on the next-to-highest rack for 1 minute more or until cheese is melted. Serve with lemon wedges.

Variation: Other white fish fillets, such as cod, halibut or tilapia, will work well with this method.

Pan-Seared Cod with Toasted Almond Sauce

Prep time: 5 minutes • Cook time: 6 minutes • Serves: 4

Each serving has: 370 calories • 36 g protein • 31 g animal protein • 5 g vegetable protein • 5 g carbohydrates • 2 g dietary fiber • 3 g net carbohydrates • 25 g fat • 3½ g saturated fat • 74 mg cholesterol • 116 mg sodium • Exchanges: 5 very-lean meat, 4 fat

3 TB. butter or olive oil

1½ lb. cod fillets (number of fillets will vary depending upon the size of fish)

½ tsp. ground black pepper

¾ cup sliced almonds

⅓ cup light sour cream

2 TB. light cream

1 TB. cognac or brandy (optional)

Pinch salt

Heat butter in a large skillet over medium heat. Thoroughly rinse fillets in cold water, pat dry with paper towels, and sprinkle both sides with black pepper. Cook in a skillet (a spatter screen is a good idea) for 3 minutes per side or until done. Remove fish to a warm plate and cover with foil to keep warm. Turn the heat to high and add almonds to remaining butter in the skillet. If necessary, add a little more butter to prevent burning. Cook, stirring rapidly, for 1 minute or until nuts begin to brown lightly. Turn off heat. Add sour cream, light cream, cognac (if using), and salt and stir. Distribute fish to serving plates and distribute toasted almond sauce along with each plate.

Variation: Other whitefish fillets, such as halibut, tilapia, or haddock, will also work well with this method.

Tuna-Stuffed Tomatoes

Prep time: 5 minutes • Cook time: 10 minutes • Serves: 4

Each serving has: 218 calories • 16 g protein • 15 g animal protein • 1 g vegetable protein • 6 g carbohydrates • 1 g dietary fiber • 5 g net carbohydrates • 16 g fat • 2 g saturated fat • 28 mg cholesterol • 622 mg sodium • Exchanges: 1½ very-lean meat, ½ medium-fat meat, 1 vegetable, 2½ fat

1 (6-oz.) can chunk white tuna in water, drained

½ cup celery, chopped into ¼-inch chunks (about ½ stalk)

½ cup water-packed artichoke hearts, drained and chopped into ¼ inch pieces

¼ cup real mayonnaise

¼ cup toasted pine nuts

1 TB. freshly squeezed lemon juice

1 tsp. Italian seasoning

Dash hot pepper sauce

½ tsp. salt

Pinch freshly ground black pepper

4 medium-size tomatoes (about baseball size), top ½ inch removed, insides scooped out and discarded

½ cup shredded mozzarella cheese

In a bowl, mix tuna, celery, artichoke pieces, mayonnaise, pine nuts, lemon juice, Italian seasoning, hot pepper sauce, salt, and pepper. Stuff each tomato with an equal amount of tuna salad and arrange tomatoes in a microwave- and oven-safe dish. Preheat the broiler. Microwave on high for 4 minutes or until filling is hot, turning once or twice if your microwave does not have a turntable (times vary depending on microwave power). Remove tomatoes from the microwave, top each with shredded cheese, and slide under the broiler for 3 minutes or until cheese is melted and bubbling.

Sole Amandine

Prep time: 5 minutes • Cook time: 10 minutes • Serves: 4

Each serving has: 224 calories • 32 g protein • 30 g animal protein • 2 g vegetable protein • 2 g carbohydrates • 1 g dietary fiber • 1 g net carbohydrates • 10 g fat • 4 g saturated fat • 94 mg cholesterol • 224 mg sodium • Exchanges: 5 very-lean meat, 1½ fat

1½ lb. whitefish fillets (such as sole, cod, or haddock) (number of fillets will vary depending upon the size of fish)

2 TB. lemon juice

Pinch salt

Pinch ground black pepper

¼ cup heavy or whipping cream

¼ cup sliced almonds

Preheat your oven to 350°F. Thoroughly rinse fillets in cold water, pat dry with paper towels, and set into a baking dish. Drizzle with lemon juice and sprinkle with salt and pepper. Spread cream and then almonds over fillets. Bake for 10 minutes or until fish is cooked and divide among serving plates.

Serve with steamed green beans and a glass of dry white wine, and enjoy life.

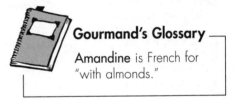

Gourmand's Glossary

Amandine is French for "with almonds."

Broiled Soy Salmon

Prep time: 10 minutes • Cook time: 8 minutes • Serves: 4

Each serving has: 314 calories • 34 g protein • 34 g animal protein • < 1 g vegetable protein • 0 g carbohydrates • 0 g dietary fiber • 0 g net carbohydrates • 26 g fat • 5 g saturated fat • 98 mg cholesterol • 775 mg sodium • Exchanges: 5 lean meat, 1½ fat

2 TB. olive oil

3 TB. soy sauce

1½ lb. salmon fillet (number of fillets will vary depending upon the size of fish)

3 scallions, roots and dark green parts removed, sliced into very thin rings

Preheat the broiler. Mix olive oil and soy sauce in a bowl. Thoroughly rinse fillets in cold water, pat dry with paper towels, and put into an oven-proof baking dish. Pour oil-soy sauce mixture over fillets, turning fish to coat both sides. Broil for 4 minutes, skin side up, then turn and sprinkle with scallion slices. Broil for another 4 minutes or until flesh just turns opaque and distribute to serving plates.

Variation: You can also prepare this salmon dish on an indoor or outdoor grill, although you'll need to take care not to lose your scallion slices.

Grilled Southwest Tuna Steaks

Prep time: 10 minutes • Cook time: 10 minutes • Serves: 4

Each serving has: 300 calories • 45 g protein • 45 g animal protein • 0 g vegetable protein • 0 g carbohydrates • 0 g dietary fiber • 0 g net carbohydrates • 13 g fat • 2 g saturated fat • 88 mg cholesterol • 349 g sodium • Exchanges: 6 very-lean meat, 2 fat

1½ lb. tuna steaks (number of fillets will vary depending upon the size of fish)	½ tsp. ground cumin
	½ tsp. ground black pepper
Juice of ½ lime	½ tsp. chili powder
3 TB. olive oil	½ tsp. salt

Start up the grill. Thoroughly rinse steaks in cold water and pat dry with paper towels. Put tuna steaks into a dish, drizzle with lime juice and then oil, turning to coat all sides. Mix cumin, pepper, chili powder, and salt in a cup and sprinkle over steaks, turning to coat all sides. Grill for 4 minutes per side or until barely done (fish will continue to cook after you remove it from heat).

Variation: For a less-intense seasoning, omit cumin. Other fish steaks, such as halibut, salmon, or shark, will work well with this method, too.

Carb Alert

Some people prefer to cook tuna for a much shorter period of time, say 2 minutes per side, resulting in a rare pink interior. The flavor of tuna prepared this way is delicious; however, you'll need to be comfortable with the increased risk of consuming uncooked fish.

Salmon Burgers with Lemon-Caper Mayonnaise

Prep time: 5 minutes • Cook time: 8 minutes • Serves: 4

Each serving has: 309 calories • 36 g protein • 33 g animal protein • 3 g vegetable protein • 7 g carbohydrates • 3 g dietary fiber • 4 g net carbohydrates • 15 g fat • 4 g saturated fat • 94 mg cholesterol • 880 mg sodium • Exchanges: 5 lean meat, 1 fat

4 (6-oz.) cans pink salmon meat, drained, skin and bones discarded, if necessary	½ tsp. salt
3 scallions, roots and dark green tops removed, minced	¼ tsp. ground black pepper
	3 TB. whole-wheat flour
2 tsp. olive oil	3 TB. *unprocessed bran*
½ tsp. dried dill	Lemon-Caper Mayonnaise (recipe follows)

Thoroughly chop salmon meat and combine in a bowl with scallion, olive oil, dill, salt, and pepper. Form into four patties. Spread flour and bran on a plate and roll burger to thoroughly coat.

Gourmand's Glossary

Unprocessed bran is a wheat product useful for its crunchy texture, similar in usage in this recipe to breadcrumbs. Yet instead of containing carbs and preservatives, it brings vitamins and fiber. Not a bad trade! Find it near the hot cereals in most grocery stores.

Heat a nonstick skillet over medium heat and cook burger for 3 minutes per side or until cooked and coating is crisp. Serve with Lemon-Caper Mayonnaise.

Variation: Fresh dill is even better than dried dill. Use 1 teaspoon if you're going with fresh. You can substitute breadcrumbs for bran, although this will increase the carb count. Also, this is the world's best use for leftover salmon (be sure to remove skin and bones and break fish into small pieces). If you've got fresh skinless salmon, so much the better than canned (prep and cooking will take a bit longer, though).

Lemon-Caper Mayonnaise

Prep time: 5 minutes • Cook time: 8 minutes • Serves: 2 (double as necessary)

Each serving has: 102 calories • 0 g protein • 0 g animal protein • 0 g vegetable protein • 0 g carbohydrates • 0 g dietary fiber • 0 g net carbohydrates • 24 g fat • 1 g saturated fat • 2 mg cholesterol • 164 mg sodium • Exchanges: 5 fat

¼ cup mayonnaise	⅛ tsp. dried dill
1 TB. small capers, drained and rinsed	Pinch ground black pepper
1½ tsp. lemon juice	

Mix mayonnaise, capers, lemon juice, dill, and pepper in a bowl. Keep refrigerated until use.

Rosemary-Lemon Halibut

Prep time: 5 minutes • Cook time: 8 minutes • Serves: 4

Each serving has: 200 calories • 30 g protein • 30 g animal protein • 0 g vegetable protein • 0 g carbohydrates • 0 g dietary fiber • 0 g net carbohydrates • 9 g fat • 1 g saturated fat • 73 mg cholesterol • 92 mg sodium • Exchanges: 5 very-lean meat, 1½ fat

1½ lb. halibut steaks (usually about 2 steaks)	½ tsp. Italian seasoning
Juice of ½ lemon	½ tsp. salt
2 TB. olive oil	½ tsp. ground black pepper
1 TB. fresh chopped rosemary or 1 tsp. dried	Fresh parsley (optional)

Preheat the broiler. Thoroughly rinse steaks in cold water and pat dry with paper towels. Put halibut steaks into an oven-proof baking dish and drizzle with lemon juice and then oil, turning to coat all sides. Sprinkle rosemary, Italian seasoning, salt, pepper, and parsley (if using) over all sides of the steaks. Broil on the second-from-the-top rack for 4 minutes per side or until flesh has just barely turned opaque.

Variation: Halibut steaks can also be grilled. Other whitefish fillets, such as cod, haddock, and even sole, will also work with this method under the broiler, although thinner cuts will cook much more quickly.

Carb Smarts

Watch these broiling steaks carefully, and remove them quickly so they don't dry out.

Many versions of Italian seasoning contain rosemary. This recipe, with its additional rosemary, doubles that delicious flavor.

Crisp Fried Haddock

Prep time: 8 minutes • Cook time: 6 minutes • Serves: 4

Each serving has: 315 calories • 35 g protein • 31 g animal protein • 4 g vegetable protein • 11 g carbohydrates • 3 g dietary fiber • 8 g net carbohydrates • 16 g fat • 2 g saturated fat • 74 mg cholesterol • 642 mg sodium • Exchanges: 5 very-lean meat, ½ starch, 3 fat

1½ lb. haddock or other whitefish fillets (number of fillets will vary according to the size of fish)

⅓ cup unprocessed bran

⅓ cup whole-wheat flour

½ tsp. salt

1 tsp. Italian seasoning

½ cup milk

¼ cup olive oil

Lemon wedges

Thoroughly rinse fillets in cold water and pat dry with paper towels. Mix bran, flour, salt, and Italian seasoning in a bowl and spread mixture on a plate. Pour milk into a bowl, dip fillets in milk, and then dredge them in flour, turning to coat all sides. Heat oil in a large skillet over medium heat. Place fillets in the skillet and cook for 3 minutes per side or until cooked through. Serve with lemon wedges.

 Carb Alert

You'll note that the recipes in this chapter do not include breading for fried fish. That breading includes ... bread, and often lots of it. Keep that in mind the next time you're in a restaurant as well. A nice piece of broiled fish will taste a lot better than a deep-fried one, as well as be better for you. Of course, when the ingredients are under your control, you can be creative, such as using unprocessed bran.

Quick Fish Chowder

Prep time: 5 minutes • Cook time: 15 minutes • Serves: 6

Each serving has: 187 calories • 25 g protein • 24 g animal protein • 1 g vegetable protein • 6 g carbohydrates • 1 g dietary fiber • 5 g net carbohydrates • 7 g fat • 3½ g saturated fat • 57 mg cholesterol • 208 mg sodium • Exchanges: 3½ very-lean meat, ½ skim milk, 1 fat

1½ lb. white fish, such as flounder, cod, haddock, sole, or tilapia

3 slices bacon, cooked and crumbled

1 medium onion, peeled and chopped into ½-inch chunks

2 cups milk

½ cup light cream

½ cup fresh parsley, finely chopped (optional)

Salt and ground black pepper

Thoroughly rinse fillets in cold water and pat dry with paper towels. Cook bacon in a large saucepan or skillet over medium heat until crispy and fat is rendered. Remove bacon and save it on a paper-towel–lined plate. Drain most of the fat from the skillet, leaving just enough to coat the bottom. Add onion to the skillet and cook for 5 minutes, stirring. Add milk and heat until barely beginning to boil; then add fish. Cook for 3 to 4 minutes, stirring occasionally, until fish is opaque and flakes easily. Add cream and parsley (if using), and heat for 1 minute, stirring. Ladle into serving bowls, crumbling bacon over each bowl, and serve, salting to taste and seasoning generously with pepper.

Variation: Without parsley, this chunky chowder is white and creamy. With parsley, fresh greens add texture, color, and flavor.

Carb Alert _____

Whenever the words *milk* and *boil* appear in the same sentence, that's an alert to watch closely! Milk boils over easily, creating a big, hard-to-clean mess.

Sautéed Shrimp and Artichokes

Prep time: 4 minutes   •   Cook time: 5 minutes   •   Serves: 4

Each serving has: 240 calories   •   27 g protein   •   25 g animal protein   •   2 g vegetable protein   •   6 g carbohydrates   •   3 g dietary fiber   •   3 g net carbohydrates   •   13 g fat   •   2 g saturated fat   •   223 mg cholesterol   •   607 mg sodium   •   Exchanges: 4 very-lean meat, 1 vegetable, 2 fat

3 TB. olive oil	1 lb. (31 to 40 count) cooked shrimp, tail off
1 (9-oz.) pkg. frozen artichoke hearts, thawed	½ tsp. kosher salt
1 tsp. Italian seasoning	2 TB. shredded Parmesan cheese
1 TB. chopped garlic	

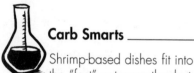

Carb Smarts

Shrimp-based dishes fit into the "fast" category thanks to time-saving options available at the grocery store. Buy shrimp that is already cleaned, or to really get moving in a hurry, purchase precooked "tail-off" shrimp.

Heat oil in a large skillet over medium heat. Add artichokes, Italian seasoning, and garlic and cook for 3 minutes, stirring. Add shrimp and heat thoroughly, stirring, for another 1 to 2 minutes. Distribute shrimp and artichokes to serving plates, sprinkle with salt and Parmesan cheese, and serve.

Variations: For a hearty meal, stir 1 (15-oz.) can drained and rinsed chickpeas in along with the shrimp.

Grilled Shrimp Scampi

Prep time: 10 minutes • Cook time: 5 minutes • Serves: 4

Each serving has: 202 calories • 24 g protein • 24 g animal protein • 0 g vegetable protein • 0 g carbohydrates • 0 g dietary fiber • 0 g net carbohydrates • 12 g fat • 2 g saturated fat • 221 mg cholesterol • 254 mg sodium • Exchanges: 3½ very-lean meat, 2 fat

1 TB. garlic, minced

¼ cup olive oil

1 lb. (31 to 40 count) fresh shrimp, peeled, and thawed, if frozen

¼ cup chopped fresh parsley

Skewers (soak wooden skewers prior to use to prevent burning)

Salt and ground black pepper to taste

Lemon wedges

Preheat the grill. Mix garlic and olive oil in a bowl, add shrimp, and toss to coat. Sprinkle shrimp with parsley. Slide 4 or 5 shrimp onto each skewer, sprinkle with salt and pepper, and grill for 2 to 3 minutes per side. Serve with lemon wedges.

Gourmand's Glossary

Scampi, originally from the Italian word for "shrimp," is commonly used to refer to shrimp that has been cooked in olive oil and garlic.

Mussels in Wine

Prep time: 5 minutes • Cook time: 10 minutes • Serves: 4

Each serving has: 312 calories • 40 g protein • 40 g animal protein • 0 g vegetable protein • < 1 g carbohydrates • 0 g dietary fiber • 0 g net carbohydrates • 8 g fat • 1 g saturated fat • 96 mg cholesterol • 860 mg sodium • Exchanges: 7 very-lean meat, 1 fat

3 lb. mussels, cleaned	Pinch salt
1 cup dry white wine	Pinch ground black pepper
½ cup water	Freshly squeezed lemon juice
1 TB. chopped garlic	Parsley to garnish
1 tsp. Italian seasoning	

Discard any mussels that are open prior to cooking. Bring wine, water, garlic, Italian seasoning, salt, and pepper to a boil in a large saucepan over medium-high heat. Add mussels, cover, and cook for 5 minutes or until mussels have opened. Discard any mussels that have not opened.

To serve, scoop mussels into large serving bowls, drizzling with broth from the pan. Drizzle with fresh lemon juice and garnish with parsley.

A chilled glass of Sauvignon Blanc alongside makes this picture complete.

Variation: It's decadent but sometimes irresistible to drizzle cooked mussels with melted butter (or to dip them, like lobster meat). You won't be adding carbs, but you will be adding saturated fat!

Carb Smarts

Mussels and other mollusks live on the ocean bottom, so cleaning is important. Scrub them with a stiff brush under cold running water. Remove any fibers (the "beard") coming from the concave side. Discard any mussels that are open (they're dead already—not a good thing).

Don't feel the need to add lots of seasonings to seafood. Most fish and shellfish dishes succeed because they allow fresh seafood flavors to shine through.

Ginger Scallops

Prep time: 10 minutes • Cook time: 6 minutes • Serves: 4

Each serving has: 195 calories • 29 g protein • 29 g animal protein • 0 g vegetable protein • < 1 g carbohydrates • 0 g dietary fiber • 0 g net carbohydrates • 4 g fat • 2 g saturated fat • 66 mg cholesterol • 276 mg sodium • Exchanges: 5 very-lean meat, 1 fat

3 TB. butter or olive oil	2 TB. lemon juice
1½ lb. fresh bay scallops or 1½ lb. fresh sea scallops, quartered	2 TB. heavy cream
	Pinch nutmeg
1 TB. freshly grated ginger	Salt and ground black pepper
½ cup white wine	

Melt butter in a large skillet over medium heat. Thoroughly rinse scallops in cold water, pat dry with paper towels, and cook with ginger for 3 minutes or until cooked, stirring. Remove to a warm plate and cover with foil.

Turn the heat to high and add wine and lemon juice to the skillet. Boil for 2 minutes or until liquid is reduced by half. Remove from heat and stir in cream, nutmeg, salt, and pepper.

Distribute scallops to serving plates, pour sauce over each serving, and serve.

Scallop and White Bean Stew

Prep time: 8 minutes • Cook time: 10 minutes • Serves: 4

Each serving has: 332 calories • 29 g protein • 19 g animal protein • 10 g vegetable protein • 22 g carbohydrates • 6 g dietary fiber • 16 g net carbohydrates • 13 g fat • 2 g saturated fat • 39 mg cholesterol • 525 mg sodium • Exchanges: 5 very-lean meat, 1 starch, ½ vegetable, 2 fat

3 TB. olive oil

4 scallions, roots and dark green tops removed, white and light green parts chopped into ¼-inch pieces

1 lb. fresh bay scallops, or 1 lb. fresh sea scallops, quartered

1 large sweet red pepper, seeds and ribs removed and chopped

1 tsp. Italian seasoning

1 tsp. freshly grated ginger

1 (14-oz.) can chicken broth

1 (15-oz.) can cannellini beans, drained and rinsed

Juice of ½ lemon

2 TB. shredded Parmesan cheese

Salt and ground black pepper

Heat oil in a large skillet over medium heat and sauté scallions, stirring, for 4 minutes. Thoroughly rinse scallops in cold water and pat dry with paper towels. Add scallops, red pepper, Italian seasoning, and ginger and cook for 3 minutes, stirring, or until scallops are just done. Add broth, cannellini beans, and lemon juice and heat, stirring, for 2 more minutes. Serve, seasoning with Parmesan, salt, and pepper to taste.

Quick Seafood Stew

Prep time: 5 minutes • Cook time: 8 minutes • Serves: 6

Each serving has: 230 calories • 20 g protein • 19 g animal protein • 1 g vegetable protein • 6 g carbohydrates • 1 g dietary fiber • 5 g net carbohydrates • 10 g fat • 1½ g saturated fat • 37 mg cholesterol • 192 mg sodium • Exchanges: 3 very-lean meat, 1 vegetable, 2 fat

2 cups tomato sauce (your sugar-free favorite)	¼ cup olive oil
¾ cup dry red wine	2 TB. chopped garlic
2 TB. tomato paste	1½ lb. assorted scallops, shrimp, calamari, and fish chunks
2 tsp. Italian seasoning	
½ tsp. crushed red pepper	

Heat tomato sauce, wine, tomato paste, Italian seasoning, and crushed red pepper in a saucepan over medium heat, stirring, for 10 minutes.

Meanwhile, cook olive oil and garlic in a large skillet over medium heat for 2 minutes. Add scallops, shrimp, calamari, and fish chunks and cook, stirring, for 3 minutes or until just done. Add seafood to sauce.

Serve in bowls with a garden salad alongside and a wine. Don't forget candles.

Carb Smarts

Some grocery stores sell frozen seafood mixes that include shrimp, scallops, and calamari and are perfect to keep in the freezer to jump-start Quick Seafood Stew.

Carbohistory

Every maritime region has a rich stew that makes the most of locally caught seafood. This version, resplendent with olive oil, tomatoes, and herbs, takes its inspiration from Italian-style seafood stews. To accelerate this dish, I cook the seafood in the skillet and add it to the sauce cooking in a separate saucepan.

Quick Crab Cakes

Prep time: 15 minutes • Cook time: 6 minutes • Serves: 4

Each serving has: 319 calories • 22 g protein • 21 g animal protein • 1 g vegetable protein • 6 g carbohydrates • 2 g dietary fiber • 4 g net carbohydrates • 24 g fat • 3 g saturated fat • 159 mg cholesterol • 329 mg sodium • Exchanges: 3½ very-lean meat, 1 vegetable, 4 fat

3 (5-oz.) cans or 1 (15-oz.) can crabmeat, drained, and picked over to discard any shell fragments

⅔ cup unprocessed bran

3 scallions, roots and dark green parts removed, minced

1 egg

2 TB. mayonnaise

1 tsp. Worcestershire sauce

1 tsp. Dijon-style mustard

Dash hot red pepper sauce (optional)

4 TB. (¼ cup) butter or canola oil

Lemon wedges

Mix crabmeat, bran, scallions, egg, mayonnaise, Worcestershire sauce, mustard, and hot pepper sauce (if using) in a large bowl. Mixture should be moist enough to stick together. If not, add a little more bran. Shape into 8 cakes, each about 2 inches across and ¾ inch thick (the spatula will help to flatten them in the skillet). Heat the butter or oil in a large skillet over medium heat. Cook cakes for 3 minutes per side or until crisp and golden. If necessary, cook cakes in batches, keeping the cooked ones on a plate tented with aluminum foil to keep them warm. Serve 2 per person with lemon wedges.

Variations: Fresh crabmeat is delicious in place of the canned crab. You can also use finely chopped salmon or lobster meat in place of the crabmeat.

The Least You Need to Know

- Microwave cooking enables ultra-fast, tasty, low-carb seafood dishes.
- Fresh seafood is perfect for quick cooking.
- Simple seafood dishes are quick but can also be elegant.
- Fast, delicious, low-carb fish and shellfish dishes can be prepared in a range of styles.

Chapter 8

White Meats: Poultry and Pork

In This Chapter

- ◆ Inexpensive, low-fat, and low-carb meats
- ◆ Super-fast chicken and pork recipes
- ◆ Leftover magic

Poultry and pork, the so-called "white meats," are, in many forms, health-ful, low-fat, nutritious meats with few or no carbohydrates. Many forms of poultry and pork are extremely versatile, lending themselves to a range of cuisines. Culinary traditions worldwide are based on poultry and pork. Plus, these meats are also often quick-cooking and tend to be downright cheap compared to other meats and seafoods.

In this chapter, you'll see why poultry and pork earn a firm place in fast, carb-conscious cooking.

Carb Smarts

Cooks in a hurry do not want to sacrifice flavor for the sake of speed. For this reason, we seek out ingredients that bring appealing flavor and texture and seasonings that, while easy to use, also bring richness to a dish. Also, we make smart use of the concept of "pairing": combining ingredients that result in flavor greater than the sum of its parts. Many of the recipes in this chapter make good use of this notion and help create elegance from simplicity.

Poultry-Based Recipes

The recipes in this chapter start with some of the many manifestations of the chicken breast. These quick-cooking morsels are low in carbohydrates and fat, and high in nutrition—another ideal food well worth crossing the road for!

Pork Barrel Cuisine

Pork, the other white meat in this chapter, is equally low carb, versatile, and easy to prepare. In fact, many of these poultry recipes will work with pork as well.

Broiled Lemon-Rosemary Chicken

Prep time: 4 minutes • Cook time: 8 minutes • Serves: 4

Each serving has: 247 calories • 39 g protein • 39 g animal protein • 0 g vegetable protein • 0 g carbohydrates • 0 g dietary fiber • 0 g net carbohydrates • 10 g fat • 1½ g saturated fat • 98 mg cholesterol • 242 mg sodium • Exchanges: 6 very-lean meat, 1½ fat

1½ lb. boneless, skinless chicken breasts	2 tsp. chopped garlic
Juice of 1 lemon	½ tsp. dried rosemary
2 TB. olive oil	Salt and ground black pepper

Preheat the broiler. Thoroughly rinse breasts in cold water and pat dry with paper towels. Place breasts into a bowl and drizzle with lemon juice. In a measuring cup, combine olive oil and garlic, pour over chicken, and turn to coat. (If you're not a garlic fan, omit it.) Sprinkle rosemary, salt, and pepper over chicken and lay chicken in an oven-proof baking dish in a single layer. Broil for 8 minutes or until done, turning once.

Variation: Cooking this chicken in an oiled skillet will result in a slightly crispier exterior.

Carb Smarts

Black pepper is one of the world's best all-purpose seasonings, but it loses much of its flavor soon after it's been ground. To get the best pepper flavor, pick up a pepper mill and freshly grind your pepper.

Chicken with Garlicky Wine Sauce

Prep time: 5 minutes • Cook time: 10 minutes • Serves: 4

Each serving has: 287 calories • 40 g protein • 40 g animal protein • 0 g vegetable protein • < 1 g carbohydrates • 0 g dietary fiber • 0 g net carbohydrates • 11½ g fat • 3 g saturated fat • 104 mg cholesterol • 396 mg sodium • Exchanges: 6 very-lean meat, 1½ fat

2 TB. olive oil

1 TB. chopped garlic

1½ lb. skinless, boneless chicken breasts, rinsed, dried, and cut into 1-inch-thick strips

Salt and freshly ground black pepper

¼ cup dry white wine

1 TB. freshly squeezed lemon juice

¼ cup light sour cream

 Carb Alert

Sour cream is versatile in cooking, but don't let it boil. It curdles, and that's not pretty.

Heat olive oil in a large skillet over medium heat and cook garlic for 2 minutes, stirring. Season chicken strips with salt and pepper to taste, add to the skillet with garlic, and cook for 6 minutes or until done, turning once. Remove chicken to a plate and cover with foil to keep warm. Turn the heat under the skillet to high and add wine and lemon juice. Boil for 1 minute, stirring. Turn off heat and stir in sour cream. Arrange chicken strips on serving plates and spoon creamy sauce over chicken.

Mustard-Glaze Chicken Breasts

Prep time: 5 minutes • Cook time: 8 minutes • Serves: 4

Each serving has: 277 calories • 39 g protein • 39 g animal protein • 0 g vegetable protein • 0 g carbohydrates • 0 g dietary fiber • 0 g net carbohydrates • 13½ g fat • 2 g saturated fat • 99 mg cholesterol • 195 mg sodium • Exchanges: 6 very-lean meat, 2 fat

1½ lb. skinless, boneless chicken breasts

3 TB. olive oil

2 TB. Dijon-style mustard

1 TB. balsamic vinegar

Salt and ground black pepper

Thoroughly rinse breasts in cold water and pat dry with paper towels. Heat 2 tablespoons oil in a large skillet over medium heat. Mix mustard, remaining 1 tablespoon oil, and vinegar in a bowl and brush chicken with mustard mixture. Cook chicken for 6 minutes or until done, turning once. Serve, seasoning with salt and pepper to taste.

Variation: Substitute red wine or cider vinegar for balsamic vinegar.

Carb Smarts

Is it done? To be sure your meat is cooked, make a cut with a sharp knife into the thickest part. If the juices run clear, it's done.

Chili-Crust Chicken Breasts

Prep time: 5 minutes • Cook time: 15 minutes • Serves: 4

Each serving has: 291 calories • 42 g protein • 41 g animal protein • 1 g vegetable protein • 6 g carbohydrates • 2 g dietary fiber • 4 g net carbohydrates • 11 g fat • 1½ g saturated fat • 151 mg cholesterol • 111 mg sodium • Exchanges: 6 very-lean meat, ⅓ starch, 1½ fat

1½ lb. skinless, boneless chicken breasts

1 egg

2 TB. olive oil

3 TB. unprocessed bran

3 TB. whole-wheat flour

1 TB. chili powder

½ tsp. salt

Carb Smarts

Vary the amount of chili powder to suit your taste in this tasty, savory chicken dish.

Thoroughly rinse breasts in cold water and pat dry with paper towels. Preheat oven to 400°F. Crack egg into a bowl and add olive oil. Mix bran, flour, chili powder, and salt on a plate next to the bowl. Spray a baking tray with cooking oil. Dip each piece of chicken into egg mixture, dredge in chili-flour mix, and set on the baking tray. Bake for 15 minutes or until done.

Chicken, Vegetable, and White Bean Stew

Prep time: 5 minutes • Cook time: 10 minutes • Serves: 8

Each serving has: 237 calories • 27 g protein • 22 g animal protein • 5 g vegetable protein • 18 g carbohydrates • 5 g dietary fiber • 13 g net carbohydrates • 5 g fat • 1 g saturated fat • 52 mg cholesterol • 642 mg sodium • Exchanges: 3 very-lean meat, ½ starch, 2 vegetable, ½ fat

4 TB. olive oil

1 medium onion, peeled and chopped into ¼-inch pieces

1 TB. chopped garlic

2 large carrots, scraped and cut into ¼-inch rounds

4 large celery stalks, washed and cut into ¼-inch pieces

1½ lb. boneless, skinless chicken breasts, rinsed, dried, and cut into ½-inch pieces

½ tsp. salt

Ground black pepper

1 tsp. Italian seasoning

2 (15-oz.) cans fat-free chicken broth

1 (15-oz.) can cannellini beans, drained and rinsed

1 cup tomato sauce or 1 cup crushed tomatoes with liquid

Shredded Parmesan cheese

Heat 2 tablespoons olive oil in a large saucepan over medium heat and cook onion for 2 minutes, stirring. Add garlic, carrots, and celery and cook for 3 more minutes.

Meanwhile, heat remaining 2 tablespoons oil in a large skillet over medium-high heat. Add chicken pieces, sprinkle with salt and pepper, and cook, stirring, for 5 minutes or until done.

When chicken is cooked, add it to the saucepan along with Italian seasoning, broth, cannellini beans, and tomato sauce. Cook, stirring occasionally, for 5 minutes.

Serve in bowls with Parmesan cheese.

Carbohistory

This farmhouse-style stew tastes great now and will be even better tomorrow. To accelerate the dish, cook the chicken in a separate skillet, then add it to the rest of the stew. If you have another few minutes, you can prepare the whole stew in one pot.

Chicken Sautéed with Olives, Lemon, and Capers

Prep time: 5 minutes   •   Cook time: 10 minutes   •   Serves: 4

Each serving has: 296 calories   •   39 g protein   •   39 g animal protein   •   0 g vegetable protein   •   1 g carbohydrates   •   < 1 g dietary fiber   •   1 g net carbohydrates   •   15 g fat   •   2 g saturated fat   •   99 mg cholesterol   •   174 mg sodium   •   Exchanges: 6 very-lean meat, 1½ fat

2 TB. olive oil	Salt and ground black pepper
1 TB. chopped garlic	3 TB. capers, drained and rinsed
2 tsp. Italian seasoning	½ cup pitted kalamata olives
1½ lb. boneless, skinless chicken breasts, rinsed, dried, and cut into 1-inch thick strips	Juice of ½ lemon
	3 TB. toasted pine nuts

Heat oil in a large skillet over medium heat. Add garlic and Italian seasoning and cook, stirring, for 2 minutes. Add chicken strips and cook for 4 minutes, turning once. Sprinkle with salt and pepper as they cook. Add capers and olives and cook, stirring, for 3 minutes or until chicken is done. Scoop to serving plates, drizzling each serving with lemon juice and sprinkling with pine nuts. Taste before adding additional salt, as capers are salty.

Sesame-Scallion Chicken Stir-Fry

Prep time: 10 minutes • Cook time: 5 minutes • Serves: 4

Each serving has: 312 calories • 43 g protein • 39 g animal protein • 4 g vegetable protein • 9 g carbohydrates • 3 g dietary fiber • 6 g net carbohydrates • 11 g fat • 1½ g saturated fat • 98 mg cholesterol • 467 mg sodium • Exchanges: 6 very-lean meat, 1½ vegetable, 1½ fat

1½ lb. skinless, boneless chicken breasts, rinsed, dried, and cut into 1-inch chunks

¼ cup canola oil

3 TB. sesame seeds

4 scallions, roots and dark green leaves removed, chopped into ¼-inch pieces

½ tsp. crushed red pepper

1 (6-oz.) can sliced water chestnuts, drained

2 cups snow peas, stemmed and rinsed

⅓ cup fresh chives, cut into ¼-inch pieces

3 TB. soy sauce

Place chicken in a bowl, pour oil over, and turn to coat. Sprinkle chicken with sesame seeds. Heat a wok or large skillet over medium-high heat; add chicken, scallions, and red pepper; and cook, stirring, for 2 minutes. Add water chestnuts, snow peas, and chives and continue to cook, stirring, for an additional 3 minutes or until chicken is cooked. Pour soy sauce over, stir, and serve.

Variation: Serve over brown rice (this will add to the good-carb count).

Chicken Paprika

Prep time: 5 minutes • Cook time: 10 minutes • Serves: 4

Each serving has: 307 calories • 40 g protein • 40 g animal protein • 0 g vegetable protein • 2 g carbohydrates • 0 g dietary fiber • 2 g net carbohydrates • 14½ g fat • 4½ g saturated fat • 114 mg cholesterol • 433 mg sodium • Exchanges: 6 very-lean meat, 2 fat

2 TB. olive oil	¼ tsp. salt
1½ lb. boneless, skinless chicken breasts, rinsed, dried, and cut into 1-inch-thick strips	Pinch ground black pepper
	1 cup fat-free chicken broth
1 TB. paprika	⅔ cup light sour cream

Heat oil in a large skillet over medium heat. Sprinkle chicken with ½ tablespoon paprika, salt, and pepper and cook for 5 minutes or until done, turning once. Remove to a serving plate and cover with foil to keep it warm. Turn the heat under the skillet to high and add chicken broth and remaining ½ tablespoon paprika. Bring to a boil and cook for 5 minutes until broth is reduced by half or more. Remove the skillet from the heat and stir in sour cream, allowing it to warm from the skillet.

Carb Smarts

To accelerate dishes that call for chicken pieces, use that good pantry standby, canned chunk white chicken meat (drained).

Distribute chicken to serving plates and spoon creamy paprika sauce over each serving (while humming "Blue Danube").

Chicken-Crab Curry

Prep time: 5 minutes   •   Cook time: 15 minutes   •   Serves: 4

Each serving has: 348 calories   •   50 g protein   •   48 g animal protein   •   2 g vegetable protein   •   12 g carbohydrates   •   2 g dietary fiber   •   10 g net carbohydrates   •   10 g fat   •   1½ g saturated fat   •   126 mg cholesterol   •   908 mg sodium   •   Exchanges: 7 very-lean meat, 1 vegetable, ¼ skim milk, ¼ starch, 1½ fat

2 TB. olive oil

1 lb. boneless, skinless chicken, rinsed, dried, and cut into 1-inch cubes

3 TB. butter

1 medium onion, peeled and finely chopped

2 large bell peppers, seeds and ribs removed, and chopped into ½-inch pieces

1½ tsp. curry powder

3 TB. whole-wheat flour

¼ tsp. ground ginger

1 cup chicken broth or 1 chicken bouillon cube dissolved in 1 cup hot water

1 cup milk

1 (6-oz.) can crabmeat, drained and picked over to discard any shell fragments

1 tsp. lemon juice

Salt

Heat oil in a medium-size skillet over medium heat and cook chicken, stirring, for 6 minutes or until cooked through. Turn off heat.

While chicken is cooking, melt butter over medium heat in a large skillet. Sauté onion, pepper, and curry powder for 5 minutes; then stir in flour and ginger and cook, stirring, until bubbling and smooth. Add chicken broth and milk and, stirring, bring to a boil. Boil 1 minute before adding cooked chicken, crabmeat, and lemon juice. Heat mixture for 2 to 3 minutes and serve in bowls, either as is or over ½ cup brown rice (this will increase the good-carb count). Season with salt to taste.

Variations: Curry powder is the flavor throttle in this dish. Some mixes are more intense than others. If you're new to spicy foods, start with less. Also, using two skillets accelerates this recipe.

Carb Alert

Overcooked pork and poultry becomes dry and unappetizing. Watch your meal closely to prevent overcooking!

Stir-Fried Peanut Chicken

Prep time: 5 minutes • Cook time: 11 minutes • Serves: 4

Each serving has: 319 calories • 43 g protein • 39 g animal protein • 4 g vegetable protein • 8 g carbohydrates • 3 g dietary fiber • 5 g net carbohydrates • 14 g fat • 2 g saturated fat • 98 mg cholesterol • 1,174 mg sodium • Exchanges: 6 very-lean meat, 1 vegetable, 1½ fat

2 TB. vegetable oil

1 TB. chopped garlic

1½ tsp. fresh ginger root, peeled and grated

Dash hot red pepper sauce

4 TB. soy sauce

2 TB. "natural" peanut butter

1½ lb. boneless, skinless chicken breasts, rinsed, dried, and cut into ¾-inch cubes

3 cups green beans, stemmed and cut in half crosswise

Heat oil in a wok or large skillet over medium heat and cook garlic, ginger, hot pepper sauce, soy sauce, and peanut butter, stirring, for about 3 minutes or until peanut butter blends smoothly with the other ingredients. Add chicken and cook, stirring, for 5 minutes or until just done. Add beans and cook until slightly crisp, about 3 minutes.

Serve as is or over ½ cup brown rice (this will raise the good-carb count).

Grilled Chicken with Spiced Chickpea Purée

Prep time: 5 minutes • Cook time: 10 minutes • Serves: 4

Each serving has: 421 calories • 36 g protein • 28 g animal protein • 8 g vegetable protein • 30 g carbohydrates • 6 g dietary fiber • 24 g net carbohydrates • 17 g fat • 4 g saturated fat • 77 mg cholesterol • 618 mg sodium • Exchanges: 5 very-lean meat, 1½ starch, ½ vegetable, 2 fat

2 TB. olive oil

1 lb. boneless, skinless chicken breasts, rinsed, dried, and cut into 1-inch chunks

½ medium onion, peeled and chopped into ¼-inch pieces

1 tsp. ground cumin

½ (15-oz.) can (1 cup) *chickpeas*, drained and rinsed

1 TB. chopped garlic

3 TB. diced prosciutto

½ cup light sour cream

¼ cup milk

½ tsp. salt

¼ tsp. ground black pepper

¼ cup sliced almonds, toasted if possible

Heat oil in a large skillet over medium heat and cook chicken and onion, stirring, for 5 minutes or until chicken is cooked. Sprinkle chicken with cumin as it cooks.

Meanwhile, blend chickpeas, garlic, prosciutto, sour cream, milk, salt, and pepper in a food processor fitted with a steel blade to an almost-creamy consistency.

Remove chicken to serving plates and scrape chickpea purée into the skillet. Cook over medium heat for 2 minutes, stirring, then distribute equal amounts over the chicken. Sprinkle with sliced almonds and serve.

Variation: This purée is also delicious over grilled pork.

Gourmand's Glossary

Chickpeas (also known as garbanzo beans) are the base ingredients in hummus and many other dishes. Chickpeas are high in fiber and low in carbohydrates and fat, making this bean a delicious and healthful component of many appetizers and main dishes.

Chicken Marsala

Prep time: 5 minutes   •   Cook time: 15 minutes   •   Serves: 4

Each serving has: 360 calories   •   40 g protein   •   39 g animal protein   •   1 g vegetable protein   •   2 g carbohydrates   •   1 g dietary fiber   •   1 g net carbohydrates   •   16 g fat   •   5 g saturated fat   •   114 mg cholesterol   •   690 mg sodium   •   Exchanges: 6 very-lean meat, 2 fat

2 TB. butter	2 TB. olive oil
¼ cup unprocessed bran	1 cup chicken broth
½ tsp. salt	½ cup marsala wine
½ tsp. ground black pepper	¼ lb. fresh white mushrooms, wiped with a damp paper towel and sliced
1½ lb. boneless, skinless chicken breasts, rinsed, dried, and cut in half lengthwise	Juice of ½ lemon

Melt butter in a large skillet over medium heat. In a bowl, mix bran, salt, and pepper. Dredge chicken in bran mixture, arrange in the skillet, and cook for 6 minutes or until done, turning once. Remove the chicken to a warm plate and cover with foil to keep warm.

Turn up heat under the skillet and add olive oil, broth, wine, mushrooms, and lemon juice. Cook, stirring, for 5 minutes or until reduced by half. Distribute chicken breasts to serving plates and spoon sauce over.

Grilled Cumin-Ginger Pork Chops

Prep time: 5 minutes   •   Cook time: 8 minutes   •   Serves: 4

Each serving has: 344 calories   •   32 g protein   •   32 g animal protein   •   0 g vegetable protein   •   0 g carbohydrates   •   0 g dietary fiber   •   0 g net carbohydrates   •   22 g fat   •   7 g saturated fat   •   89 mg cholesterol   •   1,278 mg sodium   •   Exchanges: 5 lean meat, 1½ fat

1½ lb. center-cut pork chops	1 tsp. ground cumin
Juice of ½ lime	1 tsp. ground ginger
2 TB. olive oil	1 tsp. salt

Thoroughly rinse chops in cold water and pat dry with paper towels. Start the grill. Put pork chops in a dish and drizzle with lime juice, then olive oil, turning to coat. Sprinkle all sides with cumin, ginger, and salt. Grill for 8 minutes, turning once, or until cooked through.

Grilled Apple Chops

Prep time: 5 minutes   •   Cook time: 10 minutes   •   Serves: 4

Each serving has: 405 calories   •   33 g protein   •   33 g animal protein   •   0 g vegetable protein   •   5 g carbohydrates   •   0 g dietary fiber   •   5 g net carbohydrates   •   28 g fat   •   10 g saturated fat   •   100 mg cholesterol   •   222 mg sodium   •   Exchanges: 5 lean meat, 2 fat

1½ lb. center-cut pork chops	½ cup unsweetened applesauce
2 TB. olive oil	½ cup light sour cream
Salt and ground black pepper	2 TB. Dijon-style mustard

Thoroughly rinse chops in cold water and pat dry with paper towels. Heat oil in a skillet over medium heat. Sprinkle pork chops with salt and pepper on both sides and cook for 8 minutes or until cooked through, turning once. Move sizzling chops to serving plates. Add applesauce, sour cream, and mustard to the skillet and heat for 1 minute or until hot. Distribute sauce over chops.

Variation: Grilled chops are also delicious with this sauce.

Pork Kebabs

Prep time: 10 minutes • Cook time: 8 minutes • Serves: 4

Each serving has: 376 calories • 35 g protein • 32 g animal protein • 3 g vegetable protein • 7 g carbohydrates • 2½ g dietary fiber • 5 g net carbohydrates • 22 g fat • 7 g saturated fat • 88 mg cholesterol • 447 mg sodium • Exchanges: 5 lean meat, 1½ fat

Skewers (soak wooden skewers prior to use to prevent burning)

1½ lb. center-cut pork chops, rinsed, dried, and cut into 1-inch chunks

1 (8-oz.) pkg. small white mushrooms, wiped with a damp paper towel and cut in half lengthwise

1 large sweet onion, such as Vidalia, peeled and cut into 1-inch-square pieces

2 large bell peppers, seeds and ribs removed and cut into 1-inch-square pieces

⅓ cup Italian dressing

Carb Alert

Be careful to read the ingredients of marinades and dressings. Many are loaded with sugar.

Start the grill. Assemble kebabs on the skewers, alternating pieces of pork, mushroom, onion, and pepper. Lay kebabs in a baking dish or platter and drizzle with Italian dressing. Grill for 8 minutes, turning once, or until pork is fully cooked.

Variation: Use chicken or beef cubes in place of pork. You can use a wide range of marinades, or even simple olive oil, in place of Italian dressing.

Carb Smarts

Wooden (often bamboo) skewers are inexpensive but flammable. To solve that problem, soak them in water for a few minutes before assembling your kebabs. Another option is to purchase reusable metal skewers. You can find both in grocery stores.

Choucroute Garni

Prep time: 5 minutes • Cook time: 15 minutes • Serves: 4

Each serving has: 502 calories • 14 g protein • 13 g animal protein • 1 g vegetable protein • 13 g carbohydrates • 4 g dietary fiber • 9 g net carbohydrates • 39 g fat • 13 g saturated fat • 68 mg cholesterol • 1,472 mg sodium • Exchanges: 3 high-fat meat, ½ fruit, ½ vegetable, 3 fat

2 TB. cooking oil

1 medium-size onion, peeled and cut into ½-inch pieces

2 carrots, scraped and cut into ½-inch sections

1 crisp apple, such as Granny Smith, cored, seeded, and chopped into ½-inch pieces

1 lb. cooked knockwurst, kielbasa, or pork sausage, cut into ½ inch slices

1 (14.5-oz.) can sauerkraut, drained and rinsed

1 bay leaf

1 cup dry white wine

1 tsp. caraway seeds

Mustard (your sugar-free favorite)

Heat oil in a large skillet over medium heat and cook onion and carrots for 5 minutes, stirring. Add apple, knockwurst, sauerkraut, bay leaf, wine, and caraway seeds and cook, stirring, for another 10 minutes. Remove bay leaf, distribute to serving bowls, spread with mustard, and enjoy.

 **Carb Alert**

Canned sauerkraut can have an unpleasantly sharp flavor. To soften this assault on your palate, simply rinse the sauerkraut in a colander under cold running water, drain, and use.

 Gourmand's Glossary

Choucroute Garni is an Alsatian dish that comes in many forms but commonly includes sauerkraut (*choucroute* is French for "sauerkraut"), caraway, white wine, potatoes, vegetables, and cooked meats. Omit the potatoes, and you've got a hearty, low-carb meal.

Curried Pork

Prep time: 5 minutes • Cook time: 10 minutes • Serves: 4

Each serving has: 427 calories • 33 g protein • 32 g animal protein • 1 g vegetable protein • 13 g carbohydrates • 2 g dietary fiber • 11 g net carbohydrates • 28 g fat • 8 g saturated fat • 89 mg cholesterol • 682 mg sodium • Exchanges: 5 lean meat, 1 fruit, 2 fat

3 TB. olive oil

1½ lb. boneless center-cut pork chops, rinsed, dried, and cut into ½-inch pieces

1 medium onion, peeled and chopped into ½-inch pieces

2 tsp. curry powder

1 (15-oz.) can fat-free chicken broth

½ cup dried apricots, cut into ¼-inch pieces

1 crisp apple, such as Granny Smith, cored and cut into ½-inch pieces

1 tsp. salt

¼ tsp. ground black pepper

Heat oil in a large skillet over medium heat and sauté pork, onion, and curry powder for 5 minutes, stirring. Add broth, apricots and apple and cook for an additional 3 minutes or until pork is cooked through. Sprinkle with salt and pepper and stir. Serve over brown rice for a hearty, good-carb meal.

Carb Smarts

To peel, or not to peel? That is the question when it comes to using some vegetables and fruits in cooking. Before you reach for that peeler, though, consider keeping the peel on such fruits as apples and such vegetables as new potatoes. Those peels (appropriately scrubbed, of course) add color, texture, flavor, and, perhaps most important, nutrition. You also save time—a good thing in my book.

Pork and Broccoli Stir-Fry

Prep time: 5 minutes • Cook time: 10 minutes • Serves: 4

Each serving has: 256 calories • 23 g protein • 21 g animal protein • 2 g vegetable protein • 5 g carbohydrates • 2 g dietary fiber • 3 g net carbohydrates • 16 g fat • 5 g saturated fat • 59 mg cholesterol • 837 mg sodium • Exchanges: 3½ lean meat, 1 vegetable, 1 fat

1 lb. boneless center-cut pork chops, rinsed, dried, and cut into 1-inch pieces	1 medium onion, peeled and chopped into ½-inch pieces
3 TB. soy sauce	2 cups broccoli florets, about 1-inch in size
1 TB. olive oil	1 TB. freshly grated ginger, peeled (optional)
	1 TB. sesame seeds

Mix pork with soy sauce in a bowl. Heat oil in a wok or large skillet over medium heat. Cook onion and pork for 5 minutes, stirring. Add broccoli and ginger (if using) and cook for an additional 5 minutes or until pork is cooked through and broccoli is tender-crisp. Serve, sprinkling with sesame seeds.

Variation: Several Asian sauces will work in place of soy sauce, including teriyaki and hoisin (although watch how much sugar you're adding).

Carb Smarts

Is it done (part 2)? To check for doneness, pierce the center of the piece of pork. When liquid runs slightly pink (for rare) or clear (well done), the meat is cooked. If the liquid is red, keep cooking!

Grilled Rosemary and Garlic Pork Tenderloin

Prep time: 5 minutes • Cook time: 8 minutes • Serves: 4

Each serving has: 374 calories • 32 g protein • 32 g animal protein • 0 g vegetable protein • 0 g carbohydrates • 0 g dietary fiber • 0 g net carbohydrates • 27 g fat • 8 g saturated fat • 89 mg cholesterol • 125 mg sodium • Exchanges: 5 lean meat, 2 fat

3 TB. olive oil

1 TB. chopped garlic

1½ lb. *pork tenderloin*, rinsed, dried, and cut into *medallions*

Juice of ½ lime

1 TB. fresh, or 1 tsp. dried rosemary

1 tsp. salt

½ tsp. ground black pepper

Start the grill. Mix olive oil and garlic in a cup. Place pork tenderloin medallions in a bowl. Pour lime juice and then garlic-olive oil over pork, turning to coat. Sprinkle rosemary, salt, and pepper over the medallions, turning the pieces with a fork to cover all sides.

Grill for 8 minutes or until done, turning once.

Gourmand's Glossary

In my opinion, **pork tenderloin** is one of the most delicious cuts of pork in the store. The tenderloin generally is a 2- to 3-pound piece (not to be confused with a pork *loin*, which is also delicious, but much bigger). For quick cooking, slice your tenderloin into 1-inch medallions.

The Least You Need to Know

- The boneless, skinless chicken breast provides an extremely versatile, low-carb, and low-fat starting point for an exciting variety of dishes.
- Grilling, skillet cooking, and broiling are some of the fastest cooking methods for pork and poultry.
- Rich mixtures of meat, vegetables, and liquid often taste as good, if not better, as leftovers the next day.
- Pork and poultry are terrific building blocks for hearty, delicious, low-carb meals.

Chapter 9

Red Meats: Beef and Lamb

In This Chapter

- High in flavor, low in carbs
- Tips for fast preparation
- Lamb specialties
- Stir (fry) it up

Fans of beef and lamb love the rich flavor of these meats, which bring to mind luxuriant feasts—hardly the image of "diet food"! Yet beef and lamb can be an important part of a carb-conscious diet.

One advantage of beef and lamb is the rich flavor inherent in the meat. Pork or poultry might need seasoning, but you can get away with cooking a steak *au naturale*. We'll have some seasoning fun in this chapter, of course, but keep in mind that there's a lot of flavor in that sirloin to begin with. Your objective is to emphasize existing flavor, not create it.

Let's also dispel the notion that these richer meats take longer to prepare and are not appropriate for the cook in a hurry. True, we won't be roasting. Cooking methods and cuts of meat are important when time is of the essence.

Beef-Based Recipes

When it comes to beef, stick with thin cuts such as tips, fillets, steaks, and strips—and ground beef, of course. Within these limits, there is a world of opportunity. Some of my favorites are in this chapter.

Carb Alert

Rich meats are low in carbohydrates, but they also tend to be higher in saturated fat than lean cuts of poultry and pork. For this reason, enjoy beef and lamb in moderation as one source of protein among many in a balanced carb-conscious diet.

Lamb It Up

Lamb is an incredibly flavorful, rich meat that deserves more attention. Give one of the recipes in this chapter a try, and you'll see what I mean.

Carb Smarts

Some of these dishes recommend marinating time. This is time where you're doing something else and not stuck in the kitchen, but it does mean that some planning ahead is necessary. The best way to prepare Steak with Red Wine Sauce, for example, is to set up the meat in a marinade a couple hours in advance—or even better, in the morning when you leave for work. This will take about 3 minutes. Upon your return, chemistry will have done its work, and you'll have a flavorful, tender piece of meat, just waiting to go.

Spiced Steak Tips

Prep time: 5 minutes plus marinating time   •   Cook time: 8 minutes   •   Serves: 2

Each serving has: 656 calories   •   84 g protein   •   84 g animal protein   •   0 g vegetable protein   •   0 g carbohydrates   •   0 g dietary fiber   •   0 g net carbohydrates   •   24 g fat   •   8 g saturated fat   •   313 mg cholesterol   •   816 mg sodium   •   Exchanges: 12 lean meat

½ cup Worcestershire sauce   1½ lb. steak tips, sliced ½-inch thick

Pour Worcestershire sauce over steak tips in a bowl. Turn steak pieces in marinade to cover all sides. Cook immediately or, if you have time, cover the bowl and refrigerate for up to 8 hours.

When you're ready to cook, start the grill. Grill for 4 minutes per side or until done.

Variations: Your local grocery store has a wide variety of marinades perfect for steak tips. Just pass over the ones with added sugar. I like grilling for the flavor, but broiling or even skillet-frying will work.

Gourmand's Glossary

A **marinade** is a seasoned sauce, usually high in acid content. The acids break down the muscle of the meat, making it tender and adding flavor.

Steak and Onions

Prep time: 3 minutes • Cook time: 12 minutes • Serves: 4

Each serving has: 448 calories • 42 g protein • 42 g animal protein • 0 g vegetable protein • 0 g carbohydrates • 0 g dietary fiber • 0 g net carbohydrates • 27 g fat • 9 g saturated fat • 172 mg cholesterol • 670 mg sodium • Exchanges: 6 lean meat, 3 fat

2 TB. butter	1½ lb. steak, such as sirloin
2 TB. olive oil	1 tsp. salt
1 medium onion, peeled and sliced thin into ¼-inch pieces	½ tsp. ground black pepper

Carb Alert

Heat varies from stovetop to stovetop. If your skillet gets hot enough to burn the onions (in spite of the butter and oil in the skillet), take them out before you cook your steak.

Heat butter and oil in a large skillet over medium heat. Cook onion for 4 minutes, stirring. Meanwhile, sprinkle steak with salt and pepper. Turn the heat to high, move onions to the edge of the skillet, and place steak in the middle. Cook steak for 8 minutes or to your desired doneness, turning once.

Top each serving of steak with onions.

Grilled Steak with Red Wine Sauce

Prep time: 5 minutes plus marinating time • Cook time: 10 minutes • Serves: 4

Each serving has: 485 calories • 42 g protein • 42 g animal protein • 0 g vegetable protein • < 1 g carbohydrates • 0 g dietary fiber • 0 g net carbohydrates • 28 g fat • 10 g saturated fat • 180 mg cholesterol • 736 mg sodium • Exchanges: 6 lean meat, 3 fat

½ cup dry red wine

2 TB. olive oil

2 TB. chopped garlic

1 TB. Italian seasoning

1 tsp. salt

½ tsp. ground cumin

½ tsp. ground black pepper

1½ lb. tenderloin, T-bone, or your favorite steak

3 TB. butter

In a large zipper-type bag or large bowl, mix wine, oil, garlic, Italian seasoning, salt, cumin, and pepper. Place steak in the bag (or bowl), seal, and refrigerate for between 2 and 8 hours.

When you're ready to cook, start the grill. Remove steak from marinade, reserve marinade, and grill steak 4 minutes per side or to your preferred level of doneness. While steak is grilling, heat marinade and butter in a skillet over high heat, stirring occasionally, for 5 minutes or until sauce *reduces* by about half. Serve steak, spooning sauce over each serving.

Variation: You can prepare this recipe using the broiler rather than a grill, although you'll sacrifice some grill flavor. For the most points for presentation, slice your grilled steak across the grain in strips about ½ inch wide, arrange them on a plate, and drizzle with the wine sauce.

Carb Alert

The reason for heating the red wine sauce is twofold: to intensify the flavor and, even more important, to cook a liquid that has been in contact with raw meat. Don't even think about using this marinade uncooked!

Gourmand's Glossary

To **reduce** is to heat a broth or sauce to remove some of the water content, resulting in more concentrated flavor and color.

Tenderloin Strips with Pepper Cream

Prep time: 5 minutes • Cook time: 8 minutes • Serves: 4

Each serving has: 429 calories • 43 g protein • 43 g animal protein • 0 g vegetable protein • 1 g carbohydrates • 0 g dietary fiber • 1 g net carbohydrates • 23 g fat • 7 g saturated fat • 168 mg cholesterol • 386 mg sodium • Exchanges: 6 lean meat, 2 fat

2 TB. butter or olive oil

1½ lb. tenderloin steak, sliced into ½-inch strips

1½ tsp. ground cumin

½ tsp. salt

¼ tsp. ground black pepper

½ cup light sour cream

Carb Smarts

Is it done? With steak, red in the middle is rare, pink is medium, gray all the way is well done. For me, between rare and medium is perfect. I find that a well-done steak loses its flavor and isn't as tender.

Melt butter in a large skillet over medium heat. Dust steak with cumin, salt, and pepper. Cook for 3 minutes per side or to your preferred doneness. Distribute strips to serving plates and turn off the heat. Scrape sour cream into the skillet and mix it thoroughly with any butter and spices remaining. Spoon cream mixture over each serving.

Meat Loaf

Prep time: 10 minutes • Cook time: 45 minutes • Serves: 6

Each serving has: 265 calories • 21 g protein • 21 g animal protein • 0 g vegetable protein • 2 g carbohydrates • 1 g dietary fiber • 1 g net carbohydrates • 19 g fat • 10 g saturated fat • 116 mg cholesterol • 140 mg sodium • Exchanges: 1½ medium-fat meat, 2 high-fat meat

½ cup unprocessed bran	2 eggs
1 TB. Italian seasoning	1 cup (4 oz.) shredded cheddar cheese
1 tsp. ground cumin	2 TB. chopped garlic
1 lb. ground beef	2 TB. Worcestershire sauce
1 lb. ground pork	

Preheat the oven to 375°F. Mix bran, Italian seasoning, and cumin in a large bowl. Add ground beef, pork, eggs, cheese, garlic, and Worcestershire sauce and mix thoroughly (your hands are the best kitchen tool for this messy job). The mixture should cling together. Shape into an elongated loaf shape and lay on a baking tray. Bake for 45 minutes or until done (a meat thermometer should register 170° for pork, 160° to 170° for all-beef). Serve slices with sautéed vegetables for a great cold-weather meal (or any weather, for that matter).

 Carbohistory

Meat loaf is one of those comfort foods that bring back warm memories. With minor adjustments to traditional methods such as removing the breadcrumbs, this classic becomes a *piece de resistance* of carb-conscious cuisine.

For years, though, I thought this dish was complicated. I learned differently at 5:15 one afternoon when I learned that guests were coming at 6 for a casual dinner. In the fridge I had ground beef, sun-dried tomatoes, and roasted red peppers. I got that meatloaf in the oven in less than 5 minutes. Even better, our guests asked for the recipe. Now I understand why Mom used to love making meat loaf.

I include it here for two reasons. The first is that your time commitment is about 10 minutes (I was rushing for the 5-minute version). The second is that a meatloaf can easily cover two or three meals; meaning a bit of extra time tonight pays dividends of an "instant" low-carb meal tomorrow and maybe the next night.

Meatballs

Prep time: 10 minutes • Cook time: 8 minutes • Serves: 4

Each serving has: 389 calories • 35 g protein • 35 g animal protein • 0 g vegetable protein • 0 g carbohydrates • 0 g dietary fiber • 0 g net carbohydrates • 28 g fat • 16 g saturated fat • 110 mg cholesterol • 692 mg sodium • Exchanges: 5 medium-fat meat, 2 fat

3 TB. canola oil	1 tsp. salt
1½ lb. ground beef	½ tsp. ground black pepper
1 TB. chopped garlic	Dash hot red pepper sauce
1 TB. Italian seasoning	

Heat oil in a large skillet over medium heat. Thoroughly mix beef, garlic, Italian seasoning, salt, black pepper, and hot pepper sauce in a large bowl. Then shape 1-inch meatballs using your hands or a melon-baller. Cook meatballs in hot oil, rotating once or twice, for 8 minutes or until done.

Variations: Preheat the oven to 400°F. Arrange meatballs on a baking tray and bake for 15 minutes or until done. This method takes longer, but is neater and requires no oil.

The pepper and hot pepper sauce make these spicy. To tone down that spice, reduce or eliminate the pepper.

Quick-Grilled Beef Satay

Prep time: 15 minutes • Cook time: 5 minutes • Serves: 4

Each serving has: 664 calories • 51 g protein • 42 g animal protein • 9 g vegetable protein • 8 g carbohydrates • 3 g dietary fiber • 5 g net carbohydrates • 28 g fat • 8 g saturated fat • 156 mg cholesterol • 941 mg sodium • Exchanges: 6 lean meat, 3 fat

½ cup natural-style "crunchy" peanut butter

2 TB. soy sauce

2 TB. canola oil

Double dash hot red pepper sauce

1½ lb. sirloin steak tips, cut into ¾-inch pieces

2 TB. hot pepper oil, or 2 TB. canola oil mixed with ¼ tsp. hot red pepper sauce

2 TB. teriyaki sauce

Skewers (soak wooden skewers prior to use to prevent burning)

3 TB. sesame seeds

Start the grill. Mix peanut butter, soy sauce, canola oil, and hot pepper sauce in a small serving bowl until smooth.

Place steak in a bowl and toss with hot pepper oil and teriyaki sauce to coat. Spear two beef morsels on the tip of each skewer. Arrange beef on grill with skewer extending off the grill to minimize burning and facilitate turning. Grill for 5 minutes or until done, turning once. Arrange skewers on a serving platter in a circle with meat in the center, surrounding the bowl of dipping sauce. Sprinkle sesame seeds over beef and serve so diners can lift a skewer, dip, and devour.

Gourmand's Glossary

A **satay** is a popular Southeast Asian dish of broiled skewers of fish or meat, often served with peanut sauce.

Turkish Beef Pockets

Prep time: 10 minutes • Cook time: 6 minutes • Serves: 4

Each serving has: 354 calories • 36 g protein • 32 g animal protein • 4 g vegetable protein • 19 g carbohydrates • 11 g dietary fiber • 8 g net carbohydrates • 14 g fat • 4 g saturated fat • 89 mg cholesterol • 507 mg sodium • Exchanges: 4 lean meat, 1 starch, ½ vegetable, 1 fat

1 lb. sirloin steak, cut into ¼-inch strips

1 tsp. ground cumin

Salt and ground black pepper

1 TB. olive oil

½ cup plain yogurt

2 tsp. lemon juice

2 tsp. chopped garlic

½ cup peeled and finely chopped cucumber

¼ tsp. ground black pepper

2 small whole-wheat pita bread loaves, sliced in half (4 halves)

1 cup (¼-inch strips) purple or green cabbage

Sprinkle beef with cumin, salt, and pepper. Heat oil in a large skillet over medium heat and cook steak strips for 6 minutes or until done, turning once.

Meanwhile, combine yogurt, lemon juice, garlic, cucumber, and ¼ teaspoon pepper in a bowl.

Cut each piece of pita in half. Distribute beef between each pita half, arranging them lengthwise. Top beef with cabbage and yogurt.

Citrus Stir-Fry

Prep time: 10 minutes • Cook time: 10 minutes • Serves: 4

Each serving has: 390 calories • 31 g protein • 28 g animal protein • 3 g vegetable protein • 10 g carbohydrates • 4 g dietary fiber • 6 g net carbohydrates • 16 g fat • 4 g saturated fat • 104 mg cholesterol • 854 mg sodium • Exchanges: 4 lean meat, 1 fat, 1 vegetable

2 TB. sesame or olive oil	1 (6-oz.) can sliced water chestnuts, drained
1 lb. steak tips, cut into ¾-inch pieces	2 TB. lime juice
½ tsp. salt	2 TB. soy sauce
1 large onion, peeled and chopped into ¼-inch pieces	2 TB. orange zest
1 TB. chopped garlic	¼ tsp. ground black pepper
2 cups fresh sugar snap peas, stemmed and rinsed, or 1 (9-oz.) pkg. frozen sugar snap peas, thawed	Lime slices to garnish (optional)

Heat oil in a wok or large skillet over medium-high heat. Sprinkle beef with salt and cook 4 minutes or until done, turning once. Remove beef to a separate plate. Reduce heat to medium. Add onion to the wok and cook for 2 minutes, stirring. Add garlic and cook for 1 additional minute. Add snap peas and water chestnuts and cook for an additional 3 minutes, stirring, or until pods are tender-crisp. Return beef to wok or skillet and add lime juice, soy sauce, orange zest, and pepper. Cook, stirring, for 1 minute, and serve, garnished with lime slices.

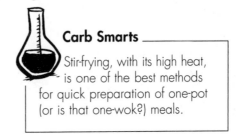

Carb Smarts

Stir-frying, with its high heat, is one of the best methods for quick preparation of one-pot (or is that one-wok?) meals.

Variation: Serve over ½ cup brown rice (this will increase the good-carb count).

Garlic Beef and Asparagus Stir-Fry

Prep time: 10 minutes • Cook time: 6 minutes • Serves: 4

Each serving has: 327 calories • 32 g protein • 28 g animal protein • 4 g vegetable protein • 6 g carbohydrates • 3 g dietary fiber • 3 g net carbohydrates • 18 g fat • 4 g saturated fat • 104 mg cholesterol • 582 mg sodium • Exchanges: 4 lean fat meat, 1½ fat

2 TB. sesame or olive oil	2 TB. chopped garlic
1 lb. steak tips, cut into ¾-inch pieces	3 TB. teriyaki sauce
1 lb. fresh asparagus, rinsed, tough bottoms removed, cut into 1-inch sections	2 TB. sesame seeds

Heat oil in a wok or large skillet over medium-high heat. Cook beef for 2 minutes. Add asparagus and garlic and cook for 4 minutes, stirring, or until beef is done. Drizzle with teriyaki sauce and serve, sprinkling each serving with sesame seeds.

Variation: Serve over ½ cup brown rice (this will increase the good-carb count).

Fast Stuffed Peppers

Prep time: 5 minutes • Cook time: 12 minutes • Serves: 4

Each serving has: 315 calories • 29 g protein • 26 g animal protein • 3 g vegetable protein • 14 g carbohydrates • 5 g dietary fiber • 9 g net carbohydrates • 16 g fat • 10 g saturated fat • 59 mg cholesterol • 415 mg sodium • Exchanges: 4 medium-fat meat, ½ high-fat meat, 1 vegetable

1 lb. lean ground beef	2 tsp. Italian seasoning
1 medium onion, peeled and chopped into ½-inch pieces	½ tsp. salt
2 tsp. chopped garlic	¼ tsp. ground black pepper
1 (14.5-oz.) can diced tomatoes, drained with juice reserved	2 large green bell peppers, sliced in half lengthwise, seeds and ribs removed
¼ cup unprocessed bran	Water
1 TB. Worcestershire sauce	½ cup (2 oz.) shredded cheddar cheese

Preheat the broiler.

Cook ground beef, onion, and garlic in a large skillet over medium heat, stirring, for 5 minutes or until done. Drain fat from the skillet and mix in tomatoes, bran, Worcestershire sauce, Italian seasoning, salt, and pepper. Cook for 4 minutes, stirring. If mixture is too dry to cling together, use some of reserved tomato juice.

Meanwhile, microwave pepper halves, cut side up, in a microwave- and oven-safe (Pyrex type) baking dish with ¼ inch water in the bottom for 3 to 4 minutes or until softened. Remove peppers from microwave and stuff with cooked ground beef mixture (keep a little water in the bottom of the baking dish). Top each pepper with some cheese and slide under the broiler for 3 minutes or until cheese has melted.

Variation: Use ground pork, turkey, or sausage in place of the ground beef.

Mediterranean Beef Skewers

Prep time: 10 minutes   •   Cook time: 6 minutes   •   Serves: 6

Each skewer has: 253 calories   •   20 g protein   •   19 g animal protein   •   1 g vegetable protein   •   5 g carbohydrates   •   2 g dietary fiber   •   3 g net carbohydrates   •   15 g fat   •   3 g saturated fat   •   39 mg cholesterol   •   678 mg sodium   •   Exchanges: 2½ lean meat, 1 vegetable, 1 fat

Skewers (soak wooden skewers prior to use to prevent burning)	1 (8-oz.) pkg. button mushrooms, stems removed and wiped with a damp paper towel
1 lb. steak tips, cut into 1-inch pieces	2 TB. olive oil
1 medium sweet onion, peeled and cut into 1-inch pieces	2 tsp. Italian seasoning
1 cup large pimiento-stuffed olives	Salt and ground black pepper
1 pint grape tomatoes	Lemon juice

Preheat the grill. On each skewer, slide alternating pieces of steak, onion, olive, tomato, and mushroom. Stack the loaded skewers on a large plate, drizzle with olive oil, and sprinkle with Italian seasoning, salt, and pepper. Grill kebabs for 6 minutes or until meat is cooked, turning once. Drizzle with lemon juice and serve.

Variation: Use hot peppers, squash, or bell peppers (green, yellow, or red) on your skewers.

 Carb Alert

Onions don't cook completely in these dishes, so you'll get a blast of unwelcome sharp flavor with sharp onions. Stick with the sweet, mild varieties, like Vidalia, Bermuda, or Maui. (Sweet onions don't completely cook either, but the mild flavor makes the kebabs a success.)

Fast Start Chili

Prep time: 5 minutes • Cook time: 20 minutes • Serves: 8

Each serving has: 273 calories • 19 g protein • 12 g animal protein • 7 g vegetable protein • 23 g carbohydrates • 8 g dietary fiber • 15 g net carbohydrates • 12 g fat • 5 g saturated fat • 42 mg cholesterol • 453 mg sodium • Exchanges: 2 lean meat, 1 starch, 1 vegetable, 1½ fat

2 TB. olive oil	2 TB. chili powder
1 lb. lean ground beef	1 TB. ground cumin
1 (16-oz.) can refried beans	1 tsp. salt
1 (15-oz.) can red kidney beans, drained and rinsed	½ tsp. ground black pepper
1 (14-oz.) can diced tomatoes with juice	½ cup (4 oz.) light sour cream

Heat oil in a large skillet over medium heat and cook ground beef for 5 minutes or until browned, stirring. Stir in refried beans, kidney beans, tomatoes, chili powder, cumin, salt, and pepper and cook for 10 minutes, stirring. Serve, topping with a dollop of sour cream.

Variations: Use ground chicken, pork, or turkey in place of ground beef. Add sliced mushrooms or canned corn. Few will object to shredded cheese on top, either.

For a chili that benefits from longer cooking (but doesn't take any more of your time), take a look at Chapter 11.

 Carbohistory

The definition of chili varies from region to region, and even from house to house. I recently organized a competition that included 17 versions of chili. Each one was delicious, and each one distinct. The only common components were chili seasoning and perhaps beans. Go to another region of the country, and you won't even find beans (as a friend of mine from Texas pointed out). Speaking of beans, buy the fat-free version if you want to avoid lard.

Lamb Chops on Wilted Greens with Balsamic Drizzle

Prep time: 8 minutes • Cook time: 12 minutes • Serves: 4

Each serving has: 457 calories • 32 g protein • 31 g animal protein • 1 g vegetable protein • 2 g carbohydrates • 1 g dietary fiber • 1 g net carbohydrates • 36 g fat • 13 g saturated fat • 112 mg cholesterol • 379 mg sodium • Exchanges: 6 medium-fat meat, 1 vegetable, 1 fat

3 TB. canola oil	1 (8-oz.) pkg. fresh baby spinach, stemmed, rinsed, and dried
1½ lb. lamb loin chops	1 TB. crushed garlic
Salt and ground black pepper	3 TB. balsamic vinegar

Heat 1 tablespoon oil in a large skillet over medium-high heat. Rub lamb chops with salt and pepper and brown for 1 minute on each side. Reduce heat to medium and cook for 6 more minutes or until done, turning once. Remove chops to a plate and cover with foil. Add 1 tablespoon oil to the skillet, add spinach, cover, and cook for 1 minute or until spinach is wilted. Distribute spinach to serving plates and top with a lamb chop. Add remaining 1 tablespoon oil to the skillet along with garlic and vinegar and cook for 1 minute. Drizzle vinegar mixture over lamb chops and spinach on each plate and serve.

Serve with a salad, and maybe a glass of red Bordeaux, and all is right with the world.

Moroccan Lamb Kebabs

Prep time: 10 minutes   •   Cook time: 8 minutes   •   Serves: 4

Each serving has: 472 calories   •   33 g protein   •   31 g animal protein   •   2 g vegetable protein   •   5 g carbohydrates   •   2 g dietary fiber   •   3 g net carbohydrates   •   35 g fat   •   13 g saturated fat   •   112 mg cholesterol   •   1,200 mg sodium   •   Exchanges: 6 lean fat meat, 1 vegetable, 2 fat

Skewers (soak wooden skewers prior to use to prevent burning)

1½ lb. lamb steak, cut into 1-inch chunks

2 large bell peppers (different colors look nice), seeds and ribs removed and cut into 1-inch-square pieces

1 (8-oz.) pkg. small white mushrooms, stems trimmed, wiped with a damp paper towel, and cut in half lengthwise

1 large sweet onion, such as Vidalia, peeled and cut into 1-inch-square pieces

3 TB. olive oil

1 tsp. salt

1 tsp. cumin

½ tsp. ground black pepper

¼ tsp. ground cardamom

¼ tsp. ground cinnamon

Preheat the grill. On each skewer, slide alternating pieces of lamb, bell pepper, mushroom, and onion. Stack the loaded skewers on a large plate and drizzle with olive oil. Mix salt, cumin, black pepper, cardamom, and cinnamon in a small bowl and sprinkle over kebabs. Grill kebabs for 8 minutes or until meat is cooked, turning once.

Variation: Use cubes of steak, chicken, or pork. Experiment with grape tomatoes and vegetables.

Carb Smarts

Many grills, especially when you're using charcoal, will have hot and cold spots. Rotate food on your grill if it has a hot spot. When turning your kebabs, rotate the less-done ones to the hot spot and the more-done ones out to cooler areas of the grill so all the kebabs will be done at about the same time.

The Least You Need to Know

♦ Beef dishes can be perfect for the cook in a hurry, if you're careful about the cut you choose (hint: avoid 10-pound roasts).

♦ Rich meats such as beef and lamb bring terrific flavor on their own but can also stand up to aggressive seasoning.

♦ Ground beef is a versatile, easy-to-use ingredient, whether its destination is simple (meat balls) or more complex (stuffed peppers).

♦ Stir-frying is not only a fun and appetizing method of cooking, but it's also extremely fast.

Chapter 10

Bean Cuisine

In This Chapter

- ◆ Bean recipes from around the world
- ◆ New, delicious uses for familiar bean-y friends
- ◆ Nutritious hot and cold bean recipes

Beans form the foundation of many healthy meals across the globe. They bring a hearty consistency and a nutrition profile that is perfect for the carb-conscious cook.

In these recipes, I've specified *shell beans* most commonly found canned in grocery stores, such as:

- ◆ White beans (also known as cannellini beans)
- ◆ Chickpeas (also called garbanzo beans)
- ◆ Black beans
- ◆ Red beans (or kidney beans)

Many other types of delicious shell beans are out there, including, among others:

◆ Black-eyed peas

◆ Pinto beans

◆ Fava beans

◆ Adzuki beans

If you find them, give them a try!

As an added bonus: Many of the dishes in this chapter are also quick, one-pot meals.

A World Tour with Mr. Bean

Several bean dishes in this chapter have clear roots in the culinary traditions of specific parts of the world, making dinner time an opportunity to experience part of a different culture than our own. Not bad for a quick, low-carb meal.

Classic Bean

We'll have some fun exploring some different ways to prepare beans, from somewhat unusual (pancakes) to pure comfort food (ham and beans). The bean-based dishes in this chapter show how flexible, and delicious, bean cuisine can be.

Bean Salads

Finally, I wrap up the chapter with some of my favorite salads that make good use of beans. These are terrific for dinner or for lunch.

For more on salads, many with beans, visit Chapter 14.

Black Bean Stew

Prep time: 5 minutes • Cook time: 15 minutes • Serves: 6

Each serving has: 193 calories • 8 g protein • 1 g animal protein • 7 g vegetable protein • 21 g carbohydrates • 8 g dietary fiber • 13 g net carbohydrates • 6 g fat • 2 g saturated fat • 8 mg cholesterol • 562 mg sodium • Exchanges: 1 very-lean meat, 1 starch, 1 vegetable, 1 fat

2 TB. olive oil	1 (14-oz.) can chopped tomatoes, with juice
1 large onion, peeled and chopped	½ cup fresh cilantro, chopped
1 TB. chili powder	2 TB. lime juice
1 tsp. ground cumin	⅔ cup light sour cream
2 (15-oz.) cans chicken broth	½ tsp. freshly ground black pepper
2 (15-oz.) cans black beans, drained	Salt

Heat oil in a large stockpot over medium heat and cook onion for 3 minutes, stirring. Add chili powder and cumin and cook 2 minutes, stirring. Add 1 can broth, 1 can beans, and tomatoes to the saucepan and cook for 10 minutes. Meanwhile, pour remaining can broth and remaining can beans into a blender and purée to a smooth consistency. Add puréed beans to soup in stockpot for the remainder of the cooking time. Stir in cilantro and lime juice and serve in bowls with a dollop of sour cream. Season to taste with pepper and salt, if desired (there's salt in chicken broth, so it might not be necessary).

Carb Smarts

Soups and stews traditionally use flour or cornstarch for thickening. A quick purée of cooked beans can serve this same delicious purpose while adding fiber and nutrition instead of empty carbohydrates.

Cassoulet

Prep time: 10 minutes • Cook time: 15 minutes • Serves: 6

Each serving has: 330 calories • 15 g protein • 7 g animal protein • 8 g vegetable protein • 28 g carbohydrates • 7 g dietary fiber • 21 g net carbohydrates • 16 g fat • 6 g saturated fat • 33 mg cholesterol • 850 mg sodium • Exchanges: 2 high-fat meat, 1 very-lean meat, 1½ starch, ½ vegetable

1 lb. pork sausage links, cut into 1-inch pieces

3 TB. olive oil

1 medium onion, peeled and chopped into ½-inch pieces

2 large carrots, scraped and cut into ½-inch pieces

1 TB. chopped garlic

2 (15-oz.) cans white beans, drained and rinsed

2 (15-oz.) cans chicken broth

¼ cup dry white wine

1 TB. fresh basil, chopped

1 tsp. fresh oregano

1 tsp. fresh sage, chopped

1 tsp. fresh rosemary leaves

2 tsp. ground mustard

1 bay leaf (optional)

½ tsp. ground black pepper

Salt

Carb Smarts

To accelerate rich meat and bean dishes, cook the meat in a separate skillet while cooking the vegetables in a stockpot next door. If you've got a few extra minutes, though, you can save cleaning by cooking the chicken in the stockpot, then adding your vegetables and cooking them in one pot.

Cook sausage in a large skillet over medium heat for 5 minutes or until done, stirring. Meanwhile, heat oil in a large stockpot over medium heat and cook onion and carrots for 4 minutes. Add garlic and cook for another minute. Using a slotted spoon, lift sausage into the stockpot with onion and carrots. Add beans, broth, wine, basil, oregano, sage, rosemary, mustard, bay leaf (if using), and pepper and cook for 10 minutes, stirring. Remove bay leaf and serve in big bowls with additional salt, if desired (there's salt in chicken broth, so it might not be necessary).

Variation: Substitute 2 teaspoons Italian seasoning for fresh herbs. If you've got the time, use half pork and half sausage in the skillet; then put everything in a slow cooker for 6 to 8 hours on low.

North African Bean Stew

Prep time: 8 minutes   •   Cook time: 15 minutes   •   Serves: 6

Each serving has: 303 calories   •   11 g protein   •   1 g animal protein   •   10 g vegetable protein   •   42 g carbohydrates   •   10 g dietary fiber   •   32 g net carbohydrates   •   10 g fat   •   2½ g saturated fat   •   8 mg cholesterol   •   1,358 mg sodium   •   Exchanges: 2 very-lean meat, 1½ starch, ½ fruit, ½ vegetable, 2 fat

3 (15-oz.) cans chicken stock

3 TB. olive oil

1 medium onion, peeled and chopped into ½-inch pieces

2 celery stalks, rinsed and chopped into ½-inch pieces

2 TB. chopped garlic

½ cup dried apricots, quartered

2 tsp. ground cinnamon

2 tsp. ground paprika

1 tsp. ground cumin

1 tsp. ground coriander

1 tsp. salt

Dash hot red pepper sauce

1 (15-oz.) can black beans, drained and rinsed

1 (15-oz.) can chickpeas, drained and rinsed

1 (14-oz.) can diced tomatoes with juice

½ cup fat-free plain yogurt

Heat chicken stock over high heat in a large pot until near boiling. Meanwhile, heat oil in a large frying pan over medium heat and cook onion, celery, and garlic, stirring, for 4 minutes. Add apricots, cinnamon, paprika, cumin, coriander, salt, and hot sauce and cook, stirring constantly, for another 2 to 3 minutes. Reduce the heat under broth to medium and add black beans, chickpeas, tomatoes with juice, and contents of the large frying pan to the heated broth. Cook for 5 minutes, stirring occasionally to mix the ingredients. Serve in bowls topped with a dollop of yogurt.

Quick Wok Chickpeas and Chicken

Prep time: 5 minutes • Cook time: 5 minutes • Serves: 4

Each serving has: 400 calories • 35 g protein • 27 g animal protein • 8 g vegetable protein • 28 g carbohydrates • 7 g dietary fiber • 21 g net carbohydrates • 17 g fat • 2½ g saturated fat • 66 mg cholesterol • 198 mg sodium • Exchanges: 5 very-lean meat, 1 starch, 1 vegetable, 2 fat

3 TB. sesame or olive oil

1 lb. boneless, skinless chicken breasts, rinsed and dried, and cut into ¾-inch pieces

½ (10-oz.) head broccoli, broken into 1-inch florets, stems discarded

2 TB. chopped garlic

Dash hot red pepper sauce

1 (15-oz.) can chickpeas, drained and rinsed

2 TB. lemon juice

1 TB. grated fresh peeled ginger

2 TB. sesame seeds

Salt

Heat oil in a wok or large skillet over medium-high heat. Add chicken, broccoli, garlic, and hot pepper sauce and cook, stirring, for 4 minutes or until chicken is just done. Add chickpeas and cook for 1 minute, stirring. Turn off heat, drizzle with lemon juice, then sprinkle with ginger. Toss to coat and serve, sprinkling each serving with sesame seeds and seasoning to taste with salt.

Italian Farmhouse Stew

Prep time: 5 minutes   •   Cook time: 15 minutes   •   Serves: 4

Each serving has: 451 calories   •   48 g protein   •   39 g animal protein   •   9 g vegetable protein   •   37 g carbohydrates   •   9 g dietary fiber   •   28 g net carbohydrates   •   11 g fat   •   2 g saturated fat   •   99 mg cholesterol   •   1,017 mg sodium   •   Exchanges: 7 very-lean meat, 1 starch, 2 vegetable, 1½ fat

4 TB. olive oil

1½ lb. boneless, skinless chicken breasts, rinsed, dried, and chopped into ½-inch cubes

1 medium onion, peeled and chopped

2 large celery stalks, rinsed and cut into ¼-inch slices

2 large carrots, scraped and cut into ¼-inch rounds

1 TB. crushed garlic

1 (16-oz.) can white (cannellini) beans, drained and rinsed

2 (15-oz.) cans chicken broth

1 (14-oz.) can crushed tomatoes with juice

1 TB. fresh basil, chopped

1 tsp. fresh oregano

1 tsp. fresh sage, chopped

1 tsp. fresh rosemary leaves

Crushed red pepper

1 TB. balsamic vinegar

Parmesan cheese

Salt and ground black pepper

Heat 2 tablespoons oil in a large skillet over medium heat and cook chicken, stirring, for 5 minutes or until done. Meanwhile, heat remaining 2 tablespoons oil in a large stockpot over medium heat and cook onion, celery, and carrots for 4 minutes. Add garlic and cook for another minute. When chicken is done, add it to the stockpot with vegetables. Add beans, broth, tomatoes, basil, oregano, sage, rosemary, and red pepper and cook for 10 minutes, stirring. Turn off heat, stir in vinegar, and serve in big bowls, sprinkling with Parmesan and seasoning with additional salt, if desired (there's salt in chicken broth, so it might not be necessary), and pepper.

As with many stews of this type, leftovers will taste even better the next night.

Red Beans and Rice

Prep time: 5 minutes • Cook time: 15 minutes • Serves: 4

Each serving has: 372 calories • 10 g protein • 0 g animal protein • 10 g vegetable protein • 55 g carbohydrates • 10 g dietary fiber • 45 g net carbohydrates • 12½ g fat • 2 g saturated fat • 0 mg cholesterol • 425 mg sodium • Exchanges: 1 very-lean meat, 3½ starch, 2 fat

1 cup uncooked brown rice

3 TB. butter or olive oil

1 medium onion, peeled and chopped into ½-inch pieces

2 tsp. Cajun seasoning

2 TB. chopped garlic

1 cup chicken broth

1 (15-oz.) can red kidney beans, drained and rinsed

½ tsp. crushed red pepper (optional)

½ tsp. ground black pepper

1 TB. lime juice

Salt to taste

Cook rice according to package directions.

Meanwhile, heat butter in a large skillet over medium heat and cook onions and Cajun seasoning for 5 minutes, stirring. Add garlic and cook for another minute. Add broth, kidney beans, crushed red pepper (if using), and black pepper. Cook, stirring, for 8 minutes. Serve hot red beans over cooked rice, drizzling with fresh lime juice and seasoning with salt, if desired (there's salt in chicken broth, so it might not be necessary).

Carb Alert

Beans get a bad rap when it comes to gas. All high-fiber foods, including cabbage, broccoli, onions, and many fruits, often result in gas in the lower intestine (the gas is the result of normal bacteria doing its work). For many people, gas results when beans are not a normal part of the diet. For people who eat beans regularly, according to Sally and Martin Stone, authors of *The Instant Bean,* gas is much less of a problem. Rinsing beans before cooking them also removes much of the problem. Finally, there's that little container of Beano.

Minestra

Prep time: 5 minutes • Cook time: 10 minutes • Serves: 4

Each serving has: 293 calories • 11 g protein • 1 g animal protein • 10 g vegetable protein • 30 g carbohydrates • 7 g dietary fiber • 23 g net carbohydrates • 16 g fat • 2½ g saturated fat • 1 mg cholesterol • 220 mg sodium • Exchanges: 1 very-lean meat, 1½ starch, 1 vegetable, 3 fat

1 bunch (about 1 lb.) greens such as chard, kale, or escarole, rinsed	1 (15-oz.) can cannellini beans, drained and rinsed
4 TB. olive oil	Salt and ground black pepper
1½ TB. crushed garlic	Freshly shredded Parmesan cheese

Chop greens. If using chard, add it directly into the recipe; if using kale or escarole, blanch greens for 1 minute in boiling water before using.

Heat oil in a large skillet over medium heat and cook garlic, stirring, for 2 minutes or until garlic begins to turn golden. Add greens and cook for 5 minutes, stirring. Add beans and heat for another 2 minutes. Distribute to serving plates, seasoning with salt and pepper to taste and sprinkling with Parmesan.

Mediterranean Skillet Meal

Prep time: 5 minutes • Cook time: 10 minutes • Serves: 4

Each serving has: 341 calories • 10 g protein • 3 g animal protein • 7 g vegetable protein • 34 g carbohydrates • 7 g dietary fiber • 27 g net carbohydrates • 21 g fat • 4 g saturated fat • 17 mg cholesterol • 863 mg sodium • Exchanges: 1 very-lean meat, ½ medium-fat meat, 1½ starch, 1 vegetable, 2 fat

3 TB. olive oil	1 (14-oz.) can chopped tomatoes, drained
1 medium onion, peeled and chopped into ½-inch pieces	½ cup pitted kalamata olives
2 TB. chopped garlic	½ cup chopped fresh parsley
1 tsp. Italian seasoning	½ cup (2 oz.) crumbled feta cheese
1 (14-oz.) can chickpeas, drained and rinsed	Salt and ground black pepper to taste

Heat olive oil in a large skillet over medium heat and cook onion, stirring, for 4 minutes. Add garlic and Italian seasoning and cook for another minute. Add chickpeas, tomatoes, and olives and cook for another 5 minutes, stirring. Stir in parsley and serve, topping with crumbled feta cheese and seasoning with salt and pepper to taste.

White Bean Vegetable Pancakes

Prep time: 10 minutes • Cook time: 8 minutes • Serves: 4

Each serving has: 339 calories • 13 g protein • 4 g animal protein • 9 g vegetable protein • 28 g carbohydrates • 2 g dietary fiber • 26 g net carbohydrates • 21 g fat • 4 g saturated fat • 105 mg cholesterol • 416 mg sodium • Exchanges: 1 very-lean meat, ½ medium-fat meat, 1½ starch, 1 vegetable, 3 fat

1 (15-oz.) can cannellini beans, drained and rinsed	1 small (8 × 1-inch) zucchini squash, rinsed and trimmed
1 TB. chopped garlic	1 portobello mushroom, stemmed and wiped with a damp paper towel
½ tsp. salt	
¼ tsp. ground black pepper	2 large eggs, whisked
¼ tsp. ground cumin	4 TB. olive oil
¼ tsp. dried thyme	½ cup light sour cream

In a food processor fitted with a steel blade, process beans, garlic, salt, pepper, cumin, and thyme just enough to break up beans but leave plenty of texture. Scrape beans into a large bowl. Switch out the steel blade with the shredder wheel (don't bother cleaning the bowl). Cut zucchini into pieces to fit into the feed tube, shred zucchini, then do the same with mushroom on top of zucchini. Pour shredded mushroom and zucchini on top of beans. Add eggs and stir mixture thoroughly.

Heat oil in a large skillet over medium heat. Using a ¼-cup measure, spoon lumpy batter into the skillet and cook for approximately 3 minutes on one side, then 1 minute on the other (watch for the point when the pancakes are solid enough to flip: too early and they tend to break apart). Serve hot, with a spoonful of sour cream on top.

Carbohistory

I first made these because a friend challenged me to make what he called an "edible" pancake based on beans. I can never resist a challenge, so I came up with these savory, crisp-creamy burgers. The consistency is somewhat like crab cakes. These, apparently, are more than "edible": My challenging friend had thirds.

Two-Bean Ham Stew

Prep time: 5 minutes • Cook time: 15 minutes • Serves: 8

Each serving has: 193 calories • 14 g protein • 7 g animal protein • 7 g vegetable protein • 21 g carbohydrates • 6 g dietary fiber • 15 g net carbohydrates • 6 g fat • 1 g saturated fat • 15 mg cholesterol • 431 mg sodium • Exchanges: 2 very-lean meat, 1 starch, 1 vegetable, 1 fat

3 TB. olive oil

2 tsp. mustard seed

1 medium onion, peeled and chopped into ½-inch pieces

3 celery stalks, including leafy tops, rinsed and cut into ½-inch pieces

1 bay leaf

2 (15-oz.) cans chicken broth

1 (15-oz.) can white navy beans or cannellini beans, drained and rinsed

1 (15-oz.) can black beans, drained and rinsed

1 (14-oz.) can diced tomatoes with juice

1 (¾-lb.) ham steak, cut into ½-inch cubes

Dash hot red pepper sauce

Salt and ground black pepper

Heat oil in a large stockpot over medium heat and add mustard seed, onion, celery, and bay leaf. Cook, stirring, for 5 minutes. Add chicken broth, white and black beans, tomatoes, ham, and hot sauce and cook for 10 minutes. Remove bay leaf and serve, seasoning to taste with salt, if desired (there's salt in broth and ham, so it might not be necessary), and pepper.

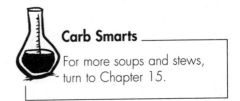

Carb Smarts

For more soups and stews, turn to Chapter 15.

Herbed White Beans with Baby Spinach

Prep time: 5 minutes • Cook time: 10 minutes • Serves: 4

Each serving has: 395 calories • 21 g protein • 3 g animal protein • 18 g vegetable protein • 51 g carbohydrates • 13 g dietary fiber • 38 g net carbohydrates • 13 g fat • 3 g saturated fat • 5 mg cholesterol • 363 mg sodium • Exchanges: 2 very-lean meat, ½ medium-fat meat, 2½ starch, 1 vegetable, 2 fat

3 TB. olive oil	1 (7-oz.) pkg. fresh baby spinach, rinsed and stemmed
1 medium onion, peeled and chopped into ½-inch pieces	2 TB. balsamic vinegar
2 TB. chopped garlic	⅓ cup shredded Parmesan cheese
1 TB. chopped fresh rosemary or 1 tsp. dried	½ tsp. ground black pepper
2 (15-oz.) cans white beans, drained and rinsed	Salt to taste

Heat oil in a large skillet over medium heat and cook onion for 4 minutes, stirring. Add garlic and rosemary and cook, stirring, for 1 minute. Add white beans and cook, stirring, for 3 minutes. Finally, add spinach, cover, and cook for 2 minutes. Spinach will wilt. Turn off heat and drizzle with balsamic vinegar. Stir to coat and serve, sprinkling each serving with Parmesan and seasoning with pepper and salt to taste.

Variation: Substitute 1 pound boneless, skinless chicken breasts, cut into ¾-inch pieces, for 1 can white beans. Add chicken after onions have cooked for 4 minutes and add about 5 minutes to the cooking time before adding beans and spinach to give chicken time to cook. Substitute frozen spinach, thawed, drained, and pressed dry, for fresh spinach. Substitute lemon juice for balsamic vinegar (this will change the dish, but it's delicious).

White Beans with Olive Oil, Gorgonzola, and Fresh Sage

Prep time: 5 minutes   •   Cook time: 10 minutes   •   Serves: 4

Each serving has: 404 calories   •   20 g protein   •   4 g animal protein   •   16 g vegetable protein   •   48 g carbohydrates   •   12 g dietary fiber   •   36 g net carbohydrates   •   15 g fat   •   4 g saturated fat   •   16 mg cholesterol   •   422 mg sodium   •   Exchanges: 2 very-lean meat, ½ high-fat meat, 3 starch, 2 fat

4 cups water

2 (15-oz.) cans white beans, drained and rinsed

3 TB. extra-virgin olive oil

1 TB. minced fresh sage leaves or ½ tsp. dried

½ cup crumbled *Gorgonzola dolce* cheese

Salt and ground black pepper

Bring water to a boil and add beans. Bring just to a boil again, then drain beans. Toss with olive oil, sage, and Gorgonzola and serve warm, seasoning to taste with salt and pepper.

Variation: Use regular crumbled blue cheese in place of Gorgonzola. The taste will not be the same, but it will be in the same ballpark.

Gourmand's Glossary

Gorgonzola dolce is a creamy and rich Italian blue cheese. *Dolce* means "sweet," and that's the kind you want.

White Beans with Mushrooms, Olives, and Sun-Dried Tomatoes

Prep time: 5 minutes • Cook time: 5 minutes • Serves: 4

Each serving has: 334 calories • 15 g protein • 2 g animal protein • 13 g vegetable protein • 33 g carbohydrates • 9 g dietary fiber • 24 g net carbohydrates • 18 g fat • 5 g saturated fat • 3½ mg cholesterol • 784 mg sodium • Exchanges: 2 starch, 2 very-lean meat, 3 fat

3 TB. olive oil

2 TB. chopped garlic

1½ tsp. fresh oregano or ½ tsp. dried

1½ tsp. fresh chopped basil or ½ tsp. dried

1 bay leaf

1 lb. button mushrooms, trimmed, wiped with a damp paper towel, and sliced in half lengthwise

1 (15-oz.) can white beans, drained and rinsed

½ cup pitted *kalamata olives*

½ cup oil-packed sun-dried tomatoes, drained and chopped

2 TB. red wine vinegar

¼ cup shredded Parmesan cheese

Gourmand's Glossary

Kalamata olives, traditionally from Greece, are a medium-small, long black olive with a smoky, rich flavor—very different from run-of-the-mill canned black olives. Try them and you'll be hooked.

Heat oil in a large skillet over medium heat and cook garlic, oregano, basil, and bay leaf for 2 minutes, stirring. Add mushrooms and cook for 5 minutes, stirring. Add beans, olives, and sun-dried tomatoes and cook for 1 minute more. Remove from heat, remove bay leaf, toss with vinegar, and serve, topping with Parmesan and seasoning to taste with salt.

Variation: If you can find fava beans to use in place of the white beans, they are a natural.

Pan-Broiled White Bean, Bacon, and Scallop Dinner

Prep time: 5 minutes • Cook time: 11 minutes • Serves: 6

Each serving has: 359 calories • 29 g protein • 23 g animal protein • 6 g vegetable protein • 18 g carbohydrates • 5 g dietary fiber • 13 g net carbohydrates • 18 g fat • 7 g saturated fat • 72 mg cholesterol • 913 mg sodium • Exchanges: 1½ high-fat meat, 2 very-lean meat, 2 fat

½ lb. bacon

1 bunch scallions, roots and dark green parts removed, minced

2 TB. sherry

1½ tsp. fresh thyme or ½ tsp. dried

1 tsp. fresh sage, minced, or ¼ tsp. ground

½ lb. bay scallops

1 (15-oz.) can white beans, drained and rinsed

½ cup shredded Swiss cheese

Ground black pepper and salt to taste

Preheat the broiler.

Cook bacon in a large skillet over medium heat for 2 minutes per side or until crisp. Remove bacon to a paper-towel–lined plate and pour off most fat, leaving enough to coat the bottom of the skillet. Add scallions, sherry, thyme, and sage and cook for 3 minutes, stirring. Add scallops to the skillet and cook for 3 minutes or until done, stirring. Crumble bacon. Add beans and crumbled bacon to the skillet and stir to thoroughly combine. Heat for 1 minute. Turn off the stove and sprinkle cheese over the top of bean mixture. Slide skillet under the broiler for 2 minutes or until cheese melts. Remove from oven and serve, seasoning with pepper to taste. You might not need salt, as bacon will already have introduced salt to the dish.

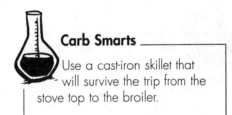

Carb Smarts

Use a cast-iron skillet that will survive the trip from the stove top to the broiler.

Garbanzo Bisque

Prep time: 5 minutes • Cook time: 12 minutes • Serves: 4

Each serving has: 238 calories • 10 g protein • 3 g animal protein • 7 g vegetable protein • 32 g carbohydrates • 6 g dietary fiber • 26 g net carbohydrates • 9 g fat • 2 g saturated fat • 2 mg cholesterol • 897 mg sodium • Exchanges: 2 starch, ¼ milk, 1½ fat

2 TB. butter or olive oil

1 medium onion, peeled and chopped into ½-inch pieces

1 TB. curry powder

1 (15-oz.) can chicken broth

1 (15-oz.) can chickpeas, drained and rinsed

1 TB. marsala cooking wine (optional)

1 tsp. salt

¼ tsp. ground black pepper

Double dash hot red pepper sauce

1 cup heavy cream or plain yogurt

2 TB. fresh chives, minced

Heat oil in a large saucepan over medium heat and cook onion for 5 minutes, stirring. Add curry powder and cook, stirring, for 2 minutes. Add broth, chickpeas, wine, salt, pepper, and hot pepper sauce to the saucepan and cook for 5 minutes, stirring.

Gourmand's Glossary

A **bisque** is a creamy, thick soup made with puréed vegetables, meats, and especially seafood.

Working in batches, put *bisque* in a blender and purée to a smooth consistency. Return bisque to the saucepan. Stir in cream or yogurt and heat for another minute or until soup is hot (if using yogurt, be careful not to bring it to a boil). Serve in bowls with a sprinkling of chives.

Variation: Use Garam masala in place of the curry powder. The result will be slightly less spicy, but just as rich.

White Bean Salad

Prep time: 10 minutes   •   Serves: 4

Each serving has: 303 calories   •   18 g protein   •   3 g animal protein   •   15 g vegetable protein   •   44 g carbohydrates   •   22 g dietary fiber   •   22 g net carbohydrates   •   8 g fat   •   2 g saturated fat   •   8 mg cholesterol   •   649 mg sodium   •   Exchanges: ½ high-fat meat, 1 very-lean meat, 1 starch, 3 vegetable, 1½ fat

1 (15-oz.) can cannellini beans, drained

1 medium fresh tomato, rinsed, seeded, and chopped into pieces about ¼ inch across, or about 10 grape tomatoes, quartered

1 cup fresh basil leaves, rinsed and chopped into ¼-inch pieces

¼ sweet onion, peeled and chopped (about ⅓ cup chopped)

¼ cup shredded Parmesan cheese

1 TB. balsamic vinegar

1 TB. olive oil

½ tsp. salt

⅛ tsp. ground black pepper

4 Belgian endive heads, broken into leaves

3 pieces cooked bacon as garnish (optional)

Additional salt and pepper (optional)

Additional olive oil as dressing

In a bowl, mix beans, tomato, basil, onion, Parmesan, vinegar, oil, salt, and black pepper, being sure to preserve the shape of most beans. Arrange endive leaves on 4 serving plates, ends touching at the center and tips pointing out flower style. Distribute bean salad among plates, crumbling bacon (if using) over each serving, seasoning, if desired, with additional salt, pepper, and olive oil as dressing.

Variation: Substitute red wine vinegar for the balsamic vinegar. For a more hearty salad, add 1 (6-ounce) can chunk white tuna in water (drained).

Carb Smarts

If you're careful how you scoop the salad onto the endive leaves, the tips will rise slightly from the weight of the salad in the center, creating a "flower" effect. It's always fun to play with your food.

Presto Pesto Chickpea Salad

Prep time: 8 minutes • Serves: 4

Each serving has: 239 calories • 8 g protein • 0 g animal protein • 8 g vegetable protein • 30 g carbohydrates • 8 g dietary fiber • 22 g net carbohydrates • 11 g fat • 1½ g saturated fat • 0 mg cholesterol • 320 mg sodium • Exchanges: 2 very-lean meat, 2 starch, 2 fat

1 (15-oz.) can chickpeas, drained and rinsed

1 large red bell pepper, seeds and ribs removed, and chopped into ¼-inch pieces

1 large celery stalk, rinsed and cut into ¼-inch pieces

¼ sweet onion, peeled and chopped (about ⅓ cup chopped)

¼ cup prepared pesto sauce

3 TB. toasted pine nuts

2 TB. lemon juice

Toss chickpeas, red pepper, celery, onion, pesto, and pine nuts in a bowl. Distribute to serving plates, drizzle with lemon juice, and sprinkle with Parmesan.

The Least You Need to Know

- ◆ Beans have been used across the world for generations as a flexible, delicious food.
- ◆ Shell beans are naturally high in protein and fiber and are a terrific good-carb food for the carb-conscious gourmand.
- ◆ Beans can be the focus of a dish, a flavorful component, or an unexpected foundation (as in pancakes, or as a thickener). Magical fruit, indeed.
- ◆ Canned beans provide a fast option for quick meals.

Chapter 11

Vegetarian Favorites

In This Chapter

- ◆ Naturally fast vegetarian cuisine
- ◆ Hearty casseroles
- ◆ Go for a power wok
- ◆ Savory tofu delicacies

When it comes to vegetarian cuisine, time is on your side. Many of the dishes in this chapter rely on bright flavors from fresh ingredients—flavors that would be dulled or destroyed by long cooking.

My family is not vegetarian, but many of our meals fall into the vegetarian category anyway. Flavorful and packed with nutrition, these vegetarian dishes are a must-make part of a carb-conscious diet.

The recipes in this chapter comply with a definition of vegetarianism that does not include fish, white or red meat, but can include eggs, milk, and cheese.

Vegetarian Comfort Food

If the term *vegetarian* makes you think of lentils and brown rice, you're in for a pleasant surprise. The main course dishes in this chapter are savory and hearty and include everything from stuffed vegetables to casseroles.

Vegetarian cuisine can easily be adapted to the needs of the carb-conscious cook. An added bonus: Many dishes are naturally lower in saturated fat than their meat-based counterparts.

Vegetarian World Tour

Our country is unusual in its reliance on meat. Many culinary traditions in other parts of the world are largely vegetarian, so exploring vegetarian dishes leads us, inescapably, on a tasty world tour.

Some of my favorite recipes take their influence from other parts of the (culinary) world as you will see with the recipes in this chapter.

Tofu

I wrap up this chapter with some tofu recipes. Tofu, that versatile, cheeselike soy product made from soybeans and soy milk, has long been included in cuisines of the Far East. Its meaty texture and mild flavor make it easy to use. Tofu is a good low-carb source of fiber and protein. For added interest, use a flavored tofu, available at your grocery store. Firm tofu will hold its shape in your recipe.

Stuffed Tomatoes

Prep time: 5 minutes • Cook time: 12 minutes • Serves: 4

Each serving has: 313 calories • 11 g protein • 3 g animal protein • 9 g vegetable protein • 37 g carbohydrates • 8 g dietary fiber • 29 g net carbohydrates • 15 g fat • 3 g saturated fat • 10 mg cholesterol • 740 mg sodium • Exchanges: 1 starch, 3 vegetable, 3 fat

4 medium ripe tomatoes

2 TB. olive oil

1 medium onion, peeled and chopped into ½-inch pieces

2 tsp. chopped garlic

1 (15-oz.) can chickpeas, drained and rinsed

½ (14.5-oz.) can (1 cup) diced tomatoes

¼ cup unprocessed bran

¼ cup chopped walnuts

¼ cup fresh basil, chopped

1 tsp. fresh oregano leaves

½ tsp. fresh thyme

½ tsp. fresh rosemary

½ tsp. ground cumin

½ tsp. salt

¼ tsp. ground black pepper

¼ cup plus 2 TB. shredded Parmesan cheese

Preheat the oven to 375°F. Slice off the top ⅓ of each tomato, scoop out the insides, and discard insides. Place tomatoes, cut side up, in an oven-safe baking dish with ¼ inch water in the bottom and slide tomatoes into the oven to begin to cook for 7 to 10 minutes while you prepare the other ingredients.

Meanwhile, heat oil in a large skillet over medium heat and cook onion and garlic, stirring, for 3 minutes. Mix in chickpeas, diced tomatoes, reserved tomato flesh, bran, walnuts, basil, oregano, thyme, rosemary, cumin, salt, and pepper. Cook for 4 minutes, stirring. Stir in ¼ cup Parmesan cheese. Remove tomatoes from the oven and stuff them with the skillet mixture (keep a little water in the bottom of the baking dish). Top with remaining Parmesan. Slide tomatoes in their baking tray back into the oven and heat for 4 minutes, or until cheese begins to melt.

Variation: Fresh flavors from fresh herbs are delicious, but to save even more time, use 2 teaspoons Italian seasoning in place of fresh basil, oregano, thyme, and rosemary.

Cheesy Stuffed Peppers

Prep time: 5 minutes • Cook time: 12 minutes • Serves: 4

Each serving has: 283 calories • 13 g protein • 11 g animal protein • 2 g vegetable protein • 15 g carbohydrates • 4 g dietary fiber • 11 g net carbohydrates • 21 g fat • 6 g saturated fat • 27 mg cholesterol • 642 mg sodium • Exchanges: 1½ medium-fat meat, ½ high-fat meat, 2 vegetable, 2 fat

3 TB. olive oil

1 medium onion, peeled and chopped into ½-inch pieces

2 tsp. chopped garlic

½ (14-oz.) can (1 cup) diced tomatoes, juice reserved

¼ cup unprocessed bran

1 TB. Worcestershire sauce

½ tsp. salt

¼ tsp. ground black pepper

⅛ tsp. ground nutmeg

1 cup part-skim ricotta cheese

4 medium red bell peppers, top 1 inch cut off, seeds and ribs removed

½ cup (2 oz.) shredded cheddar cheese

Preheat the broiler.

Heat oil in a large skillet over medium heat and cook onion and garlic, stirring, for 4 minutes. Mix in tomatoes, bran, Worcestershire sauce, salt, pepper, and nutmeg. Cook for 4 minutes, stirring. Turn off heat, and stir in ricotta.

Carb Alert

Prevent burnt sacrifices by closely watching broiling and grilling dishes. The difference between "done" and "unrecognizable" is only a minute or two with these quick-cooking methods.

Meanwhile, microwave peppers, cut side up, in a microwave- and oven-safe baking dish with ½ inch water in the bottom for 4 to 5 minutes or until softened. Remove and stuff peppers with tomato-ricotta mixture (keep a little water in the bottom of the baking dish). Top each pepper with some shredded cheddar and then slide under the broiler on the second rack for 3 minutes or until cheese has melted.

Portobello Pizza

Prep time: 3 minutes • Cook time: 9 minutes • Serves: 2

Each serving has: 408 calories • 21 g protein • 18 g animal protein • 3 g vegetable protein • 9 g carbohydrates • 2 g dietary fiber • 7 g net carbohydrates • 33 g fat • 10 g saturated fat • 48 mg cholesterol • 652 mg sodium • Exchanges: 3 medium lean meat, 2 vegetable, 4 fat

2 large (about 4-inch) flat portobello mushroom caps, stems and gills removed and wiped with a damp paper towel	½ tsp. dried tarragon
	½ cup pizza sauce
3 TB. olive oil	⅔ cup shredded part-skim Mozzarella cheese
	Salt and ground black pepper

Preheat the broiler; if your broiler has multiple settings, select the medium setting. Place mushroom caps on a baking tray, top side up. Brush each with some oil and broil on the next-to-highest rack for 3 minutes. Flip caps, drizzle each with ½ remaining olive oil, sprinkle with tarragon, and broil for 3 more minutes. Slide sizzling mushrooms out of the oven and divide sauce and then cheese between each mushroom, spreading each layer smooth. Slide your pizzas back under the broiler and broil for 3 minutes or until cheese is melted.

Place each pizza on a serving plate and serve with a knife and fork, seasoning to taste with salt and pepper.

Carb Smarts

Your favorite vegetarian pasta sauce will work in place of the pizza sauce.

This method is for a basic cheese version. As for toppings, anything that you like on regular pizza is fair game.

Sautéed Mushroom Enchiladas

Prep time: 5 minutes • Cook time: 5 minutes • Serves: 2

Each serving has: 379 calories • 25 g protein • 14 g animal protein • 11 g vegetable protein • 24 g carbohydrates • 15 g dietary fiber • 9 g net carbohydrates • 28 g fat • 5 g saturated fat • 12 mg cholesterol • 530 mg sodium • Exchanges: 1 starch, 1 vegetable, 2 lean meat, 4 fat

3 TB. olive oil	2 large whole-wheat or low-carb soft tortillas
1 TB. chopped garlic	Pinch salt
1 tsp. Italian seasoning	Pinch ground black pepper
2 cups sliced white mushrooms	1 cup (4 oz.) shredded low-fat cheddar cheese

Heat oil in a large skillet over medium heat. Cook garlic and Italian seasoning for 1 minute, stirring. Add mushrooms and cook for 3 minutes, stirring, or until mushrooms are soft. Lay each tortilla on a microwave-safe serving plate and place ½ mushrooms in a line along one side. Sprinkle mushrooms with salt and pepper. Top mushrooms with about ¼ cup cheese per tortilla and roll tortilla over its filling. Top with another ¼ cup cheese per tortilla. Microwave for 1 minute or until cheese on top is melted; serve.

Variation: Top with sour cream.

Fast Ricotta-Spinach Casserole

Prep time: 10 minutes • Cook time: 10 minutes • Serves: 6

Each serving has: 358 calories • 20 g protein • 10 g animal protein • 10 g vegetable protein • 26 g carbohydrates • 7 g dietary fiber • 19 g net carbohydrates • 22 g fat • 7 g saturated fat • 31 mg cholesterol • 216 mg sodium • Exchanges: 2 very-lean meat, 1 medium-fat meat, 1½ starch, ½ vegetable, 3 fat

3 TB. olive oil	½ cup light sour cream
1 medium onion, peeled and chopped into ½-inch chunks	1 (15-oz.) can cannellini beans, drained and rinsed
1 TB. chopped garlic	1 cup part-skim ricotta cheese
1 (10-oz.) pkg. frozen chopped spinach, thawed and squeezed dry	½ cup chopped walnuts
1 tsp. paprika	½ tsp. freshly ground black pepper
¼ tsp. nutmeg	½ cup shredded part skim mozzarella cheese

Heat oil in a large skillet and cook onion and garlic, stirring, for 5 minutes. Meanwhile, spread spinach on the bottom of a 9 × 9 casserole pan. Stir paprika and nutmeg into sour cream and spread sour cream over spinach. Add cannellini beans and spread in an even layer. Mix ricotta cheese, walnuts, and pepper and spread over cannellini beans. Scrape sautéed onions on top of ricotta, and top with mozzarella. Microwave for 5 minutes or until cheese is melted and casserole is bubbling.

Variation: Cook in a preheated 350°F oven for 25 minutes.

Chunky Zucchini Casserole

Prep time: 10 minutes • Cook time: 30 minutes • Serves: 8

Each serving has: 213 calories • 9 g protein • 5 g animal protein • 4 g vegetable protein • 20 g carbohydrates • 6 g dietary fiber • 14 g net carbohydrates • 13 g fat • 4 g saturated fat • 13 mg cholesterol • 403 mg sodium • Exchanges: 1 starch, 1 vegetable, 1 very-lean meat, 2½ fat

1 eggplant, peeled, stem removed, cut into ½-inch chunks

1 tsp. salt

3 TB. olive oil

1 medium onion, peeled and chopped into ½-inch chunks

1 TB. chopped garlic

2 tsp. Italian seasoning

1 (14-oz.) can artichoke hearts, drained

1 lb. zucchini squashes, ends cut off, chopped into ½-inch chunks

1 cup light sour cream

1 (10.75-oz.) can condensed cream of mushroom soup (do not add liquid)

1 cup shredded light cheddar cheese

½ cup unprocessed bran

Carb Smarts

This casserole takes longer than many of the other recipes in this book, but because it will last for multiple meals, it's a good investment of time!

Place eggplant in a bowl, sprinkle with salt, and set aside. Preheat the oven to 400°F. Heat oil in a large skillet and cook onion, garlic, and Italian seasoning, stirring, for 2 minutes. Add eggplant and artichokes and cook for 5 minutes, stirring. Meanwhile, put zucchini in a saucepan with just enough water to cover and bring to a boil over high heat. Boil for 4 minutes and drain. Oil a large baking dish. Spread ½ skillet vegetables on the bottom of the pan, then top with sour cream, zucchini, condensed soup, and remainder of skillet vegetables. Top with shredded cheese, then bran. Bake for 20 minutes or until cheese on top melts.

Ratatouille

Prep time: 10 minutes   •   Cook time: 20 minutes   •   Serves: 8

Each serving has: 108 calories   •   4 g protein   •   2 g animal protein   •   2 g vegetable protein   •   10 g carbohydrates   •   4 g dietary fiber   •   6 g net carbohydrates   •   7 g fat   •   2 g saturated fat   •   4 mg cholesterol   •   384 mg sodium   •   Exchanges: ½ high-fat meat, 2 vegetable, 1 fat

3 TB. olive oil

1 medium onion, peeled and chopped into ½-inch pieces

1 TB. chopped garlic

1 large bell pepper, seeds and ribs removed, chopped into ½-inch pieces

2 small zucchini, ends removed, cut into ½-inch pieces

1 eggplant, peeled, stem removed, cut into ½-inch chunks

3 large tomatoes, rinsed, cored, and roughly chopped, or 1 (28-oz.) can whole tomatoes, roughly chopped, with juice

2 tsp. Italian seasoning

1 tsp. salt

½ tsp. ground black pepper

½ cup shredded Parmesan cheese

Heat oil in a large skillet over medium heat and cook onion, stirring, for 4 minutes. Add garlic and cook for 1 minute. Then add bell pepper, zucchini, eggplant, tomatoes, Italian seasoning, salt, and pepper and cook, stirring constantly, for 15 minutes.

Serve in bowls and top with Parmesan.

Carb Smarts _____

If you've got fresh herbs, you've got a chance to make something great even better. In place of the Italian seasoning, use ¼ cup chopped fresh basil leaves and 1 teaspoon fresh oregano. It wouldn't hurt to put in ½ teaspoon each fresh thyme and fresh rosemary, either. (This fresh herb observation goes for the other recipes in this chapter, and this book, for that matter.)

Grilled Vegetable Kebabs

Prep time: 10 minutes • Cook time: 6 minutes • Serves: 8

Each serving has: 101 calories • 5 g protein • 0 g animal protein • 5 g vegetable protein • 5 g carbohydrates • 1 g dietary fiber • 4 g net carbohydrates • 5 g fat • 1 g saturated fat • 0 mg cholesterol • 39 mg sodium • Exchanges: ½ very-lean meat, 1 vegetable, 1 fat

Skewers (soak wooden skewers prior to use to prevent burning)

1 medium sweet onion, peeled and cut into 1-inch pieces

1 (16-oz.) pkg. extra-firm tofu, drained and cut into 1-inch cubes

1 large bell pepper, seeds and ribs removed, cut into 1-inch pieces

1 pt. grape tomatoes, stemmed and rinsed

2 TB. olive oil

Lemon juice

2 tsp. Italian seasoning

Salt and ground black pepper

Preheat the grill. On each skewer, slide alternating pieces of onion, tofu, bell pepper, and tomato. Stack the loaded skewers on a large plate, drizzle with olive oil and lemon juice, and sprinkle with Italian seasoning, salt, and pepper. Grill for 6 minutes, turning and circulating kebabs around those inevitable hot spots.

Variations: Use mushrooms, hot peppers, or zucchini squash on your skewers.

Carb Smarts

Tofu producers are pretty good these days about making their "extra-firm" product solid enough to survive a skewer and a grill. But just to be on the safe side, I like to bracket each piece of tofu between onion and pepper. The naturally curved shape of these two pieces of vegetable hold that tofu chunk in place.

Sautéed Vegetable Medley

Prep time: 5 minutes • Cook time: 10 minutes • Serves: 4

Each serving has: 372 calories • 10 g protein • 3 g animal protein • 7 g vegetable protein • 37 g carbohydrates • 9 g dietary fiber • 28 g net carbohydrates • 23 g fat • 4 g saturated fat • 17 mg cholesterol • 1,269 mg sodium • Exchanges: 1 very-lean meat, ½ medium-fat meat, 1½ starch, 2 vegetable, 4 fat

3 TB. olive oil	½ tsp. ground cumin
1 medium onion, peeled and chopped into ½-inch pieces	1 (15-oz.) can chickpeas, drained and rinsed
1 large green bell pepper, seeds and ribs removed, chopped into ½-inch pieces	1 (14.5-oz.) can diced tomatoes with juice
	½ cup pitted kalamata olives
1 TB. chopped garlic	2 TB. fresh chopped basil or 2 tsp. dried
½ tsp. crushed red pepper	½ tsp. salt
	½ cup crumbled feta cheese

Heat oil in a large skillet over medium heat and cook onion and bell pepper, stirring, for 4 minutes. Add garlic, red pepper, and cumin and cook for 1 minute. Then add chickpeas, tomatoes, olives, basil, and salt and cook, stirring once or twice, for 5 minutes. Serve, topped with feta cheese.

Carb Smarts

Sautéed Vegetable Medley can take many forms, all of them tasty, fast, and flexible. You don't have chickpeas? White or black beans will work. No feta? Parmesan will do the trick. No kalamata olives? Use another olive—but go for the pitted ones. Like less heat? Omit the crushed red pepper. The journey is half the fun.

South-of-the-Border Eggs

Prep time: 3 minutes • Cook time: 5 minutes • Serves: 2

Each serving has: 274 calories • 13 g protein • 12 g animal protein • 1 g vegetable protein • 5 g carbohydrates • 1 g dietary fiber • 4 g net carbohydrates • 22 g fat • 5 g saturated fat • 373 mg cholesterol • 157 mg sodium • Exchanges: 2 medium-fat meat, 1 vegetable, 2½ fat

2 TB. canola or olive oil	1 TB. fresh chopped basil or 1 tsp. dried
4 large eggs	2 tsp. fresh chopped cilantro
¼ cup skim milk	1 tsp. chili powder
1 tomato, cored, seeded, and diced	Salt and ground black pepper

Heat oil in a small skillet over medium-low heat. Mix eggs, milk, tomatoes, basil, cilantro, and chili powder in a bowl. Pour egg mixture into the skillet and cook, stirring slowly to bring uncooked eggs in contact with the skillet, for 4 minutes, or to your desired consistency. Distribute to serving plates and season with salt and pepper.

Variation: If you don't have fresh cilantro, just omit it.

Vegetable Stir-Fry

Prep time: 5 minutes • Cook time: 10 minutes • Serves: 4

Each serving has: 160 calories • 8 g protein • 2 g animal protein • 6 g vegetable protein • 14 g carbohydrates • 4 g dietary fiber • 10 g net carbohydrates • 10 g fat • 2 g saturated fat • 47 mg cholesterol • 585 mg sodium • Exchanges: 1 very-lean meat, 2 vegetable, 2 fat

2 TB. sesame or olive oil	½ (14-oz.) pkg. (7 oz.) seasoned extra-firm tofu, drained and cut into ½-inch cubes
1 large onion, peeled and chopped into ¼-inch pieces	1 (6-oz.) can sliced water chestnuts, drained
2 cups fresh broccoli, cut into 1-inch florets	1 egg
1 TB. chopped garlic	2 TB. soy sauce

Heat oil in a wok or large skillet over medium heat. Cook onion for 2 minutes, stirring. Add broccoli and garlic and cook for 3 minutes, stirring. Add tofu and water chestnuts and cook, stirring, for 3 more minutes. Whisk egg and soy sauce in a measuring cup and pour over vegetables in the wok. Cook for 1 minute or until egg is cooked and broccoli florets are tender-crisp.

Variation: Serve over ½ cup brown rice (this will increase the good-carb count).

Tostadas

Prep time: 6 minutes • Cook time: 4 minutes • Serves: 4

Each serving has: 356 calories • 19 g protein • 13 g animal protein • 6 g vegetable protein • 19 g carbohydrates • 9 g dietary fiber • 10 g net carbohydrates • 27 g fat • 13 g saturated fat • 69 mg cholesterol • 1,635 mg sodium • Exchanges: 2 high-fat meat, 1 starch, 2 fat

4 small whole-wheat tortillas or low-carb tortillas

1 cup salsa (your sugar-free favorite), spooned with a slotted spoon (or drained) to remove excess liquid

1 (8-oz.) pkg. shredded Mexican-style or Monterey Jack cheese

1 (4-oz.) can sliced black olives, drained

½ cup light sour cream

Preheat the broiler. Arrange tortillas on a large baking tray or two and broil on the top rack for 1 minute to crisp a bit. Remove and divide salsa among tortillas; top salsa with shredded cheese, then sliced olives. Broil for 3 minutes or until cheese melts. Slice pizza-style and serve each with a *dollop* of sour cream.

Variation: Tostadas also make a terrific hot appetizer.

Gourmand's Glossary

I probably carry an analogy too far by calling a **tostada** a sort of pizza, but you get the idea. These simple, open-faced broiled delights with a tortilla base come in an infinite variety and are incredibly fast to make. A **dollop** is a spoonful of something creamy and thick, like sour cream or whipped cream.

Vegetarian Chili

Prep time: 5 minutes • Cook time: 15 minutes • Serves: 8

Each serving has: 142 calories • 9 g protein • 0 g animal protein • 9 g vegetable protein • 27 g carbohydrates • 9 g dietary fiber • 18 g net carbohydrates • 2 g fat • 0 g saturated fat • 5 mg cholesterol (with sour cream; 0 mg without) • 639 mg sodium • Exchanges: 1½ very-lean meat, 1½ starch, 1 vegetable

3 TB. olive oil

1 large onion, peeled and coarsely chopped

1 (28-oz.) can plum tomatoes, with juice, roughly chopped

1 (15-oz.) can black beans, drained and rinsed

1 (15-oz.) can fat-free refried beans

1 (8-oz.) pkg. sliced white mushrooms

2 TB. chili powder

1 TB. ground cumin

1 TB. fresh chopped cilantro (optional)

1 tsp. salt

½ tsp. ground black pepper

Sour cream (optional)

Heat oil in a large skillet over medium heat and cook onion for 5 minutes, stirring. Add tomatoes with juice, black beans, refried beans, mushrooms, chili powder, cumin, cilantro (if using), salt, and pepper and stir to mix. If chili is too thick, add a little water. Cook for 10 minutes, stirring. Serve in bowls, topping with a dollop of sour cream (if using).

Carb Smarts

Use fat-free refried beans to avoid the lard used in some versions of refried beans.

A dose of Beano in bean-intensive dishes such as chili helps to prevent a gas crisis.

Sizzling Tofu and Asparagus Stir-Fry

Prep time: 5 minutes • Cook time: 8 minutes • Serves: 4

Each serving has: 175 calories • 8 g protein • 0 g animal protein • 8 g vegetable protein • 10 g carbohydrates • 3 g dietary fiber • 7 g net carbohydrates • 11 g fat • 2 g saturated fat • 0 mg cholesterol • 583 mg sodium • Exchanges: 1½ very-lean meat, 1½ vegetable, 2 fat

2 TB. sesame or olive oil

1 lb. fresh asparagus, rinsed, tough bottoms removed, cut into 1-inch sections

1 (14-oz.) pkg. extra-firm plain tofu, drained and cut into ¾-inch pieces

3 scallions, roots and dark green leaves removed, cut into ¼-inch segments

1 TB. chopped garlic

3 TB. teriyaki sauce

2 TB. sesame seeds

Gourmand's Glossary

Tender-crisp is a magic point in the cooking of vegetables where they are no longer raw, but still keep a slight appetizing crunch. Different vegetables will reach this point at different times (for example, broccoli will take longer than pea pods).

Heat oil in a wok or large skillet over medium-high heat. Cook asparagus for 4 minutes, stirring. Add tofu, scallions, and garlic and cook for 3 minutes, stirring occasionally, or until asparagus is *tender-crisp*. Drizzle with teriyaki sauce and serve, sprinkling each serving with sesame seeds.

Variation: Serve over ½ cup brown rice (this will increase the good-carb count).

Sautéed Artichoke Hearts and Tofu

Prep time: 5 minutes • Cook time: 10 minutes • Serves: 4

Each serving has: 320 calories • 12 g protein • 1 g animal protein • 11 g vegetable protein • 13 g carbohydrates • 6 g dietary fiber • 7 g net carbohydrates • 27 g fat • 3 g saturated fat • 2 mg cholesterol • 585 mg sodium • Exchanges: 1½ very-lean meat, 1½ vegetable, 5 fat

2 TB. olive oil	½ cup pitted kalamata olives
1 (9-oz.) pkg. frozen artichoke hearts, thawed	¼ cup chopped walnuts, toasted if possible
1 TB. chopped garlic	2 TB. shredded Parmesan cheese
2 tsp. Italian seasoning	Salt and ground black pepper
1 (14-oz.) pkg. extra-firm plain tofu, drained and cut into ¾-inch pieces	

Heat oil in a wok or large skillet over medium heat. Cook artichoke hearts, garlic, and Italian seasoning for 2 minutes, stirring. Add tofu and cook, stirring, for 4 minutes. Add olives and walnuts and cook, stirring, for 1 minute more. Serve, sprinkling with Parmesan and seasoning with salt and pepper to taste.

Skillet Tofu Scramble

Prep time: 3 minutes • Cook time: 5 minutes • Serves: 2

Each serving has: 284 calories • 17 g protein • 7 g animal protein • 10 g vegetable protein • 7 g carbohydrates • 0 g dietary fiber • 7 g net carbohydrates • 21 g fat • 4 g saturated fat • 6 mg cholesterol • 185 mg sodium • Exchanges: 1½ very-lean meat, 1 medium-fat meat, 1 vegetable, 3 fat

2 TB. canola or olive oil

1 tsp. Italian seasoning

1 (15-oz.) pkg. firm tofu

½ cup (2 oz.) shredded low-fat cheddar cheese

Dash hot red pepper sauce

Salt and ground black pepper

Carb Smarts

For more tasty vegetarian recipes, check out the chapters on vegetable dishes, salads, and soups.

Heat oil and Italian seasoning in a small skillet over medium heat. Mix tofu, cheese, and hot pepper sauce in a bowl. Scrape tofu mixture into the skillet and cook, stirring, for 3 to 4 minutes. Distribute to serving plates, and season with salt and pepper to taste.

Variation: Add fresh herbs, such as oregano, basil, and dill, in place of Italian seasoning. Sautée ½ onion in the skillet before adding tofu. Add ½ cup of your favorite cooked vegetables, such as bell peppers.

The Least You Need to Know

- Many vegetarian dishes are not only low carb, but also naturally quick cooking.
- High-quality ingredients offer delicious, fresh flavors. These flavors are preserved through quick cooking—a bonus for the vegetarian cook in a hurry!
- Cuisines of the world offer delicious examples of how to prepare vegetarian meals.
- Hearty, nutritious tofu makes a tasty addition to many dishes.

Chapter 12

Just Kidding

In This Chapter

- ◆ Low-carb kid favorites
- ◆ Ham it up
- ◆ Fun with burgers
- ◆ Chicken dishes that will have your kids clucking with approval
- ◆ South-of-the-border kid favorites

Parents who want to keep to a carb-conscious diet face a special challenge when it comes to feeding children at the same table. They not only have to serve healthful food but also food the kids will eat!

Fortunately, many low-carb foods are natural kid favorites. You'll find those recipes here, as well as recommendations for other kid-approved dishes in other chapters.

Kid Classics

I start this chapter with several low-carb classics that both kids and adults can enjoy. With dishes like tuna melts, some of these will sound familiar from your own childhood (that's on purpose!).

What a Ham

A ham steak—and ham in general—is a beautiful thing for the carb-conscious cook in a hurry. Ham is already cooked, packed with flavor and nutrition, and has few or no carbs. In a pinch, you're practically done just by taking the ham out of the fridge.

Of course, you can't stop there ... you have to have a little fun first. My kid-tested low-carb ham recipes help with that.

Chicken Favorites

Chicken is pretty close to the ideal food for any cook in a hurry, especially boneless, skinless breasts. These are low carb, low fat, nutritious, and quick cooking. Chicken breasts offer a versatile starting point for many types of dishes, seasonings, and cooking methods.

Burgers

Most kids love burgers. I give you a couple fun, fast, tasty, and low-carb variations in this chapter.

South-of-the-Border Meals

My kids always amaze me with what they will eat or not. Things I would think would be appealing are rejected, and foods I would think of as too "spicy" (in their eyes) are favorites. Meals based on classic Mexican ingredients such as tortillas, cheese, chili, and lime are favorites in my house. I'll give you some of the winners here.

Other Kid-Tested Dishes

This book is filled with dishes kids will like. Some others that have passed the test with my two live-in food critics include the following:

◆ French toast and pancakes (no surprise here) (Chapter 2)

◆ Eggs of many kinds (Chapter 3)

◆ Ham 'n' Swiss Roll-Ups, Cheddar Chicken Wraps, and Quick Homemade Hummus (Chapter 4)

◆ Nuts, dried fruits, and jicama sticks (Chapter 5)

◆ Broiled Haddock with Mozzarella, Microwave Wine-Poached Salmon, Broiled Soy Salmon, Grilled Southwest Tuna Steaks, and Crisp Fried Haddock (Chapter 7)

◆ Chicken and pork dishes (Chapter 8)

◆ Most of the red meat recipes, especially things like Meat Loaf and Meatballs (Chapter 9)

◆ Tostadas (Chapter 11)

◆ Baked Cauliflower, Half-Pickles, Green Beans and Almonds, and Sesame Broccoli (Chapter 13)

◆ Many of the salads (Chapter 14)

◆ Almost every dessert in Chapters 16 and 17 (again, no big surprise!)

Tuna Melts

Prep time: 5 minutes   •   Cook time: 5 minutes   •   Serves: 4

Each serving has: 262 calories   •   21 g protein   •   21 g animal protein   •   0 g vegetable protein   •   8 g carbohydrates   •   3 g dietary fiber   •   5 g net carbohydrates   •   17 g fat   •   6 g saturated fat   •   33 mg cholesterol   •   449 mg sodium   •   Exchanges: 1 very-lean meat, 1 high-fat meat, ½ starch, 2 fat

1 (6-oz.) can chunk white tuna in water, drained

3 TB. mayonnaise

½ cup finely chopped celery

½ tsp. dried dill

4 slices low-carb bread

4 slices cheddar cheese

Carb Smarts

Get your kids to "help" you cook, whether it's stirring things in a bowl or measuring ingredients. When they watch dinner in progress and see something they helped make, they're a lot more likely to eat it.

Preheat the broiler. Mix tuna, mayonnaise, celery, and dill in a bowl. Lay bread in a single layer on a baking tray and broil for 1 minute or until just beginning to crisp. Remove tray from the broiler and spread an equal amount of tuna mixture on each bread slice. Cover tuna with 1 slice cheese and slide back under the broiler. Broil for 3 minutes or until cheese is melted. Distribute to plates and serve.

Variations: Substitute whole-wheat bread for low-carb bread. This will increase the good-carb count. Adults might like some minced onion, freshly ground black pepper, and a dash hot pepper sauce in their tuna. Use canned chicken, turkey, and even ham in place of tuna.

Broccoli with Cheese Sauce

Prep time: 5 minutes • Cook time: 10 minutes • Serves: 4

Each serving has: 169 calories • 8 g protein • 4 g animal protein • 5 g vegetable protein • 10 g carbohydrates • 3 g dietary fiber • 7 g net carbohydrates • 15 g fat • 6 g saturated fat • 25 mg cholesterol • 145 mg sodium • Exchanges: ½ high-fat meat, 2 vegetable, 4 fat

1 (16-oz.) head broccoli, broken into serving-size florets	½ cup shredded cheddar cheese
	2 TB. olive oil
½ cup light sour cream	Salt

Using a stovetop steamer or a saucepan with a lid, heat ½ inch water to boiling, add broccoli florets, and steam for 7 minutes or until broccoli is tender-crisp.

Meanwhile, mix sour cream, cheddar cheese, and oil in a microwave-safe measuring cup. Heat on high for 1 minute or until beginning to bubble and cheese is melted. Distribute broccoli to serving plates and pour cheese sauce over broccoli. Serve, seasoning with salt to taste.

Carb Smarts

Broccoli is a terrific, nutritious food we should all eat more of. When kids rebel, however, bring out the big gun: cheese sauce.

Grilled Cheese "Hamwiches"

Prep time: 5 minutes • Cook time: 5 minutes • Serves: 4

Each serving has: 281 calories • 26 g protein • 26 g animal protein • 0 g vegetable protein • 2 g carbohydrates • 0 g dietary fiber • 2 g net carbohydrates • 19 g fat • 8 g saturated fat • 85 mg cholesterol • 1,314 mg sodium • Exchanges: 3 very-lean meat, 1 high-fat meat, 1 fat

8 (2½-inch) round thick-cut Canadian back bacon slices (available fully cooked at many grocer stores)

4 slices cheddar (or your favorite) cheese, trimmed to fit bacon

1 TB. canola oil or butter

Set out 4 bacon pieces. Place 1 cheese slice on each ham piece and top with remaining 4 pieces of ham. Heat oil in a skillet over medium heat and cook hamwiches for 5 minutes or until cheese inside is melted, turning once.

Kids will like these as is. Adults probably will like mustard.

Carb Smarts

I've yet to find a kid who doesn't like grilled cheese. This version, made with thick bacon instead of bread, has a decent chance of being even more appealing to those little cheese fanatics (and it's ultra low carb). If you can't find back bacon, ask your deli for ⅛-inch slices of smoked ham and use those instead.

Ham 'n' Beans

Prep time: 5 minutes   •   Cook time: 15 minutes   •   Serves: 6

Each serving has: 337 calories   •   29 g protein   •   22 g animal protein   •   6 g vegetable protein   •   26 g carbohydrates   •   5 g dietary fiber   •   21 g net carbohydrates   •   12 g fat   •   3 g saturated fat   •   51 mg cholesterol   •   1,624 mg sodium   •   Exchanges: 4½ very-lean meat, 1½ starch, 2 fat

3 TB. olive oil

1 medium onion, peeled and chopped into ½-inch chunks

2 (15.5-oz.) cans small white beans, drained and rinsed

2 (¾-lb.) smoked ham steaks chopped into ¼-inch pieces

1 TB. prepared mustard

¾ cup low-carb ketchup

½ cup spoon-for-spoon sweetener, such as Splenda

½ cup water

Salt

Pinch ground black pepper

Heat oil in a large saucepan over medium heat and cook onion, stirring, for 5 minutes. Add beans, ham, mustard, ketchup, sweetener, and water and cook, stirring, for 10 minutes. If the mixture is too dry, stir in a little more water as you cook. Serve in bowls, seasoning with salt and pepper to taste.

Variations: Process half of beans in a food processor to a creamy consistency, then add them to the remaining beans and ham for a more typical baked-bean texture to the dish. If you're so inclined, rather than cooking this on the stovetop, pour everything into a slow cooker and cook for 5 to 7 hours on low.

Ham Steaks with Sweet Mustard Sauce

Prep time: 5 minutes   •   Cook time: 4 minutes   •   Serves: 4

Each serving has: 201 calories   •   23 g protein   •   23 g animal protein   •   0 g vegetable protein   •   0 g carbohydrates   •   0 g dietary fiber   •   0 g net carbohydrates   •   12 g fat   •   3 g saturated fat   •   51 mg cholesterol   •   1,481 mg sodium   •   Exchanges: 4 very-lean meat, 2 fat

2 TB. canola oil	3 TB. Dijon-style mustard
2 TB. spoon-for-spoon sweetener, such as Splenda	2 (¾-lb.) ham steaks

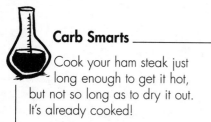

Carb Smarts

Cook your ham steak just long enough to get it hot, but not so long as to dry it out. It's already cooked!

In a bowl, mix oil, sweetener, and mustard. Place ham steak in a flat dish, such as a pie plate, and pour sauce over, turning ham to coat both sides. Heat a skillet over medium heat. Place steak in the skillet and scrape remaining sauce into the skillet. Cook for 4 minutes, turning once, then cut steak into quarters and move to serving plates. Spoon sauce over each serving.

Chicken 'n' Apples

Prep time: 10 minutes • Cook time: 15 minutes • Serves: 4

Each serving has: 342 calories • 42 g protein • 42 g animal protein • 0 g vegetable protein • 10 g carbohydrates • 2 g dietary fiber • 8 g net carbohydrates • 10 g fat • 1 g saturated fat • 64 mg cholesterol • 265 mg sodium • Exchanges: 6 very-lean meat, ½ fruit, 2 fat

3 TB. olive oil

1 medium onion, peeled and chopped into ½-inch pieces

2 celery stalks, washed and chopped into ½-inch pieces

2 tsp. chopped garlic

1½ lb. boneless, skinless chicken breasts (about 3 breasts), rinsed, dried, and cut into ½-inch pieces

1 crisp apple, such as Granny Smith, cored and cut into ½-inch pieces

10 dried apricots, quartered

½ tsp. ground ginger

½ tsp. salt

Salt and ground black pepper

Heat oil in a large skillet over medium heat and cook onion, celery, and garlic for 4 minutes, stirring. Add chicken, apples, apricots, ginger, and salt and cook, stirring, for 8 minutes or until chicken is cooked through. Serve, seasoning with salt and, if kids tolerate it, pepper to taste.

Orange Juice Chicken

Prep time: 5 minutes • Cook time: 10 minutes • Serves: 4

Each serving has: 209 calories • 28 g protein • 28 g animal protein • 0 g vegetable protein • 2 g carbohydrates • 0 g dietary fiber • 2 g net carbohydrates • 11 g fat • 2 g saturated fat • 97 mg cholesterol • 376 mg sodium • Exchanges: 4 very-lean meat, 2 fat

2 TB. olive oil

1 TB. chopped garlic

1½ lb. boneless, skinless chicken breasts (about 3 breasts), rinsed, dried, and cut into strips about ½-inch thick

½ tsp. salt

Pinch ground black pepper

¼ cup orange juice

4 thin (¼-inch), circular orange slices as garnish (optional)

Heat oil in a large skillet over medium heat and cook garlic, stirring, for 1 minute. Add chicken in a single layer to the skillet and sprinkle with salt and pepper. Cook for 3 minutes; then turn chicken strips and cook for another minute. Pour orange juice over chicken in the skillet and continue to cook until chicken is done. Remove chicken to serving plates and continue cooking orange juice for 1 more minute. Drizzle juice from skillet over chicken on the plates. Garnish each serving with an orange slice (if using) and serve.

Barbecued Chicken

Prep time: 4 minutes • Cook time: 15 minutes • Serves: 4

Each serving has: 308 calories • 56 g protein • 56 g animal protein • 0 g vegetable protein • 5 g carbohydrates • 0 g dietary fiber • 5 g net carbohydrates • 8 g fat • 3 g saturated fat • 183 mg cholesterol • 690 mg sodium • Exchanges: 8 lean meat, 1 vegetable, 1½ fat

2 lb. chicken parts	Pinch ground black pepper
1 tsp. salt	1 batch Low-Carb Barbecue Sauce (recipe follows)

Thoroughly rinse chicken in cold water and pat dry with paper towels. Preheat the grill. Place chicken in a large, microwave-safe bowl, sprinkle with salt and pepper, and cook in microwave for 10 minutes. Place partially cooked chicken on the grill and brush with Low-Carb Barbecue Sauce. Grill for 5 minutes or until chicken is done and outside is crisp.

Carb Alert

Off-the-shelf barbecue sauce often is mostly sugar, but homemade low-carb barbecue sauce only takes a few minutes.

Some kids (and adults!) like to use sauce for dipping. Be sure to keep dipping sauce separate from any sauce that has come in contact with raw chicken meat.

Low-Carb Barbecue Sauce

Prep time: 5 minutes • Serves: about 10 (2 tablespoons) servings

Each serving has: 11 calories • 0 g protein • 0 g animal protein • 0 g vegetable protein • 2 g carbohydrates • 0 g dietary fiber • 2 g net carbohydrates • 0 g fat • 0 g saturated fat • 0 mg cholesterol • 208 mg sodium • Exchanges: free

1 cup low-carb ketchup

2 TB. cider vinegar

2 TB. spoon-for-spoon sweetener, such as Splenda

1 TB. Dijon-style mustard

½ tsp. ground cumin

½ tsp. ground ginger

¼ tsp. ground black pepper

Carb Smarts

Remember, sugar is added to many "low-carb" ketchups and other condiments, such as relish and some mustards. Check the ingredient list!

Mix ketchup, vinegar, sweetener, mustard, cumin, ginger, and black pepper. This will last for at least a week in the fridge in a container with a lid.

Variation: The adults in the crowd might want to jazz up this sauce with ¼ teaspoon red pepper flakes.

Carb Alert

Traditional burgers present an obvious challenge for the carb-conscious cook: that big, fluffy, white-flour carb-laden bun. I suggest two alternatives. The first (a 0-carb option) is to serve burgers without buns. That option doesn't always go over very well, though. The second (good-carb) option is to find a source for 100 percent whole-wheat buns. A number of grocery stores sell these good-carb buns, and my kids eat them all the time. Depending on how low you want to keep carbs in your family diet, you can let the kids eat the whole-wheat buns while you focus on the meat.

Secret Cheeseburgers

Prep time: 8 minutes   •   Cook time: 8 minutes   •   Serves: 4

Each serving has: 362 calories   •   28 g protein   •   28 g animal protein   •   0 g vegetable protein   •   1 g carbohydrates   •   0 g dietary fiber   •   1 g net carbohydrates   •   26 g fat   •   13 g saturated fat   •   107 mg cholesterol   •   354 mg sodium   •   Exchanges: 4 medium-fat meat, ½ high-fat meat

1 lb. lean ground beef	2 TB. canola oil
1 tsp. Worcestershire sauce	3 TB. low-carb ketchup
1 cup (4 oz.) shredded cheddar cheese	

Mix ground beef and Worcestershire sauce in a large bowl. Shape meat into 8 thin patties about ¼ inch thick and 3½ inches across. Distribute cheese among 4 patties, centering cheese in the middle of the patty, being sure to leave at least ¼ inch exposed meat all the way around. Top cheesed patties with the remaining 4 patties and pinch the edges to bind burgers together.

Heat oil in a large skillet over medium heat and cook burgers for 6 to 8 minutes or until done, turning once. (A splatter screen is a great item to use to prevent unnecessary mess.) Distribute burgers to serving plates and serve with low-carb ketchup. Tell the kids these burgers have a secret and let the fun begin.

Variation: You can easily grill these burgers.

Feather Burgers

Prep time: 8 minutes • Cook time: 8 minutes • Serves: 6

Each serving has: 208 calories • 30 g protein • 29 g animal protein • 1 g vegetable protein • 4 g carbohydrates • 1 g dietary fiber • 3 g net carbohydrates • 10 g fat • 2 g saturated fat • 132 mg cholesterol • 235 mg sodium • Exchanges: 4 very-lean meat, ¼ starch, 1 fat

1½ lb. ground turkey or chicken (available at many grocery stores)

¼ cup unprocessed bran

1 large egg

2 tsp. Worcestershire sauce

1 tsp. salt

Pinch ground black pepper

2 TB. canola or olive oil

6 TB. low-carb ketchup

Mix ground meat, bran, egg, and Worcestershire sauce in a large bowl. Shape meat into 6 patties about ½ inch thick and 3½ inches across. Season with salt and pepper to taste.

Carb Alert

Note that ground chicken, turkey, and ostrich are low-fat meats. For this reason, you'll need to use oil in the skillet while cooking to prevent burning.

Heat oil in a large skillet over medium heat and cook burgers for 8 minutes or until done, turning once. Serve with low-carb ketchup.

Variations: There is ample opportunity for fun with these burgers. Substitute ground ostrich for ground chicken and still keep the feather theme. Then, of course, there are buffalo burgers, not to mention ground pork and ground beef.

You can also cook these burgers on the grill and prepare as cheeseburgers.

Tortilla "Pizza"

Prep time: 5 minutes • Cook time: 4 minutes • Serves: 4

Each serving has: 405 calories • 23 g protein • 23 g animal protein • 0 g vegetable protein • 16 g carbohydrates • 6 g dietary fiber • 10 g net carbohydrates • 28 g fat • 16 g saturated fat • 86 mg cholesterol • 1,141 mg sodium • Exchanges: 3 high-fat meat, 1 starch, 1 fat

4 (8-inch) soft low-carb tortillas	½ cup (2 oz.) sliced pepperoni
1 (8-oz.) pkg. shredded Mexican-style cheese	½ cup light sour cream

Preheat the broiler. Arrange tortillas on a baking tray in a single layer and broil for 1 minute, watching carefully to prevent burning. Remove tray from broiler, distribute cheese among tortillas, and spread to an even layer. Top with pepperoni slices. Broil for another 2 to 3 minutes or until cheese melts. Remove your pizzas to a cutting board, cut into wedges, and serve. Top each slice, if desired, with a dollop sour cream.

Variations: Use other shredded cheeses in place of the Mexican-style cheese. Other low-carb pizza toppings are fair game as well. Substitute whole-wheat tortillas for low-carb tortillas and increase the good-carb count.

Nachos

Prep time: 4 minutes • Cook time: 4 minutes • Serves: 4

Each serving has: 450 calories • 35 g protein • 31 g animal protein • 4 g vegetable protein • 13 g carbohydrates • 4 g dietary fiber • 9 g net carbohydrates • 32 g fat • 15 g saturated fat • 80 mg cholesterol • 1,146 mg sodium • Exchanges: 2 very-lean meat, 2 high-fat meat, ½ starch, 2 fat

4 oz. (about 60 chips) low-carb tortilla chips

1 pkg. (8 oz.) shredded Mexican-style or Monterey Jack cheese

1 cup chopped ham (¼-inch pieces)

1 tsp. chili powder

½ cup (4 oz.) light sour cream

 **Carb Alert**

Some tortilla chips are indeed very low carb compared to others, but still pay close attention to the serving size on the label. I've seen low-carb chips list a serving as 15 chips (1 ounce), which is just right for a plate of nachos.

Arrange chips in a single overlapping layer on four plates. Sprinkle cheese over chips, followed by ham and a sprinkling of chili powder. Place each plate in the microwave, and heat for about 1 minute or until cheese melts. Serve with a spoonful of sour cream on each plate.

Variation: Many grocery stores sell chopped, ready-to-use ham. If you can find this, use it in place of chopping your own. Adults often love unsweetened salsa spread on these nachos. If you can get your kids to eat it, too, let me know your secret. Chili, cooked meats, additional chili powder, green chilies, olives, and many other flavorful ingredients are all great, too.

Chicken Quesadillas

Prep time: 8 minutes • Cook time: 6 minutes • Serves: 6 (½ quesadilla each)

Each serving has: 382 calories • 30 g protein • 24 g animal protein • 6 g vegetable protein • 17 g carbohydrates • 8 g dietary fiber • 9 g net carbohydrates • 23 g fat • 13 g saturated fat • 74 mg cholesterol • 790 mg sodium • Exchanges: 1½ high-fat meat, 2 very-lean meat, 1 starch, 2 fat

1 (10-oz.) can chunk white chicken meat, drained

6 (8-inch) soft low-carb tortillas

1 (8-oz.) pkg. shredded cheddar or Monterey Jack cheese

1 tsp. chili powder

1 cup salsa (your sugar-free favorite)

1 cup light sour cream

Preheat the broiler. With a spoon or fork, break up any large chunks of chicken in the can. Place 3 tortillas on a baking tray and top each with shredded cheese, chicken meat, and a sprinkled pinch chili powder. Top with remaining 3 tortillas and broil for 3 minutes, watching carefully to prevent burning. Turn *quesadillas* and broil for another 2 minutes or until cheese is melted and tortilla is crisp. Remove quesadillas to a cutting board and cut into wedges. Serve with salsa and sour cream.

Variation: Substitute whole-wheat tortillas for low-carb tortillas. This will increase the good-carb count. Quesadillas can also be cooked in an oiled skillet over medium heat for about 2 minutes per side.

 Gourmand's Glossary

A **quesadilla** is, at its most basic, two tortillas with something in between, sort of like a grilled cheese sandwich. The "in between" is what makes all the difference. Cheese is a natural (in this country, start with Monterey Jack or cheddar; Swiss might not be what you would use first in Mexico, but it's still delicious). Also include meats, vegetables, and, of course, Southwest-style seasonings.

The Least You Need to Know

♦ Kid approval is possible for many fast, low-carb dishes.

♦ Many childhood favorites can be made low carb.

♦ This chapter focuses on kid favorites, but don't forget to use many of the other kid-tested favorites in other parts of this book.

Part 3

Finish Out the Meal

Low-carb vegetable dishes can be inherently fast and delicious, as you'll see from the range of savory options in Chapter 13. We'll take that vegetable theme just a bit further and add some other fun ingredients in Chapter 14, where we crunch into salads that are a lot more than just lettuce. Then, in Chapter 15, we'll spoon into hearty, satisfying soups and stews that have so much flavor you won't believe they were made quickly (or that they're low carb). Of course, no meal is complete without dessert. Just because you're keeping an eye on carbs doesn't mean you can't enjoy the rich, sweet chocolate desserts or luscious, juicy fruit-based treats found in Chapters 16 and 17.

Vegetable Side Dishes

In This Chapter

- ◆ The quickest way to cook (is not to cook at all)
- ◆ Fast prep for fresh vegetables
- ◆ Vegetable comfort foods
- ◆ Secrets to flavor and nutrition

Vegetable side dishes can be perfect for the carb-conscious cook. For starters, the vast majority of vegetables at your grocery store or farmers' market are naturally low carb. Many of them can be eaten raw (a very quick-cooking method!) or require minimum cooking time. And when it comes to nutrition, the less cooked, the better.

In this chapter, you'll find recipes for many of your favorite vegetables, including beans, artichokes, peppers, broccoli, and cauliflower. I'll add a slight twist to preparation, however (remember, it's all about fun, as well as low carb).

The Raw

With a bit of imagination, plain old raw vegetables aren't so plain anymore. From asparagus, carrots, cucumbers, or a crunchy combination, the "raw" recipes in this chapter make the most of fresh flavors—with no cooking at all.

Carb Alert

Fresh vegetables are mostly safe territory for carb-conscious cooks. Some vegetables do, however, bring a high number of carbohydrates per serving, and, as a result, should be avoided or treated with caution. The most common of these are the following:

- Beets
- Parsnips
- Peas
- Potatoes
- Sweet corn
- Sweet potato

To give a sense of the contrast, take a serving of potatoes (148 g) as an example, with 23 net carbs, compared to a same-size serving of peppers, with only 5. (For more on recommended vegetables, see the vegetable table in Chapter 5.)

The Cooked

Time is on your side when it comes to cooking fresh vegetables. In general, the less cooking, the better because overcooked vegetables tend to become soggy and lose flavor and nutrition. That's why, in many of the recipes in this chapter, you'll see reference to the term *tender-crisp*, which means to cook something just to the point of holding some crisp texture.

Carbohistory

Fresher is better! Not only is the flavor of fresh vegetables better, but the nutrition is better, too. Studies show that fresh vegetables lose a significant amount of their nutritional value the longer they sit on the shelf.

One of the best sources of fresh vegetables is your local farmers' market. Find one near you by visiting the U.S. Department of Agriculture's website at www.ams.usda.gov/farmersmarkets/map.htm.

Half-Pickles

Prep time: 3 minutes   •   Serves: 4

Each serving has: 15 calories   •   1 g protein   •   0 g animal protein   •   1 g vegetable protein   •   2 g carbohydrates   •   1 g dietary fiber   •   1 g net carbohydrates   •   0 g fat   •   0 g saturated fat   •   0 mg cholesterol   •   1 mg sodium   •   Exchanges: ½ vegetable

1 English-style or 2 small regular cucumbers, peeled and cut into ¼-inch slices

⅓ cup red wine vinegar

⅓ cup cold water

1 TB. fresh dill or 1 tsp. dried

Arrange cucumbers in a shallow 12-inch bowl or pie plate. Pour vinegar over cucumbers, add water, and sprinkle with dill. This 20-second cuisine will disappear in about 20 seconds.

Variation: If it's a hot day, add ice to the mix for cool cukes.

Carb Smarts

The longer crisp, half-pickled cucumbers stay in the vinegar, the stronger and more pickle-ish they get.

Roasted Asparagus

Prep time: 5 minutes   •   Cook time: 5 minutes   •   Serves: 4

Each serving has: 80 calories   •   2½ g protein   •   0 g animal protein   •   2½ g vegetable protein   •   5 g carbohydrates   •   2 g dietary fiber   •   3 g net carbohydrates   •   7½ g fat   •   2 g saturated fat   •   0 mg cholesterol   •   278 mg sodium   •   Exchanges: 1 vegetable, 1½ fat

1 lb. asparagus, tough stem ends removed, cut into 3-inch sections

2 TB. olive oil

1 TB. chopped fresh tarragon or 1 tsp. dried

Salt to taste

Preheat the broiler. Place asparagus in a large bowl, drizzle with olive oil, and turn to coat all sides. Arrange asparagus in a single layer on a baking dish or cookie sheet and sprinkle with tarragon. Broil for 3 minutes, then roll asparagus spears, and broil for 2 more minutes. Serve, sprinkling with salt to taste.

Garden Salsa

Prep time: 10 minutes • Serves: 4

Each serving has: 29 calories • 1 g protein • 0 g animal protein • 1 g vegetable protein • 6 g carbohydrates • 1 g dietary fiber • 5 g net carbohydrates • 0 g fat • 0 g saturated fat • 0 mg cholesterol • 761 mg sodium • Exchanges: 1 vegetable

2 large (8-oz.) fresh tomatoes, rinsed, cored, seeded, and chopped into ¼-inch pieces

½ cup sweet onion, such as Vidalia, peeled and chopped into ¼-inch square pieces or smaller

1 (4.5-oz.) can chopped green chilies, drained

¼ cup chopped fresh cilantro

2 TB. red wine vinegar

2 TB. lime juice

1 tsp. kosher salt

½ tsp. dried oregano

¼ tsp. hot red pepper sauce

Mix together tomatoes, onion, chilies, cilantro, vinegar, lime juice, salt, oregano, and hot pepper sauce in a serving bowl. Eat right away or keep for a day or so in the fridge.

Carb Smarts

Salsa is a terrific topping for all sorts of dishes, from Mexican-style foods to simple poultry and seafood dishes. This version, adapted from Fanny Farmer, is my favorite. Fresh tomatoes are key to the delicious flavor.

Salsa, of course, goes hand in hand with tortilla chips, but to keep carbs under control, seek out a low-net-carb chip.

Pinzimonio

Prep time: 10 minutes • Serves: 6

Each serving has: 348 calories • 1½ g protein • 0 g animal protein • 1½ g vegetable protein • 9 g carbohydrates • 3 g dietary fiber • 6 g net carbohydrates • 36 g fat • 5 g saturated fat • 0 mg cholesterol • 221 mg sodium • Exchanges: 1½ vegetable, 7 fat

4 scallions, roots and dark green parts removed, sliced into quarters lengthwise, leaves reserved

1 red bell pepper, seeds and ribs removed and cut into ¼ × 4-inch strips

1 green bell pepper, seeds and ribs removed and cut into ¼ × 4-inch strips

2 carrots, peeled and cut into ¼ × 4-inch strips

2 celery stalks, rinsed and cut into ¼ × 4-inch strips

6 long arugula or cress leaves, rinsed and stemmed

1 cup olive oil

⅓ cup balsamic vinegar

Salt and ground black pepper

Lay 1 long green scallion leaf (at least 7 inches, if possible) on a cutting board. Lay 1 red pepper strip across middle of leaf, followed by 1 green pepper strip, 1 carrot strip, 1 celery strip, and 1 arugula leaf. Gently tie scallion leaf around vegetable bunch and repeat with remaining leaves.

For dipping, distribute olive oil equally among 6 small serving bowls and top each bowl with balsamic vinegar. To eat, dip vegetable bunches in oil-vinegar mix, season, if desired, with salt and pepper, and crunch away while visualizing the Italian vegetable gardens in the distance.

Variations: Choose your own favorite vegetables that can be prepared long and skinny for bunching.

Gourmand's Glossary

Pinzimonio is an Italian vegetable dish in which combinations of sliced vegetables are served with olive oil, vinegar, salt, and pepper.

Carb Smarts

I usually advocate the freshest possible vegetables, but one exception is when you're using scallion leaves as a "tie" in this dish. Leave them out for an hour to wilt, and they will be easier to tie!

Asparagus with Tarragon-Dill Dip

Prep time: 5 minutes • Cook time: 10 minutes • Serves: 4

Each serving has: 164 calories • 4 g protein • 1 g animal protein • 3 g vegetable protein • 14 g carbohydrates • 3 g dietary fiber • 11 g net carbohydrates • 11 g fat • 4 g saturated fat • 25 mg cholesterol • 223 mg sodium • Exchanges: 1 vegetable, ½ fruit, 2 fat

¾ cup low-fat sour cream

½ cup low-fat mayonnaise

3 scallions, roots and dark green leaves removed, minced

1 TB. fresh dill or 1 tsp. dried

1½ tsp. chopped fresh tarragon or ½ tsp. dried

1 tsp. lemon juice

¼ tsp. ground black pepper

1 lb. fresh baby asparagus, tough ends removed, blanched for 1 minute in boiling water

Carb Alert

When a recipe relies on fresh vegetable texture, be sure the "star" veggie is in good shape. Pick only in-season, crisp, fresh vegetables. Anything else just isn't appealing.

Mix sour cream, mayonnaise, scallions, dill, tarragon, lemon juice, and pepper in a serving bowl. If you've got time, allow dip to sit for an hour or so for flavors to mix. Use tender-crisp asparagus to scoop up dip.

Variation: Baby carrots, snow peas, French green beans, or a combination of these are also delicious with this dip.

Garden Bruschetta

Prep time: 5 minutes • Cook time: 3 minutes • Serves: 4

Each serving has: 194 calories • 5 g protein • 2 g animal protein • 3 g vegetable protein • 9 g carbohydrates • 3 g dietary fiber • 6 g net carbohydrates • 16 g fat • 3 g saturated fat • 5 mg cholesterol • 670 mg sodium • Exchanges: ½ starch, ¼ vegetable, ¼ medium-fat meat, 3 fat

2 tsp. chopped garlic	1 tsp. salt
¼ cup olive oil	¼ tsp. ground black pepper
4 slices low-carb bread, each slice cut into 4 triangles	1 large (8-oz.) fresh tomato, rinsed, cored, seeded, and chopped into ¼-inch pieces
3 TB. fresh basil, minced	⅓ cup shredded Parmesan cheese

Preheat the broiler. Mix garlic and olive oil. Lay bread triangles on a baking tray in a single layer, brush each piece with garlic-oil mixture, and broil for 1 minute per side or until browned. While bread is toasting, mix basil, salt, pepper, and tomato. When bread is toasted, top each piece with some tomato mixture and sprinkle with Parmesan cheese. Serve to sighs of appreciation.

Variation: Use 100 percent whole-wheat bread in place of the low-carb bread and raise the good-carb count.

Gourmand's Glossary

Bite-size bread-based dishes are known by several names, including *bruschetta*, *canapés*, and *crostini*. **Canapés** (French) are bite-size hors d'oeuvres made of any number of ingredients but prepared individually and usually served on a small piece of bread or toast. **Bruschetta** and **crostini** are Italian in origin and typically involve slices of toasted or grilled bread with garlic and olive oil. The appetizers are similar to each other and similarly irresistible. Traditionally, the bread base is white bread, but there is nothing stopping us from using low-carb or whole-wheat variations.

Baked Cauliflower

Prep time: 2 minutes • Cook time: 5 minutes • Serves: 6

Each serving has: 95 calories • 3 g protein • 0 g animal protein • 3 g vegetable protein • 7 g carbohydrates • 3 g dietary fiber • 4 g net carbohydrates • 7½ g fat • 2 g saturated fat • 0 mg cholesterol • 228 mg sodium • Exchanges: 1 vegetable, 1½ fat

1 (1½-lb.) head cauliflower	Butter or margarine (optional)
3 TB. olive oil	Salt and ground black pepper
1 tsp. ground cumin	

Pour ½ inch water in the bottom of a microwave-safe baking dish. Thoroughly rinse cauliflower in cold water, pat dry with paper towels, and cut head in half lengthwise from stem to top. Place two halves flat side down in the baking dish. Drizzle cauliflower with oil, covering as much of the top as you can, then sprinkle with cumin. Microwave for 5 to 8 minutes or until cauliflower softens to tender-crisp. Remove the dish from the oven, slice each piece in 3 pieces, and distribute to serving plates. Season with butter (if using), salt, and pepper to taste.

Carb Alert

When using margarine, consider using one of the increasing number of healthful, cholesterol-oriented spreads with names such as Benecol and Smart Balance. These spreads are tasty and bring minimum saturated fat (the problem with butter) and no trans-fats (the problem with other margarines). Studies suggest that trans-fats are related to many health problems.

Green Beans with Almonds

Prep time: 5 minutes   •   Cook time: 4 minutes   •   Serves: 4

Each serving has: 120 calories   •   3 g protein   •   0 g animal protein   •   3 g vegetable protein   •   9 g carbohydrates   •   4 g dietary fiber   •   5 g net carbohydrates   •   9 g fat   •   4 g saturated fat   •   15 mg cholesterol   •   357 mg sodium   •   Exchanges: 1 vegetable, 2 fat

2 TB. butter	¼ cup slivered almonds
1 lb. fresh green beans, rinsed, stems removed, and sliced into 2-inch pieces	1 TB. fresh dill or ½ tsp. dried
	Salt to taste

Melt butter in a large skillet over medium heat and sauté beans, almonds, and dill for 4 minutes, stirring, or until tender-crisp. Season with salt to taste and distribute to serving plates.

Balsamic Green Beans

Prep time: 2 minutes   •   Cook time: 11 minutes   •   Serves: 4

Each serving has: 115 calories   •   2 g protein   •   0 g animal protein   •   2 g vegetable protein   •   9 g carbohydrates   •   3 g dietary fiber   •   5 g net carbohydrates   •   7½ g fat   •   2 g saturated fat   •   0 mg cholesterol   •   29 mg sodium   •   Exchanges: 1 vegetable, 1½ fat

3 TB. butter or olive oil	1 lb. green beans
4 scallions, roots and dark green leaves removed, cut into ¼-inch sections	Balsamic vinegar
	Salt and ground black pepper

Melt butter in a large skillet over medium heat and cook scallions for 5 minutes, stirring. Add beans and cook, stirring, for an additional 6 minutes or until beans are tender-crisp. Distribute beans to serving plates and serve, seasoning with balsamic vinegar, salt, and pepper to taste.

Variation: If you'd rather use olive oil, it will work, but the butter flavor is just terrific.

Sautéed Spinach

Prep time: 5 minutes • Cook time: 4 minutes • Serves: 4

Each serving has: 116 calories • 3 g protein • 0 g animal protein • 3 g vegetable protein • 4 g carbohydrates • 2 g dietary fiber • 2 g net carbohydrates • 11 g fat • 3 g saturated fat • 0 mg cholesterol • 281 mg sodium • Exchanges: 1 vegetable, 2 fat

3 TB. olive oil	1 lb. fresh spinach, rinsed, stemmed, and dried
1 tsp. chopped garlic	Salt and ground black pepper

Heat oil in a large skillet with a lid over medium heat and cook garlic, stirring, for 1 minute. Add spinach, cover, and cook for 3 minutes. Lift the lid (note how much spinach has shrunk) and stir to mix spinach with olive oil and garlic. Distribute to serving plates and season to taste with salt and pepper.

Variations: Balsamic vinegar is delicious on sautéed spinach. Shredded Parmesan is also very tasty.

Skillet Parmesan Artichokes

Prep time: 5 minutes • Cook time: 5 minutes • Serves: 4

Each serving has: 119 calories • 4½ g protein • 1 g animal protein • 3½ g vegetable protein • 10 g carbohydrates • 5 g dietary fiber • 5 g net carbohydrates • 8 g fat • 1½ g saturated fat • 2 mg cholesterol • 227 mg sodium • Exchanges: 1 vegetable, 1½ fat

2 TB. olive oil	2 (9-oz.) pkg. frozen artichoke hearts, thawed
1 TB. chopped garlic	2 TB. shredded Parmesan cheese
½ tsp. dried oregano	Salt and ground black pepper to taste

Heat oil, garlic, and oregano in a 12-inch skillet over medium heat. Add artichoke hearts and sauté for 4 minutes, stirring. Distribute artichokes to serving plates, sprinkle with Parmesan cheese, and season with salt and pepper to taste—and set out a lot of napkins.

Grilled Vegetables

Prep time: 5 minutes • Cook time: 6 minutes • Serves: 4

Each serving has: 194 calories • 5 g protein • 2 g animal protein • 3 g vegetable protein • 12 g carbohydrates • 4 g dietary fiber • 8 g net carbohydrates • 16 g fat • 3 g saturated fat • 4 mg cholesterol • 367 mg sodium • Exchanges: 2 vegetable, 3 fat

¼ cup olive oil

2 TB. chopped garlic

1½ tsp. Italian seasoning

2 large bell peppers (your favorite colors), seeds and ribs removed and quartered lengthwise

2 small (10-inch) fresh zucchini, rinsed, ends cut off, and quartered lengthwise

1 small eggplant, peeled and cut into ¾-inch–wide lengthwise strips

Salt and ground black pepper to taste

¼ cup shredded Parmesan cheese

Hot red pepper sauce (optional)

Start the grill. In a small cup, mix oil, garlic, and Italian seasoning. Set bell peppers, zucchini, and eggplant in a large bowl. Pour oil mixture over vegetables and turn to thoroughly coat. Lay vegetables on the grill in a single layer and cook for 3 minutes per side or until softened. Distribute to serving plates and season to taste with salt, pepper, Parmesan cheese, and hot pepper sauce (if using).

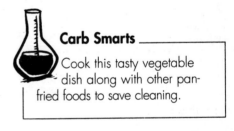

Carb Smarts

Cook this tasty vegetable dish along with other pan-fried foods to save cleaning.

Fried Red Peppers

Prep time: 5 minutes • Cook time: 4 minutes • Serves: 4

Each serving has: 236 calories • 5 g protein • 2 g animal protein • 3 g vegetable protein • 15 g carbohydrates • 7 g dietary fiber • 8 g net carbohydrates • 19 g fat • 3 g saturated fat • 53 mg cholesterol • 557 mg sodium • Exchanges: 1 vegetable, ½ starch, 4 fat

2 cups roasted red peppers (available in grocery stores in the international foods section), drained and cut into 2-inch pieces

1 egg

¼ cup milk

Dash hot red pepper sauce

⅔ cup unprocessed bran

⅓ cup olive oil

Salt and freshly ground pepper

Carb Smarts

For you gardeners, green tomatoes at the end of the season are perfect for this recipe. Of course you have to watch *Fried Green Tomatoes* (the movie) at the same time.

Place roasted pepper pieces in a large bowl. Whisk egg, milk, and hot pepper sauce in a bowl and pour egg mixture over peppers. Gently stir peppers to coat without breaking them apart more. Pour bran on a plate. Using tongs (or two forks), lift pepper pieces from the bowl, dredge in bran, and set aside. Heat oil in a large skillet over medium-high heat. Add pepper pieces to skillet in a single layer. Cook for 2 minutes per side or until coating is crispy. Distribute cooked peppers to serving plates and season to taste with salt and pepper.

Sautéed Peppers

Prep time: 5 minutes • Cook time: 5 minutes • Serves: 4

Each serving has: 120 calories • 2 g protein • 0 g animal protein • 2 g vegetable protein • 7 g carbohydrates • 3 g dietary fiber • 4 g net carbohydrates • 11 g fat • 3 g saturated fat • 0 mg cholesterol • 137 mg sodium • Exchanges: 1 vegetable, 2 fat

3 TB. olive oil

1 small onion, peeled and chopped into ½-inch pieces

1 tsp. Italian seasoning

2 tsp. crushed garlic

1 large yellow bell pepper, seeds and ribs removed and sliced crosswise into rings

1 large red bell pepper, seeds and ribs removed and sliced crosswise into rings

1 large green bell pepper, seeds and ribs removed and sliced crosswise into rings

Salt and ground black pepper

Heat oil in a large skillet over medium heat and sauté onion, Italian seasoning, and garlic for 5 minutes. Add yellow, red, and green bell peppers and cook, stirring, for 5 minutes or until tender-crisp. Season with salt and pepper to taste.

Carb Smarts

In the freezer section of some grocery stores, you'll find 1-pound bags of sliced red, yellow, and green bell peppers. Keep a bag in your freezer, and you'll have instant appeal for a side dish.

Sautéed Cabbage with Bacon

Prep time: 5 minutes • Cook time: 15 minutes • Serves: 4

Each serving has: 81 calories • 6 g protein • 4 g animal protein • 2 g vegetable protein • 6 g carbohydrates • 2½ g dietary fiber • 4 g net carbohydrates • 4 g fat • 1½ g saturated fat • 11 mg cholesterol • 231 mg sodium • Exchanges: 1 vegetable, ½ high-fat meat

½ head cabbage (about 1 lb.), sliced into ½ × 3-inch pieces

5 strips bacon

1 tsp. caraway seed

½ tsp. dried sage

Salt and ground black pepper

Carbohistory

Caraway is a popular seasoning in many German and central European dishes. One possible reason is that caraway is traditionally believed to relieve indigestion and gas—side effects associated with vegetables in the cabbage family.

Steam cabbage in a vegetable steamer for 10 minutes or until soft.

Meanwhile, cook bacon in a large skillet over medium heat until crispy. Remove bacon to a paper-towel–lined plate, add caraway and sage to bacon fat in the skillet, and heat for 1 minute. Add cabbage and cook for another minute, stirring.

Crumble bacon into cabbage, stir to mix, and season with salt and pepper to taste.

Variation: Stir in 1½ cups cooked brown rice (this will increase the good-carb count).

Sesame Broccoli

Prep time: 4 minutes • Cook time: 5 minutes • Serves: 4

Each serving has: 152 calories • 6 g protein • 0 g animal protein • 6 g vegetable protein • 12 g carbohydrates • 5 g dietary fiber • 7 g net carbohydrates • 11 g fat • 2½ g saturated fat • 0 mg cholesterol • 188 mg sodium • Exchanges: 1½ vegetable, 2 fat

1½ lb. broccoli florets	Dash hot red pepper sauce (optional)
1 TB. lemon juice	2 TB. sesame seeds
2 TB. sesame or olive oil	Salt to taste
2 tsp. grated fresh ginger, or ½ tsp. powdered	

Using a stovetop steamer or a saucepan with a lid, heat ½ inch water to boiling, add broccoli florets, and steam for 4 minutes or until tender-crisp. Scoop broccoli into a bowl. Mix lemon juice, oil, ginger, and hot pepper sauce (if using) in a cup. Pour oil mixture over broccoli and toss to coat. Serve, sprinkling each serving with sesame seeds and seasoning with salt to taste.

Variation: This method works equally well with fresh asparagus spears cut into 2-inch sections.

Carb Smarts

To save even more time, use prepackaged fresh broccoli florets, available in the vegetable section of your grocery store.

Vegetables au Gratin

Prep time: 8 minutes • Cook time: 12 minutes • Serves: 4

Each serving has: 158 calories • 5 g protein • 2 g animal protein • 3 g vegetable protein • 12 g carbohydrates • 5 g dietary fiber • 7 g net carbohydrates • 13 g fat • 1 g saturated fat • 5 mg cholesterol • 255 mg sodium • Exchanges: 1½ vegetable, ¼ high-fat meat, 2 fat

5 TB. olive oil

2 TB. chopped garlic

2 TB. fresh chopped basil or 2 tsp. dried

1 tsp. dried rosemary

½ tsp. dried marjoram

2 large celery stalks, rinsed and chopped into ½-inch pieces

2 (10-inch) zucchini squash, rinsed, ends removed, cut in half lengthwise, then cut into ½-inch sections crosswise

2 large tomatoes, rinsed, cored, seeded, and chopped into ½-inch pieces, or 1 (15-oz.) can diced tomatoes with juice

⅓ cup unprocessed bran

⅓ cup shredded Parmesan cheese

Salt and ground black pepper

Preheat the broiler. Heat 3 tablespoons oil in a large skillet over medium heat. Add garlic, basil, rosemary, and marjoram and cook, stirring, for 1 minute. Add celery and zucchini and cook for 5 minutes, stirring. Add tomatoes and cook for another 3 minutes, stirring, or until celery and zucchini are tender-crisp. Scrape herbed vegetables into a baking dish. Sprinkle vegetables with bran and Parmesan and drizzle with the remaining 2 tablespoons olive oil. Slide under the broiler for 2 minutes or until topping begins to crisp. Serve, seasoning with salt and pepper to taste.

Gourmand's Glossary

Au gratin is the quick broiling of a dish before serving to brown the top ingredients.

Sautéed Herbed Summer Squash

Prep time: 5 minutes • Cook time: 7 minutes • Serves: 4

Each serving has: 91 calories • 2½ g protein • 0 g animal protein • 2½ g vegetable protein • 7 g carbohydrates • 2 g dietary fiber • 5 g net carbohydrates • 7½ g fat • 1 g saturated fat • 0 mg cholesterol • 4 mg sodium • Exchanges: 1 vegetable, 1½ fat

2 TB. olive oil

1 TB. chopped garlic

2 (9-inch) zucchini squash, rinsed, ends removed, cut into ½-inch sections crosswise

2 (9-inch) yellow squash, rinsed, ends removed, cut into ½-inch sections crosswise

1½ tsp. fresh thyme or ½ tsp. dried

½ tsp. fresh dill or 1 pinch dried

Salt and ground black pepper

Heat oil in a large skillet over medium heat. Add garlic and cook for 2 minutes, stirring. Add zucchini, yellow squash, thyme, and dill to the skillet and cook for 5 minutes, stirring, or until squash is tender. Serve, seasoning with salt and pepper to taste.

Variation: A splash of balsamic vinegar is a delicious addition.

The Least You Need to Know

◆ Fresh vegetables require little or no cooking—perfect for the cook in a hurry.

◆ Fresh vegetables bring terrific flavor to the table, so the cook doesn't have to worry about extensive complicated seasonings.

◆ Many vegetable dishes only require 3 to 4 ingredients, yet are filled with delicious flavors.

◆ Most vegetables are fair game for the carb-conscious cook.

Chapter 14

Salad Days

In This Chapter

- The usual salad suspects—and then some
- Variations on greens
- Bean salads
- Hearty dinner salads

Of course, we've all had salads. What might surprise you, however, is the breadth and depth you can find within this food category. From a side dish to a meal, anything is possible under the catch-all *salad* term.

The beauty of a salad is its flexibility. From torn lettuce with dressing (hey, during the week, sometimes that's where we all start) to mesclun with ripe and dried fruits, nuts, balsamic vinegar and fresh chevre, there's a salad for everyone.

About once a week, I decide that if man cannot live on bread alone, he *could* live on salad alone. I usually have that epiphany as my wife and I are midway through a big bowl of greens topped with toasted nuts, a sprinkling of Parmesan, maybe chunks of fruit, and a vinaigrette or Italian dressing. We're crunching away, and life is good.

A salad needs no cooking, which saves time. Fresh ingredients bring their own terrific flavors, and it's hard to mess up something that's already good. Salad ingredients are, for the most part, unprocessed and, as a result, higher in vitamins, minerals, fiber, and good carbs, and lower in chemicals and empty carbohydrates. We could learn a healthy lesson or two just by reminding ourselves that the farm stand is a great source for dinner.

 Gourmand's Glossary

Out of curiosity, I dusted off my old dictionary (*The Random House College Dictionary*), to look up the word **salad.** I found that a salad is "any of various cold dishes consisting of vegetables, as lettuce, tomatoes, cucumbers, etc., covered with a dressing and sometimes containing seafood, meat, or eggs." This does indeed sound like a term where there's more *included* than *excluded.*

In this chapter, we'll review one or two basics but then quickly get to some of my favorites—delicious salads that take minutes to make but can easily become an addictive and truly low-carb meal. Come to think of it, I'll bet there's *more* than one salad for everyone.

The Usual Salad Suspects

These are some of the salad-bar regulars. Then we spice things up a bit with fruits, meats, and cheeses that can make a feast out of any salad.

Vegetables

- ◆ Beans (all kinds)
- ◆ Carrots
- ◆ Celery
- ◆ Cucumbers
- ◆ Lettuce
- ◆ Mesclun (a mix of greens)
- ◆ Onions
- ◆ Spinach

Dressings

- Balsamic vinegar
- Canola oil
- Cider vinegar
- Lemon juice
- Mayonnaise (except fat-free versions)
- Off-the-shelf dressings (without sugar)
- Olive oil
- Wine vinegar

Fruits

- Apples
- Apricots
- Avocados
- Grapes
- Olives
- Pears
- Tomatoes

Meat

- Chicken
- Fish
- Ham (all forms)
- Shrimp
- Steak

Cheese

- Crumbled blue (all kinds)
- Feta
- Shredded (various kinds, including cheddar, Swiss, mozzarella, Monterey Jack, Parmesan, and others)

Carb Smarts

If you have fresh lemons, by all means use fresh lemon juice on your salad. It's quick, and the flavor is much better than the bottled stuff.

Carb Alert

Fresh tomatoes are one of my favorite fruits (yes, tomatoes are fruits, not vegetables, as commonly thought). Store-bought tomatoes are not my favorites. These tomatoes, unless they are in season and grown locally, tend to have been flown economy class from far away and don't have the flavor or texture of the real (fresh) thing.

Carb Smarts

When it comes to cheese on salads, use your favorites. The key is not to over-whelm your salad, so moderate amounts in small pieces usually work best. I find that ½ cup cheese in a 4-serving side salad works great. For a dinner salad, I like a combined amount of meat and cheese to not exceed 1 or 1½ cups, and less if you've got other goodies like chopped fruit and nuts.

Nuts

- ◆ Almonds
- ◆ Peanuts
- ◆ Pecans
- ◆ Pine nuts
- ◆ Soy nuts
- ◆ Walnuts

One look at a list like this, and it becomes clear that a shorter list would be those things that *wouldn't* go well on a low-carb salad. That list would include anything with sugar or white flour and the following:

- ◆ Croutons and other flour products
- ◆ Fruits that have added sugar (such as dried cranberries) or a very high level of natural sugar (raisins)
- ◆ Sugared dressings and honey

Variations on the Salad Theme

You're home, tired, and hungry, and you don't want to take the time to cook a vegetable dish. If you've got lettuce, though, you'll be eating before you know it. I know a salad is quick and easy, but it's still one of my favorite vegetable dishes.

I'll start with the basics, then launch from this fresh, crunchy springboard to other surprisingly good and healthful salads.

Then, we start to reflect on that dictionary definition of salad that includes everything under the sun. Fruits? Slice 'em in. Nuts? Go for it. Meats and cheeses? Make yourself right at home in these dishes. Salads with little or no lettuce still have plenty of flavor from vegetables and other goodies.

Then come the shell bean salads. These hearty, tasty salads take protein and flavor from rich shell beans. With beans as an important component, these salads are high in protein and fiber, not to mention flavor.

Basic Low-Carb Salad

Prep time: 8 minutes • Serves: 4

Each serving has: 95 calories • 2 protein • 0 g animal protein • 2 g vegetable protein • 7 g carbohydrates • 1 g dietary fiber • 6 g net carbohydrates • 7½ g fat • 1 g saturated fat • 0 mg cholesterol • 278 mg sodium • Exchanges: 1½ vegetable, 1½ fat

1 medium head romaine lettuce (or your favorite)

¼ large sweet onion, peeled and cut into thin (⅛ × 1-inch) slices

1 large fresh tomato, rinsed, cored, and sliced thin and then each slice quartered, or 10 grape tomatoes, rinsed and halved

½ small cucumber, peeled, quartered lengthwise, and chopped into ¼-inch pieces

2 TB. red wine vinegar

2 TB. extra-virgin olive oil

½ tsp. kosher salt

Pepper

Wash and dry lettuce, tear into bite-size pieces, and place in a large serving bowl. Top with onion, tomato, and cucumber. Drizzle with vinegar and oil, sprinkle with salt and pepper, and toss to coat.

Variation: To make a meal out of a simple tossed salad, add ½ pound cooked chicken meat or chopped ham and ½ pound shredded Swiss or cheddar cheese. Chopped ham is ready to go in many grocery stores, as is, of course, shredded cheese.

Carb Smarts

A salad spinner, a nifty hand-driven tool that whirls moisture out of salad, is a very helpful device to have in the cabinet. You'll find one in most kitchen stores. The alternatives are to give your greens time to drip dry (hard to do in a hurry), or gently dab them dry with paper towels.

Spinach Chef Salad

Prep time: 8 minutes • Cook time: 5 minutes • Serves: 4

Each serving has: 345 calories • 17 g protein • 14 g animal protein • 3 g vegetable protein • 6 g carbohydrates • 3 g dietary fiber • 3 g net carbohydrates • 16 g fat • 3 g saturated fat • 136 mg cholesterol • 944 mg sodium • Exchanges: 1½ high-fat meat, ½ medium-fat meat, 1 vegetable, 2½ fat

¼ lb. sliced bacon

1 (7-oz.) pkg. baby spinach, rinsed, stemmed, and dried

⅓ cup dressing vinaigrette or Italian dressing (your sugar-free favorite)

2 hard-boiled eggs, peeled and cut into thin, ¼-inch slices

4-oz. fresh mushrooms (¼ lb.), trimmed, wiped with a damp paper towel, and cut into thin, ¼-inch slices

⅓ cup toasted pine nuts or toasted sliced almonds

Ground black pepper

Cook bacon in a large skillet over medium heat until crisp and drain on a paper-towel–lined plate. Place spinach in a salad bowl and toss with dressing. Arrange egg slices, mushroom slices, toasted nuts, and crumbled bacon on top. Serve, seasoning each serving with a grind of pepper.

Carb Smarts

Pine nuts and sliced almonds are often available toasted in the salad area of the grocery store. Real bacon pieces are a quick substitute for cooking the bacon. Find these in the spice section of your grocery store.

Chicken Chef Salad

Prep time: 8 minutes   •   Serves: 4

Each serving has: 345 calories   •   24 g protein   •   20 g animal protein   •   4 g vegetable protein   •   13 g carbohydrates   •   3 g dietary fiber   •   10 g net carbohydrates   •   23 g fat   •   5 g saturated fat   •   48 mg cholesterol   •   177 mg sodium   •   Exchanges: 3 very-lean meat, ½ high-fat meat, ½ fruit, 1 vegetable, 3 fat

2 (6-oz.) cans chunk white chicken meat, drained

½ cup chopped walnuts (toasted or raw)

1 (12-oz.) bag iceberg salad mix, rinsed and dried

1 crisp pear, cored and chopped into ¼-inch pieces

½ cup (2-oz.) shredded cheddar cheese (or light cheddar)

⅓ cup vinaigrette or Italian dressing (your sugar-free favorite)

In a bowl, mix chicken and walnuts with a fork, breaking up any large chunks of meat. Toss chicken with lettuce, pear, cheese, and dressing and serve.

Iceberg Nests with Avocado, Bacon, and Tomato

Prep time: 8 minutes   •   Cook time: 5 minutes   •   Serves: 2

Each serving has: 540 calories   •   13 g protein   •   7 g animal protein   •   6 g vegetable protein   •   21 g carbohydrates   •   13 g dietary fiber   •   8 g net carbohydrates   •   50 g fat   •   9 g saturated fat   •   33 mg cholesterol   •   489 mg sodium   •   Exchanges: 2 high-fat meat, 2 vegetable, 10 fat

¼ lb. sliced bacon

2 medium, ripe avocados, peeled, flesh cut into ½-inch slices

1 large head iceberg lettuce, cut in half, and carefully separated into 2 bowl-shape "nests," center of head reserved for another use

1 large fresh tomato, rinsed, cored, seeded, and chopped into ¼-inch pieces

¼ cup toasted pine nuts

2 TB. lime juice

Ground black pepper and salt

Cook bacon in a large skillet over medium heat until crisp and drain on a paper-towel–lined plate. Distribute avocado between lettuce nests, followed by tomato and pine nuts. Drizzle with lime juice and top with crumbled bacon. Serve, seasoning each nest with black pepper and salt to taste.

Variation: Use other sturdy lettuces, such as romaine, in place of iceberg. Real bacon pieces (from the spice section at your grocery store) are a quick substitute for cooking the bacon.

Flower Bed Salad

Prep time: 8 minutes • Serves: 4

Each serving has: 110 calories • 4 g protein • 0 g animal protein • 4 g vegetable protein • 15 g carbohydrates • 7 g dietary fiber • 8 g net carbohydrates • 7½ g fat • 1 g saturated fat • 0 mg cholesterol • 10 mg sodium • Exchanges: 2 vegetable, 1½ fat

1 medium head romaine lettuce, rinsed, dried, and leaves broken into bite-size pieces

1 (7-oz.) pkg. baby spinach, rinsed, stemmed, and dried

10 grape tomatoes, rinsed and halved

1 handful arugula leaves, rinsed, stemmed, and dried

2 TB. balsamic vinegar

2 TB. extra-virgin olive oil

Salt and ground black pepper

8 to 10 fresh, young Nasturtium flowers

Mix romaine, spinach, tomatoes, and arugula in a serving bowl. Drizzle with vinegar and oil, sprinkle with salt and pepper, arrange flowers on top, and present for multiple compliments.

Variation: The nasturtium is only one garden flower that is both edible and delicious. Another one of my favorites is the flower of the tiny signet marigold. (It really does taste like it smells.)

 Carbohistory

I first published this simple recipe in my book *The Complete Idiot's Guide to 20-Minute Meals* and have received several "You have to include it in this book!" suggestions. This salad changes with the season, but the ingredients here are a fair representation. This colorful mixture is filled with flavor and just shouts "Be healthy!" Use Italian or oil-based dressing in place of the vinegar and oil.

Apple and Toasted Pecan Salad

Prep time: 8 minutes • Serves: 4

Each serving has: 354 calories • 7 g protein • 4 g animal protein • 3 g vegetable protein • 13 g carbohydrates • 5 g dietary fiber • 8 g net carbohydrates • 36 g fat • 7 g saturated fat • 13 mg cholesterol • 252 mg sodium • Exchanges: ½ high-fat meat, ½ fruit, 1 vegetable, 5½ fat

6 TB. walnut oil

2 TB. sherry vinegar or wine vinegar

1 tsp. prepared Dijon-style mustard

1 TB. sherry

1 pkg. Splenda or other artificial sweetener

¼ tsp. freshly ground black pepper

1 (6-oz.) pkg. "spring mix" greens, rinsed and dried

1 crisp apple, such as Granny Smith, cored and sliced thinly

½ cup crumbled Gorgonzola or other blue cheese

½ cup toasted pecans

Mix oil, vinegar, mustard, sherry, sweetener, and black pepper in a 2-cup measure. Put greens in a serving bowl, pour dressing over, and toss to coat. Arrange apple slices in a decorative pattern on the top of salad, sprinkle with blue cheese, and top with toasted nuts.

Serve this with a glass of wine and you've got a meal to smile about.

Carbohistory

For a long time, I thought a "Greek" salad was one made with greenish tomatoes, flabby cucumbers, a token green pepper, and iceberg lettuce—all smothered under a mound of feta cheese. Then, on a trip to Greece, I saw the light. In a local restaurant, we were served a platter with generous pieces of fresh tomato, chunks of cucumber, savory onion, slices of crisp sweet peppers, kalamata olives, and a bouquet of fresh basil—all glistening with olive oil and wine vinegar and no shred of lettuce in sight. On top reclined a wedge of fresh and creamy feta. We looked around at other tables. I watched as one man carefully assembled a bite that included an olive, a bit of feta, and every vegetable. "You know," my wife whispered to me, "this is the best Greek salad I've ever tasted." It was not only the best, but it was also a link I didn't even know was missing when I crunched on lettuce in my stateside Greek salads.

Real Greek Salad

Prep time: 10 minutes • Serves: 6

Each serving has: 160 calories • 5 g protein • 3 g animal protein • 2 g vegetable protein • 10 g carbohydrates • 3 g dietary fiber • 7 g net carbohydrates • 13 g fat • 4 g saturated fat • 17 mg cholesterol • 250 mg sodium • Exchanges: ½ high-fat meat, 2 vegetable, 2 fat

2 large fresh, firm tomatoes, rinsed, cored, seeded, and chopped into 1-inch pieces, or 1 pt. grape tomatoes, rinsed and halved

2 large sweet green peppers, seeds and ribs removed and chopped into 1-inch pieces

1 large English-style cucumber (or 2 small cucumbers), *striped*, sliced in half lengthwise, and cut into ½-inch pieces

½ large sweet onion, peeled and cut into ½-inch pieces

½ cup (about 10 large leaves) fresh basil, chopped

3 TB. extra-virgin olive oil

2 TB. red wine vinegar

½ (8-oz.) pkg. feta cheese (4 oz.), sliced into ¼×3-inch pieces

½ cup kalamata olives

Salt and ground black pepper

Gourmand's Glossary

Striped here means to half peel the vegetable so there are alternating peeled and unpeeled stripes running the length of the veggie.

Put tomatoes, green peppers, cucumber, onion, and basil in a bowl, drizzle with oil and vinegar, and toss to coat. Arrange feta wedges across the top and sprinkle with kalamata olives. Serve, being careful that a slice of feta and some olives make it into each serving, and season with salt and pepper to taste.

Carb Smarts

With salads, the taste comes from the natural flavors of fresh vegetables and whatever is put on them. Use fresh, in-season vegetables to make this salad, and you'll have another low-carb favorite for the dinner table. Also, this is the place to splurge on high-quality extra-virgin olive oil. I've heard good olive oil described as "liquid sunshine." Who wouldn't want some of that on his salad?

Fresh Tomato Salad

Prep time: 5 minutes   •   Serves: 4

Each serving has: 194 calories   •   10 g protein   •   8 g animal protein   •   2 g vegetable protein   •   4 g carbohydrates   •   1 g dietary fiber   •   3 g net carbohydrates   •   17 g fat   •   6 g saturated fat   •   18 mg cholesterol   •   171 mg sodium   •   Exchanges: 1½ medium-fat meat, 1 vegetable, 2 fat

1 pt. grape tomatoes, rinsed and halved, or 2 large fresh tomatoes, rinsed, cored, seeded, and chopped into 1-inch chunks

½ cup (about 10 large leaves) fresh basil, chopped, or 1 tsp. dried

1 cup fresh small mozzarella balls, cut in half

3 TB. extra-virgin olive oil

Salt and ground black pepper

Mix tomatoes, basil, and mozzarella in a bowl and distribute to serving plates. Drizzle with oil and season with salt and pepper to taste.

Carbohistory

Mozzarella cheese comes in many varieties. When it comes to eating it in salads, however, nothing tops fresh mozzarella for flavor. Fresh mozzarella, found in the deli or cheese section of your grocery stores, comes packed in brine in small balls (about the size of cherry tomatoes) or large (about the size of an egg). Fresh mozzarella is a rich, creamy, habit-forming cheese with a mild flavor that melds perfectly with fresh tomatoes.

Warm Asparagus-Artichoke Salad with Prosciutto and Pine Nuts

Prep time: 8 minutes • Cook time: 5 minutes • Serves: 4

Each serving has: 280 calories • 12 g protein • 6 g animal protein • 6 g vegetable protein • 13 g carbohydrates • 7 g dietary fiber • 6 g net carbohydrates • 23 g fat • 4 g saturated fat • 12 mg cholesterol • 266 mg sodium • Exchanges: 1 medium-fat meat, 1 vegetable, 4 fat

3 TB. olive oil

1 TB. chopped garlic

1 lb. fresh asparagus, top 4 inches cut into 1-inch sections for the salad and the remainder reserved for another use (a stir-fry is the perfect place)

1 (9-oz.) pkg. frozen artichoke hearts, thawed

½ cup (about 2 oz.) *diced* prosciutto

¼ cup toasted pine nuts

2 TB. *balsamic vinegar*

¼ cup shredded Parmesan cheese

Salt and ground black pepper

Heat oil in a large skillet over medium heat. Add garlic and asparagus and cook, stirring, for 3 minutes or until asparagus is tender-crisp. Add artichoke hearts and heat for 1 minute. Turn off heat and stir in prosciutto and pine nuts. Distribute warm to serving plates, drizzle with balsamic vinegar, sprinkle with Parmesan, and season to taste with salt and pepper.

Gourmand's Glossary

To **dice** something is to chop it into very small pieces about ⅛-inch across.

Balsamic vinegar is produced primarily in Italy from the juice of the Trebbiano grape, then aged in wood barrels. It is heavier and darker than most vinegars and is also higher in carbohydrates than other vinegars. But because we use such small amounts in these recipes, the flavor is worth it. If necessary for strictly low-carb purposes, however, substitute red wine vinegar.

Three-Bean Salad

Prep time: 8 minutes • Serves: 6

Each serving has: 323 calories • 12 g protein • 0 g animal protein • 12 g vegetable protein • 42 g carbohydrates • 10 g dietary fiber • 32 g net carbohydrates • 13 g fat • 1½ g saturated fat • 0 mg cholesterol • 429 mg sodium • Exchanges: 2 very-lean meat, 2 starch, 1 vegetable, 2 fat

1 lb. cut fresh green beans or 1 lb. frozen, thawed

1 (15-oz.) can white beans, drained and rinsed

1 (15-oz.) can chickpeas, drained and rinsed

1 red bell pepper, seeds and ribs removed, and chopped into ¼-inch pieces

¼ large sweet onion (about ½ cup), peeled and diced

¼ cup Splenda (optional)

⅓ cup olive oil

⅓ cup red wine vinegar

½ tsp. dill

½ tsp. celery seed

½ tsp. salt

½ tsp. ground black pepper

In a container with a lid, mix green beans, white beans, chickpeas, red bell pepper, onion, Splenda (if using), oil, vinegar, dill, celery seed, salt, and black pepper. Cover and refrigerate for several hours or all day. Serve in small bowls alone or as a tasty side dish.

Carb Alert

Some artificial sweeteners such as Splenda are available in a form that can be used spoon-for-spoon or measure-for-measure as a replacement for sugar. That is the "¼ cup" in Three-Bean Salad.

Tuna-Cannellini Salad

Prep time: 8 minutes • Serves: 6

Each serving has: 244 calories • 23 g protein • 16 g animal protein • 7 g vegetable protein • 25 g carbohydrates • 5 g dietary fiber • 20 g net carbohydrates • 5 g fat • 2 g saturated fat • 31 mg cholesterol • 711 mg sodium • Exchanges: 3 very-lean meat, 1 starch, ½ fruit, 1 fat

2 (6-oz.) cans chunk white tuna, drained

1 (15-oz.) can white beans, drained and rinsed

1 celery stalk, rinsed and cut into ¼-inch pieces

1 crisp apple, such as Granny Smith, cored and chopped into ¼-inch pieces

2 cups (about 3 oz.) fresh arugula, rinsed, stemmed, and chopped

½ cup sweet onion, peeled and minced

½ cup vinaigrette or Italian dressing (your sugar-free favorite)

½ cup shredded Parmesan cheese

Place tuna, white beans, celery, apple, arugula, and onion in a salad bowl. Drizzle salad with dressing and toss to coat. Distribute to serving plates, sprinkling each serving with Parmesan cheese.

Chickpea Dinner Salad

Prep time: 8 minutes • Serves: 6

Each serving has: 293 calories • 18 g protein • 13 g animal protein • 5 g vegetable protein • 20 g carbohydrates • 4 g dietary fiber • 16 g net carbohydrates • 15 g fat • 3 g saturated fat • 35 mg cholesterol • 694 mg sodium • Exchanges: 2 very-lean meat, 1½ starch, 2½ fat

⅓ cup olive oil

2 TB. freshly squeezed lemon juice

2 anchovies

½ tsp. ground black pepper

2 (5-oz.) cans chunk white chicken meat, drained

1 (15-oz.) can chickpeas, drained and rinsed

2 celery stalks, rinsed and cut into ¼-inch pieces

1 large red bell pepper, seeds and ribs removed and chopped into ¼-inch pieces

1 cup chopped fresh parsley

½ cup sweet onion, peeled and minced

½ cup shredded Parmesan cheese

In a blender, purée oil, lemon juice, anchovies, and black pepper. Place chicken, chickpeas, celery, bell pepper, parsley, and onion in a salad bowl. Drizzle with dressing and toss to coat. Distribute salad to serving plates, sprinkling each serving with Parmesan cheese.

The Least You Need to Know

- If you start with the freshest possible vegetables, your salad is half done already.
- Salads are extremely flexible. As long as you watch out for high-carb ingredients, just about anything goes.
- A salad does not have to include lettuce.
- Meats and beans can be nutritious, low-carb components of hearty salads.

Low-Carb Soups

In This Chapter

- ◆ Tasty, ultra-fast, low-carb soups
- ◆ Low-carb versions of classic favorites
- ◆ Rich meat stews
- ◆ Savory vegetable soups
- ◆ Seasonings of the world—in your bowl

In this chapter, we explore some of the magic appeal of soups and stews. As you'll see, there's a world to explore, much of it naturally low carb.

In terms of quick, soups are a natural. Consider using canned ingredients and the microwave, and you're done with your meal almost before you start. And because a big batch of soup or stew will live happily in the fridge for a couple days—tasting better all the time—you'll have several lunches or dinners that only need warming up later.

Super Quick—and Proud of It

To get started, the first two recipes in this chapter are quicker than fast and make unashamed use of frozen and canned ingredients. When you need a tasty, low-carb meal in 10 minutes or less, start here.

Carb-Conscious Classics

Many of these soups and stews will be familiar to you, and with good reason: Soups tend to be based on meats, seafood, vegetables, and sometimes cream—all naturally low-carb foods. Where appropriate I've made some low-carb adjustments, but I don't think we've lost any flavor at all.

A World Tour in a Soup Bowl

Soups and stews abound in the cuisines of many cultures. The examples in this chapter use representative ingredients and seasoning to give just a taste of that wondrous variety.

Emergency Turkey Vegetable Soup

Prep time: 5 minutes • Cook time: 8 minutes • Serves: 4

Each serving has: 165 calories • 24 g protein • 20 g animal protein • 4 g vegetable protein • 22 g carbohydrates • 5 g dietary fiber • 17 g net carbohydrates • 2 g fat • 1 g saturated fat • 42 mg cholesterol • 1,106 mg sodium • Exchanges: 2½ very-lean meat, 3 vegetable

2 (14.5-oz.) cans chicken broth

2 (5-oz.) cans chunk turkey meat, drained

1 (16-oz.) pkg. frozen broccoli, green beans, pearl onions, and red pepper mix

1 (1.4-oz.) pkg. vegetable soup mix

Salt and ground black pepper

Carb Smarts

I always recommend fresh vegetables, but for speed and convenience, don't ignore "freezer diving" for frozen vegetables. Add that to a few choice canned items from the pantry, and you're on your way to a terrific stew.

Mix broth, turkey, frozen veggie mix, and soup mix in a large microwave-safe bowl and microwave on high for 5 to 8 minutes, stirring twice. (Cook time will vary according to microwave power.) Stir and serve, seasoning with salt and pepper to taste.

Variations: Try other canned meats, such as chicken or even diced ham.

Lightning Chicken Stew

Prep time: 5 minutes • Cook time: 15 minutes • Serves: 4

Each serving has: 239 calories • 21 g protein • 18 g animal protein • 3 g vegetable protein • 15 g carbohydrates • 3 g dietary fiber • 12 g net carbohydrates • 11 g fat • 3 g saturated fat • 33 mg cholesterol • 769 mg sodium • Exchanges: 2½ very-lean meat, 1 starch, 1 fat

1 (10-oz.) can or 2 (5-oz.) cans chunk white chicken meat, drained

1 (10.75-oz.) cans "healthy" condensed cream of mushroom soup (don't add the extra water)

1 (14.5-oz.) can cut green beans, drained

1 (6-oz.) can sliced mushrooms, drained

1 cup milk

½ tsp. ground black pepper

Dash hot red pepper sauce

Mix chicken, soup, green beans, mushrooms, milk, black pepper, and hot pepper sauce in a large microwave-safe dish with a lid. Put on the lid (leaving it loose to allow steam to escape) and microwave for 4 minutes or until stew is hot, stirring once or twice. (If your microwave does not have a turntable, stir a couple times to ensure even cooking). Ladle stew into bowls and serve.

Cream of Spinach Soup

Prep time: 5 minutes • Cook time: 15 minutes • Serves: 4

Each serving has: 127 calories • 8 g protein • 4 g animal protein • 4 g vegetable protein • 8 g carbohydrates • 4 g dietary fiber • 4 g net carbohydrates • 8 g fat • 4 g saturated fat • 23 mg cholesterol • 878 mg sodium • Exchanges: 1 vegetable, 2 fat

2 (10-oz.) pkg. frozen chopped spinach, thawed

3 cups (about 1½ [14.5-oz.] cans) chicken broth

2 tsp. sweet paprika

½ tsp. salt

½ tsp. ground black pepper

½ cup heavy cream

¼ tsp. ground nutmeg

Bring a large saucepan of water to a boil and cook spinach for 4 minutes. Drain in a colander. Working in batches, process spinach and some broth (to aid in processing) in a blender or food processor to a smooth consistency (visible pieces of leaves add appealing texture). Return creamed spinach and any remaining broth to the saucepan over medium heat and stir in paprika, salt, and black pepper. Heat for 5 minutes, stirring. Stir in cream, heat for 1 minute, and serve in big bowls, each garnished with a pinch of nutmeg.

Quick Vegetable-Beef Stew

Prep time: 5 minutes   •   Cook time: 15 minutes   •   Serves: 6

Each serving has: 385 calories   •   31 g protein   •   28 g animal protein   •   3 g vegetable protein   •   10 g carbohydrates   •   2 g dietary fiber   •   8 g net carbohydrates   •   25 g fat   •   9 g saturated fat   •   78 mg cholesterol   •   638 mg sodium   •   Exchanges: 4 lean meat, 2 vegetable, 1½ fat

3 TB. olive or canola oil

1 medium onion, peeled and chopped into ½-inch pieces

1½ lb. steak tips, cut into ½-inch pieces

Pinch salt

½ tsp. ground black pepper

1 (16-oz.) pkg. frozen green beans and pearl onions mixture

2 TB. tomato paste

1 (14.5-oz.) can beef broth

1 (14.5-oz.) can diced tomatoes with juice

2 TB. Worcestershire sauce

Carb Alert

When substituting vegetables for beef stew, keep in mind that some vegetables, especially peas, corn, and potatoes, are naturally high carb and should be avoided or used with caution. Fortunately, there are plenty of alternatives in the fresh, frozen, and canned vegetable sections of your grocery store.

Heat oil in a large skillet over medium heat. Add onion and beef and cook, stirring, for 5 minutes or until done. Season beef with salt and pepper as it cooks. While beef is cooking, thaw frozen vegetables in the microwave, and whisk tomato paste into 1 cup beef broth. When beef is done, add tomatoes to the skillet along with broth and tomato paste, pea/onion mixture, and Worcestershire sauce. Mix thoroughly and cook for 10 minutes, stirring.

Variation: For the vegetable enthusiast, substitute fresh vegetables or other interesting mixes from the freezer section such as broccoli, cauliflower, carrots, and bell peppers, or cauliflower, carrots, and peapods. After cooking beef in the skillet, you can also prepare this stew in a slow cooker for 8 to 10 hours on low.

Chunky Chicken Vegetable Soup

Prep time: 5 minutes • Cook time: 20 minutes • Serves: 8

Each serving has: 153 calories • 19 g protein • 18 g animal protein • 1 g vegetable protein • 5 g carbohydrates • 1 g dietary fiber • 4 g net carbohydrates • 9 g fat • 3 g saturated fat • 49 mg cholesterol • 805 mg sodium • Exchanges: 2 very-lean meat, 1 vegetable, 1 fat

3 TB. olive or canola oil

1 medium onion, peeled and chopped into ½-inch pieces

1 lb. boneless, skinless chicken, rinsed, dried, and cut into ½-inch pieces

2 large carrots, scraped and cut into ¼-inch slices

2 large celery stalks with leaves, rinsed and cut into ½-inch slices

3 (14.5-oz.) cans chicken broth

¼ cup prepared pesto

½ tsp. ground black pepper plus additional for seasoning

Salt

Heat oil in a stockpot or large saucepan over medium heat. Add onion and cook, stirring, for 2 minutes. Add chicken and cook for another 5 minutes or until chicken is done. Add carrots, celery, broth, pesto, and pepper and cook for 12 minutes or until carrots and celery are tender. Distribute to bowls and serve, seasoning to taste with additional salt and pepper, if desired.

Variations: This rich, flavorful soup is possible even more quickly by using canned chicken (in your grocery store next to the canned tuna). Add 1 (15-ounce) can white beans (drained) to make it a one-pot meal.

White Beans and Dark Greens

Prep time: 5 minutes • Cook time: 15 minutes • Serves: 10

Each serving has: 111 calories • 5 g protein • 1 g animal protein • 4 g vegetable protein • 12 g carbohydrates • 3 g dietary fiber • 9 g net carbohydrates • 4½ g fat • 1 g saturated fat • 1 mg cholesterol • 781 mg sodium • Exchanges: 1 very-lean meat, ½ starch, ½ vegetable, 1 fat

3 TB. olive oil

1 large onion, peeled and cut into ½-inch pieces

2 tsp. chopped garlic

4 large kale leaves, rinsed, stemmed, and chopped into 1 × 2-inch pieces

1 (10-oz.) pkg. frozen leaf spinach, thawed (don't worry about squeezing it dry)

4 (15-oz.) cans (about 7 cups) chicken broth

1 (15-oz.) can white beans, drained and rinsed

2 tsp. Italian seasoning

½ tsp. salt

¼ tsp. ground black pepper

Dash hot red pepper sauce

Heat oil in a stockpot over medium heat. Add onions and cook, stirring, for 4 minutes. Add garlic and cook for another minute. Add kale, spinach, broth, beans, Italian seasoning, salt, pepper, and hot pepper sauce and cook for 10 minutes, stirring, or until kale is tender.

Variation: Season with Parmesan cheese for even more flavor.

Carb Smarts

With stews, making extra doesn't take much extra time. That's why many of the recipes in this chapter give you a big batch. Make it tonight, and you've got a practically instant meal tomorrow (not to mention easy clean-up tomorrow, too). An added bonus with these rich dishes is that they'll probably taste even better the second time around.

Quick Seafood Vegetable Stew

Prep time: 8 minutes • Cook time: 12 minutes • Serves: 8

Each serving has: 351 calories • 29 g protein • 22 g animal protein • 7 g vegetable protein • 26 g carbohydrates • 5 g dietary fiber • 21 g net carbohydrates • 13 g fat • 2 g saturated fat • 49 mg cholesterol • 581 mg sodium • Exchanges: 4 very-lean meat, 1 starch, 1 vegetable, 2½ fat

5 TB. olive oil

1 medium onion, peeled and chopped into ½-inch pieces

2 large carrots, scraped, trimmed and cut into ¼-inch pieces

2 TB. chopped garlic

2 tsp. Italian seasoning

½ tsp. crushed red pepper

1 cup arugula, rinsed, stemmed, and coarsely chopped

1 (15-oz.) can white beans, drained and rinsed

1 (14.5-oz.) can vegetable broth

1 cup water

1 cup dry white wine

1 lb. whitefish, such as cod or haddock, rinsed in cold water, patted dry with paper towels, and cut into 1-inch chunks

½ lb. bay scallops or quartered sea scallops, rinsed

Salt and ground black pepper

Heat oil in a large skillet or stockpot over medium heat. Add onion and carrots and cook, stirring, for 5 minutes. Add garlic, Italian seasoning, and crushed red pepper and cook for 1 minute more. Add arugula, white beans, broth, water, and wine. Bring to a low boil. Add fish, cook for 2 minutes, and then add scallops and cook for another 4 minutes or until fish and scallops are just done. Serve in big bowls, seasoning with salt and pepper to taste.

Spicy Shrimp Stew

Prep time: 5 minutes • Cook time: 15 minutes • Serves: 6

Each serving has: 223 calories • 26 g protein • 24 g animal protein • 2 g vegetable protein • 8 g carbohydrates • 2 g dietary fiber • 6 g net carbohydrates • 10 g fat • 3 g saturated fat • 127 mg cholesterol • 1,229 mg sodium • Exchanges: 2½ very-lean meat, 1 vegetable, 2 fat

4 strips bacon

1 large onion, peeled and chopped into ½-inch pieces

1 tsp. garlic

½ tsp. crushed red pepper

½ tsp. ground cumin

½ tsp. ground thyme

2 (15-oz.) cans chicken broth

¼ tsp. black pepper

Dash hot red pepper sauce

1 bunch (about 1 lb.) asparagus, chopped into 1-inch segments, bottom 2 inches discarded

1 lb. (31 to 40 count) medium cooked shrimp, tail off

¼ cup Madeira or sherry

Shredded Parmesan cheese

Salt and ground black pepper

Carb Alert

Many of these recipes use canned chicken or vegetable broth for a base. You have some choices here, particularly between low-sodium and regular broth. If you use the regular, higher-salt version, taste the result before adding any additional salt. You might not need it.

Cook bacon in a large skillet over medium heat for 4 minutes or until bacon is crisp. Remove bacon to a paper-towel–lined plate. Drain most of fat, leaving enough to coat the bottom of the pot, and cook onion, garlic, crushed red pepper, cumin, and thyme for 4 minutes, stirring.

While bacon is cooking, heat broth, black pepper, and hot pepper sauce in a large saucepan or stockpot. Add asparagus and cook for 8 minutes or until asparagus is just turning from crisp to tender. Stir in cooked onion and garlic from the skillet, add shrimp and Madeira, and cook for 3 minutes. Serve topped with crumbled bacon, Parmesan, and salt and pepper to taste.

Minestrone

Prep time: 5 minutes • Cook time: 20 minutes • Serves: 10

Each serving has: 190 calories • 12 g protein • 4 g animal protein • 8 g vegetable protein • 27 g carbohydrates • 6 g dietary fiber • 21 g net carbohydrates • 3 g fat • 1 g saturated fat • 2 mg cholesterol • 1,106 mg sodium • Exchanges: 1½ very-lean meat, 1 starch, 2 vegetable, ½ fat

2 TB. olive oil

1 large onion, peeled and chopped into ½-inch pieces

2 TB. chopped garlic

4 (14.5-oz.) cans chicken broth

1 (14.5-oz.) can chopped tomatoes with juice

2 (15-oz.) cans white beans, drained and rinsed

¼ small head cabbage (about 1½ cups), sliced into thin, ½ × 2-inch pieces

2 large carrots, scraped and cut into ¼-inch slices

2 large celery stalks including leaves, rinsed and cut into ¼-inch slices

¼ cup fresh basil leaves, coarsely chopped, or 1 tsp. dried

2 tsp. fresh oregano or 1 tsp. dried

¼ tsp. crushed red pepper

1 tsp. salt

1 (10-inch) zucchini squash, rinsed, ends removed, halved lengthwise, cut into ½-inch slices

Ground black pepper

Shredded Parmesan cheese

Heat oil in a large stockpot over medium heat. Add onion and cook, stirring, for 4 minutes. Add garlic and cook for another 1 minute. Add broth, tomatoes, beans, cabbage, carrots, celery, basil, oregano, crushed red pepper, and salt and cook for 10 minutes. Add zucchini and cook for 3 minutes or until zucchini, carrots, and celery are tender. Serve in bowls, seasoning with pepper to taste and sprinkling with Parmesan cheese.

Grilled Chicken-Ginger Soup

Prep time: 5 minutes   •   Cook time: 15 minutes   •   Serves: 4

Each serving has: 265 calories   •   29 g protein   •   28 g animal protein   •   1 g vegetable protein   •   5 g carbohydrates   •   1 g dietary fiber   •   4 g net carbohydrates   •   12 g fat   •   3 g saturated fat   •   99 mg cholesterol   •   1,253 mg sodium   •   Exchanges: 4 very-lean meat, 1 vegetable, 2 fat

1 lb. boneless, skinless chicken breasts, rinsed, dried, and cut into ½-inch strips

1 TB. grated fresh ginger

½ tsp. ground black pepper

½ tsp. salt

2 TB. sesame oil

2 (15-oz.) cans chicken broth

1 tsp. dried lemongrass

1 bunch (about 6) scallions, roots and dark green parts removed, cut into thin, ⅛-inch–thick rings

4 tsp. sesame seeds

Place chicken in a bowl and sprinkle with ginger, pepper, and salt, turning to allow ginger and pepper to reach all sides. Heat oil in a large skillet or saucepan over medium heat. Add chicken and cook, stirring, for 5 minutes or until chicken is done. Add broth and lemongrass and heat, stirring, until soup just reaches a boil. Turn heat to low and simmer for 10 minutes. Stir in scallions and serve in large bowls, sprinkling each bowl with 1 teaspoon sesame seeds.

Hearty Low-Carb Chili

Prep time: 5 minutes • Cook time: 15 minutes • Serves: 6

Each serving has: 260 calories • 17 g protein • 12 g animal protein • 5 g vegetable protein • 17 g carbohydrates • 5 g dietary fiber • 12 g net carbohydrates • 16 g fat • 5 g saturated fat • 39 mg cholesterol • 745 mg sodium • Exchanges: 2 medium-fat meat, ½ very-lean meat, ½ starch, 2 vegetable, 1 fat

2 TB. olive or canola oil

1 medium onion, peeled and chopped into ½-inch pieces

1 lb. ground beef

1 (15.5-oz.) can red kidney beans, drained and rinsed

2 (14.5-oz.) cans diced tomatoes with juice

1 (4.5-oz.) can chopped green chilies

1 (4.25-oz.) can chopped ripe olives, drained

2 TB. chili powder

2 TB. unsweetened chocolate (either chopped baking chocolate or chips)

2 TB. Worcestershire sauce

1 TB. ground cumin

Heat oil in a large skillet over medium heat. Add onion and ground beef and cook, stirring, for 5 minutes or until meat is browned. Add beans, tomatoes, chilies, olives, chili powder, chocolate chips, Worcestershire sauce, and cumin and cook for 10 minutes, stirring. Serve in big bowls.

Variation: Substitute bittersweet chips for unsweetened chocolate. These contain sugar and will add carbs, but not much when spread over this batch. Leftovers will be terrific.

Carbohistory

Chocolate does not always have to be associated with sweet flavors or with dessert. In other parts of the world, chocolate is used in all kinds of sweet and savory dishes. Use of chocolate here adds authentic richness and depth the way chili is prepared in many south-of-the-border countries.

Miso Soup with Scallions, Tofu, and Carrots

Prep time: 5 minutes • Cook time: 10 minutes • Serves: 4

Each serving has: 160 calories • 8 g protein • 0 g animal protein • 8 g vegetable protein • 13 g carbohydrates • 3 g dietary fiber • 10 g net carbohydrates • 4 g fat • 1 g saturated fat • 0 mg cholesterol • 1,305 mg sodium • Exchanges: 1½ very-lean meat, 2 vegetable, 1 fat

2 (14-oz.) cans (about 3¾ cups) vegetable broth	4 scallions, roots and dark green parts removed, cut into ¼-inch rings
1 large carrot, scraped and sliced on the diagonal to form very thin, ¹⁄₁₆- to ⅛-inch–thick oval shapes	¼ (16-oz.) pkg. (about 4 oz.) soft tofu, drained and cut into ¼-inch chunks
¼ cup *miso*	2 TB. soy sauce (optional)

Gourmand's Glossary

Miso is a fermented, flavorful soybean paste and is a key ingredient in many Japanese dishes. You'll find it in larger grocery stores and stores specializing in Asian foods.

In a saucepan or stockpot, bring broth to a boil over medium-high heat. Add sliced carrots, reduce heat to low, cover, and cook for 5 minutes. Remove ½ cup broth to a heat-safe measuring cup and stir in miso until well blended. Pour miso and broth back into soup, stirring to blend. Add scallions and tofu, season with soy sauce (if using), and serve.

Variations: Use 4 cups water and 2 vegetable bouillon cubes in place of canned vegetable broth. For an interesting variation in texture and flavor, use adzuki beans in place of tofu.

Crunchy Watercress-Crab Soup

Prep time: 5 minutes • Cook time: 15 minutes • Serves: 4

Each serving has: 263 calories • 19 g protein • 13 g animal protein • 6 g vegetable protein • 18 g carbohydrates • 4 g dietary fiber • 14 g net carbohydrates • 12 g fat • 3 g saturated fat • 59 mg cholesterol • 1,202 mg sodium • Exchanges: 2 very-lean meat, 3 vegetable, 2½ fat

3 TB. sesame or olive oil

1 small onion, peeled and chopped into ½-inch pieces

1 TB. chopped garlic

1 (10-inch) zucchini squash, rinsed, ends trimmed, quartered lengthwise, cut into ¼-inch pieces

1 TB. sesame seeds

1 tsp. crushed red pepper

2 (14-oz.) cans vegetable broth

2 (4.5-oz.) cans crabmeat, drained, and picked over to discard shell fragments

1 tsp. dried lemongrass (optional)

1½ cups watercress, rinsed, stemmed, and coarsely chopped

Salt and ground black pepper

Heat oil in a large skillet or saucepan over medium heat. Add onion and cook, stirring, for 4 minutes. Add garlic, zucchini, sesame seeds, and crushed red pepper. Cover and cook for 4 minutes, removing cover to stir several times. Add broth, crabmeat, and lemongrass (if using) and heat for 4 additional minutes or until just beginning to bubble. Stir in watercress and serve, seasoning with salt (there's salt in vegetable broth, so it might not be necessary) and pepper to taste.

Carbohistory

As these recipes show, seasonings bring with them a wealth of cultural context. Sesame oil, sesame seeds, and lemongrass are all traditional ingredients in Asian dishes. Cinnamon, cloves, and saffron evoke an entirely different image. Basil, oregano, rosemary, and other herbs found in Italian seasoning, although nominally Italian, are common to many Mediterranean cuisines.

Middle Eastern Vegetable Stew

Prep time: 5 minutes   •   Cook time: 15 minutes   •   Serves: 4

Each serving has: 393 calories   •   16 g protein   •   7 g animal protein   •   9 g vegetable protein   •   43 g carbohydrates   •   10 g dietary fiber   •   33 g net carbohydrates   •   15 g fat   •   3 g saturated fat   •   9 mg cholesterol   •   1,212 mg sodium   •   Exchanges: 2 very-lean meat, 2 starch, 2 vegetable, 2½ fat

3 TB. olive oil	2 tsp. ground cinnamon
1 medium onion, peeled and chopped into ½-inch pieces	2 tsp. sweet paprika
2 celery stalks, rinsed and chopped into ½-inch pieces	1 tsp. fennel seed
	1 tsp. ground cumin
2 TB. chopped garlic	1 tsp. salt
3 (15-oz.) cans chicken broth	½ tsp. ground black pepper
1 (10-inch) zucchini squash, ends trimmed, halved lengthwise and chopped into ½-inch pieces	½ tsp. turmeric
	¼ tsp. ground cloves
1 (15-oz.) can chickpeas, drained and rinsed	Pinch saffron
1 (14-oz.) can plum tomatoes with juice, coarsely chopped	½ cup plain yogurt

Heat oil in a large stockpot over medium heat. Add onion and cook, stirring, for 4 minutes. Add celery and garlic and cook another 1 minute. Add broth, zucchini, chickpeas, tomatoes with juice, cinnamon, paprika, fennel, cumin, salt, pepper, turmeric, cloves, and saffron. Cook for 10 minutes, stirring. Serve in big bowls with a dollop of yogurt and watch the sun set over the Sahara.

Mushroom Mélange Soup

Prep time: 5 minutes • Cook time: 15 minutes • Serves: 4

Each serving has: 387 calories • 14 g protein • 8 g animal protein • 6 g vegetable protein • 26 g carbohydrates • 4 g dietary fiber • 22 g net carbohydrates • 29 g fat • 10 g saturated fat • 50 mg cholesterol • 1,544 mg sodium • Exchanges: ½ high-fat meat, 1 starch, 2 vegetable, 4½ fat

4 strips bacon

1 medium onion, peeled and chopped into ½-inch pieces

1 (8-oz.) pkg. sliced portobello mushrooms

1 TB. chopped garlic

2 TB. whole-wheat flour

3 (15-oz.) cans chicken broth

½ cup white wine

1 (4-oz.) pkg. shiitake mushrooms, stemmed, wiped with a damp paper towel, and sliced

1 (8-oz.) pkg. sliced white mushrooms

2 tsp. fresh thyme

½ tsp. ground black pepper

½ cup heavy cream

Salt to taste

Cook bacon in a large skillet over medium heat for 2 minutes per side or until crisp. Remove bacon to a paper-towel–lined plate to drain. Drain off most fat, leaving just enough to coat the bottom of the pan. Cook onions for 5 minutes, stirring. Add portobello mushrooms and garlic, sprinkle mushrooms with flour and cook, stirring, for 4 minutes.

While bacon is cooking, heat broth, wine, shiitake and white mushrooms, thyme, and black pepper in a large stockpot over medium heat. Cook for 5 minutes, stirring. Add portobello mushrooms from the skillet when they are ready. Cook for another 5 minutes, stirring. Stir in cream and serve in bowls, garnishing with crumbled bacon and seasoning to taste with additional salt.

Variation: For a delicious cream soup, process half of the soup in a blender or food processor to a creamy consistency and return it to the pot with the rest of the soup.

To save on cleaning, cook bacon in the same pot before the soup. This will add to the total time of preparation.

Gourmand's Glossary

A **mélange** is French for a mixture or blend—in this case, of mushrooms. Next time you make dinner with leftovers, don't call it *leftovers*, call it a *mélange*. There, doesn't that taste better?

The Least You Need to Know

◆ Soups and stews can be not only hearty and delicious but also quick to prepare.

◆ Soup ingredients are often naturally low carb.

◆ Many soups and stews offer the time-saving convenience of a one-pot meal.

◆ Make tasty homemade soups using canned and frozen ingredients—a big bonus for the cook in a hurry.

◆ Soups are found across the world, and many bring international flavor and interest to your dinner table.

Chapter 16

Dessert Time

In This Chapter

- ◆ Chocolate desserts
- ◆ Creamy delights
- ◆ Quick-cooked low-carb treats
- ◆ Out-of-the-box desserts

Desserts present a challenge for the carb-conscious cook. Most of us love sweet flavors, yet sugar (at least the refined, high-glycemic kind) is precisely what we need to avoid.

In this chapter, we explore solutions to this delicious challenge. We'll spoon into delicious desserts where flavor and sweetness is based on fruit sugar—generally considered a good carb. We'll bite into textures and flavors such as chocolate and cream that enable delicious desserts without necessarily containing a lot of carbs. And for the dyed-in-the-wool sweet tooth, we'll explore the potential of some of the tasty sweeteners out there. Some are based on sugar and claim to offer sweet flavor without the aftertaste that plagues other sweeteners.

And sometimes we'll combine the three—to decadent results.

Hot and Sweet

To get us started on the right note (a chocolate note, that is), I'll give you several chocolate-intensive desserts that have a minimum of carbs.

Carb Alert

The recipes in this chapter are low or good carb, but they are *not* all low in fat. If you are limiting fat intake, avoid those that are high in saturated fat (there are plenty of others). And for all of us, when it comes to a dessert indulgence, portion control is more important than ever. Too much of a good thing is not a good thing.

Then, for the cook in a hurry who doesn't have a lot of time for baking, I'll give you recipes for several delicious cooked desserts you can whip up even in a short period of time.

Think Out of the Box

In a bind for time and need a low-carb dessert? Think out of the box! These recipes play with dessert mix foundations but create dishes that might just fool guests into thinking you've been up all night making dessert.

Mocha Mousse

Prep time: 10 minutes • Serves: 4

Each serving has: 178 calories • 1 g protein • 1 g animal protein • 0 g vegetable protein • 2 g carbohydrates • 1 g dietary fiber • 1 g net carbohydrates • 19 g fat • 11 g saturated fat • 66 mg cholesterol • 21 mg sodium • Exchanges: 4 fat

1 TB. cocoa powder	1 pint (2 cups) whipping cream
2 tsp. instant espresso powder	1 tsp. pure vanilla extract
½ cup Splenda	

Mix cocoa powder, espresso powder, and sweetener in a cup measure. Whip cream, slowly adding cocoa-sweetener mixture and vanilla as you whip. When cream doubles and forms soft peaks, you're done. Serve in small bowls.

Variation: For pure chocolate flavor, use an extra tablespoon cocoa powder in place of espresso powder.

Carb Smarts

To add visual appeal, scoop the Mocha Mousse into a zipper-type freezer bag. Cut off about ½ inch from one corner of the bag and, squeezing gently, swirl servings into each bowl. Irresistible.

Cheater's Crustless Chocolate Cheesecake

Prep time: 5 minutes plus chilling time • Serves: 6

Each serving has: 322 calories • 7 g protein • 6 g animal protein • 1 g vegetable protein • 10 g carbohydrates • 2 g dietary fiber • 8 g net carbohydrates • 28 g fat • 18 g saturated fat • 90 mg cholesterol • 420 mg sodium • Exchanges: 2 high-fat meat, ½ starch, 2½ fat

2 (8-oz.) pkg. cream cheese, softened

½ cup light sour cream

1 (1.4-oz.) pkg. sugar-free and fat-free chocolate pudding mix

½ cup unprocessed bran

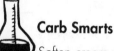

Carb Smarts

Soften cream cheese by heating it in the microwave for 15 to 30 seconds. For this cheesecake mix, it's easier to prepare the softer the cream cheese is, so heat it for about 30 seconds (depending on the power of your microwave).

Using a mixer or food processor, mix cream cheese, sour cream, and chocolate pudding mix. Spread bran into the bottom of a pie plate in a smooth layer. Scrape filling into bran-lined pie plate and smooth out mixture with the spoon and a rubber spatula. Chill for at least 1 hour, cut into pie wedges, and serve, sliding a flat knife or spatula underneath to lift one piece.

Variation: Regular cream cheese (or whipped regular cream cheese) gives this cheesecake the best texture.

Velvet Fudge

Prep time: 5 minutes   •   Cook time: 10 minutes   •   Serves: 24

Each serving has: 82 calories   •   1 g protein   •   0 g animal protein   •   1 g vegetable protein   •   7 g carbohydrates   •   0 g dietary fiber   •   7 g net carbohydrates   •   6 g fat   •   3 g saturated fat   •   31 mg cholesterol   •   30 mg sodium   •   Exchanges: ½ fruit, 1 fat

2 cups heavy cream

1 (8-oz.) box bittersweet chocolate

⅓ cup Splenda

½ tsp. pure vanilla extract

2 egg yolks

Heat cream to a simmer over medium-low heat and stir in chocolate until melted and creamy. While cream is heating, mix sweetener and vanilla into egg yolks, then line a small baking pan with wax paper.

When chocolate is completely melted, turn off heat and slowly stir in yolks until thoroughly blended. Scrape this thick mixture onto the wax paper using a rubber spatula and smooth to a flat layer. Chill until firm and cut into 1-inch squares.

Variation: Mix in ⅓ cup toasted walnuts or almonds.

Carbohistory

If chocolate is good for you, one bite of this and you'll live forever. This one's adapted from *Dr. Atkins' New Diet Revolution.*

Chocolate Macadamia Nut Clusters

Prep time: 5 minutes • Cook time: 10 minutes per batch • Makes: 24

Each serving has: 122 calories • 1 g protein • 0 g animal protein • 1 g vegetable protein • 7 g carbohydrates • 1 g dietary fiber • 6 g net carbohydrates • 10 g fat • 4 g saturated fat • 32 mg cholesterol • 30 mg sodium • Exchanges: ½ fruit, 2 fat

2 cups heavy cream	2 egg yolks, lightly beaten
1 (8-oz.) box bittersweet chocolate	½ tsp. pure vanilla extract
⅓ cup Splenda	1 cup roasted and salted macadamia nuts

Heat cream to a simmer over medium-low heat and stir in chocolate until melted and creamy. While cream is heating, mix sweetener into egg yolks, then line a baking tray with wax paper.

When chocolate is completely melted, turn off heat and slowly stir in yolks and vanilla until thoroughly blended. Stir in nuts. Scoop tablespoonfuls of chocolate-nut mixture onto the wax paper using a rubber spatula, taking care to be sure they do not touch each other. Chill clusters until firm, about 20 minutes, and cut into 1-inch squares.

Blueberry Chocolate Pudding

Prep time: 10 minutes, including cooling time • Serves: 4

Each serving has: 115 calories • 5 g protein • 5 g animal protein • 1 g vegetable protein • 16 g carbohydrates • 2 g dietary fiber • 14 g net carbohydrates • 4 g fat • 3 g saturated fat • 9 mg cholesterol • 180 mg sodium • Exchanges: 1 starch, 1 fat

1 (1.4-oz) pkg. sugar-free instant chocolate pudding	¼ cup sour cream
	½ cup fresh or frozen blueberries
Skim milk (as much as package instructions call for)	¼ tsp. vanilla extract

Prepare pudding with milk according to package instructions. Quickly stir in sour cream, blueberries, and vanilla. Distribute to small serving bowls and refrigerate for 5 minutes or until set.

Variations: Substitute small pieces of other fruits for blueberries (keep in mind that some fruits have a higher carb count). Sliced almonds and chopped walnuts are also tasty in place of fruits.

Chocolate-Chip Cookies

Prep time: 10 minutes • Cook time: 10 minutes per batch • Makes: about 24 cookies

Each serving has: 104 calories • 2 g protein • 1 g animal protein • 2 g vegetable protein • 10 g carbohydrates • 1 g dietary fiber • 9 g net carbohydrates • 7 g fat • 4 g saturated fat • 31 mg cholesterol • 67 mg sodium • Exchanges: ½ starch, ¼ fruit, 1½ fat

⅔ cup Smart Balance–type spread (suitable for baking), softened

2 large eggs

1 tsp. pure vanilla extract

1½ cups Splenda

2 cups low-carb baking mix

½ tsp. baking powder

½ tsp. salt

1 cup bittersweet chocolate chips

Preheat the oven to 375°F. In a mixing bowl, mix spread, eggs, vanilla, and sweetener. In a separate bowl, thoroughly mix baking mix, baking powder, and salt. Beat dry ingredients into egg/spread mixture. Stir in chocolate chips.

Using rounded tablespoonfuls, spoon dough onto an ungreased baking tray. Flatten each lump of cookie dough into cookie shape (this is necessary, as cookies will not naturally flatten like those loaded with sugar) and cook for 10 minutes. The more the cookies cook, the more crispy they get.

Variation: Substitute whole-wheat flour for the low-carb baking mix (this will raise the good-carb count).

Carb Smarts

For the minimum carb count in your cookies, use a low-carb baking mix. These baking mixes are increasingly available in grocery stores and can be found next to the flour or with the low-carb products. Whole-wheat cookies are higher in good carbs than the cookies made with the low-carb baking mix, but the whole-wheat versions are still a healthier bet than traditional white-flour cookies.

Chocolate-Chip Meringue Bites

Prep time: 10 minutes   •   Cook time: 1 hour unattended   •   Makes: 16 cookies

Each serving has: 18 calories   •   1 g protein   •   1 g animal protein   •   0 g vegetable protein   •   1 g carbohydrates   •   0 g dietary fiber   •   1 g net carbohydrates   •   0 g fat   •   0 g saturated fat   •   0 mg cholesterol   •   12 mg sodium   •   Exchanges: ⅛ very-lean meat, ⅛ fruit

2 egg whites, at room temperature

⅔ cup Splenda

Pinch salt

1 tsp. vanilla

1 cup *bittersweet chocolate chips*

Gourmand's Glossary

Bittersweet chocolate chips have a minimum amount of sugar and are found in grocery stores and specialty baking catalogs such as King Arthur. Unsweetened chips can be substituted, but are harder to find.

Preheat the oven to 375°F.

Beat egg whites until stiff. Beat in sweetener, salt, and vanilla. Then stir in chocolate chips.

Using a teaspoon, scoop spoonfuls onto a greased baking tray. Slide tray in the oven, close the door, and turn off the heat. Come back in an hour (or even the next morning) and these tasty morsels will be done.

Variation: Add ½ cup chopped walnuts along with chocolate chips.

Almond Oatmeal Cookies

Prep time: 10 minutes • Cook time: 10 minutes per batch • Makes : about 24 cookies

Each serving has: 95 calories • 2 g protein • 1 g animal protein • 1 g vegetable protein • 8 g carbohydrates • 1 g dietary fiber • 7 g net carbohydrates • 7 g fat • 3 g saturated fat • 31 mg cholesterol • 82 mg sodium • Exchanges: ½ starch, 1½ fat

⅔ cup (about 4 oz.) Smart Balance–type spread (suitable for baking), softened

2 large eggs

½ tsp. pure almond extract

1 cup Splenda

1 cup old-fashioned oatmeal (not instant)

1 cup low-carb baking mix

½ cup unprocessed bran

1 tsp. ground cinnamon

½ tsp. baking soda

½ tsp. salt

½ cup slivered almonds

Preheat the oven to 375°F. In a mixing bowl, mix spread, eggs, almond extract, and sweetener. In a separate bowl, thoroughly mix oatmeal, baking mix, bran, cinnamon, baking soda, and salt. Beat dry ingredients into egg-spread mixture. Add almonds and mix again.

Using a tablespoon, spoon dough onto an ungreased baking tray. Cook for 9 minutes or until cookies are just done (don't let them overcook).

Variation: Use whole-wheat flour in place of the baking mix, which will increase the good-carb count.

Carb Smarts

If you're using more than one baking tray in the oven at a time, rotate the trays halfway through the cooking time for even cooking.

When using butterlike spreads such as Smart Balance for baking, be sure to read the label. Some are appropriate for use in baking; others are not.

"Honeyed" Almonds

Prep time: 5 minutes • Cook time: 15 minutes • Serves: 8

Each serving has: 172 calories • 7 g protein • ½ g animal protein • 6½ g vegetable protein • 5 g carbohydrates • 3 g dietary fiber • 2 g net carbohydrates • 15 g fat • 1 g saturated fat • 0 mg cholesterol • 96 mg sodium • Exchanges: 1 high-fat meat, 2 fat

½ lb. roasted, lightly salted almonds

1 egg white

½ cup Splenda

1 TB. grated lemon zest

½ tsp. apple pie spice or ground cinnamon

Carb Smarts

I find that salted nuts work well for "honeyed" nuts. It might be counterintuitive to include salt in a sweet recipe, but that savory backbone seems to balance the dessert and make it even more irresistible.

Preheat the broiler. In a mixing bowl, toss nuts with egg white, then add sweetener, lemon zest, and spice. Spread nuts on a baking sheet and broil for 6 minutes, stirring a couple times, or until nuts are beginning to tan (watch carefully to prevent burning). Remove from the broiler, cool, and serve.

Variation: Use other nuts. Pecans, peanuts, and walnuts—or a mixture—work well.

Almond Chocolate Parfaits

Prep time: 10 minutes, including cooling time   •   Serves: 4

Each serving has: 165 calories   •   11½ g protein   •   10 g animal protein   •   1½ g vegetable protein   •   22 g carbohydrates   •   1½ g dietary fiber   •   21 g net carbohydrates   •   4½ g fat   •   3 g saturated fat   •   16 mg cholesterol   •   267 mg sodium   •   Exchanges: 1½ starch, ½ fat

1 (1.4-oz.) pkg. sugar-free instant chocolate pudding	1 cup light sour cream
Skim milk (as much as package instructions call for)	2 TB. Splenda
	½ tsp. pure almond extract

Prepare pudding with milk according to package instructions. In a separate bowl, mix sour cream, sweetener, and almond extract. Spoon chocolate pudding into 4 tall, slender glasses in a 1-inch layer, then add ½ inch sour cream, and repeat with pudding until glasses are filled equally. Refrigerate for 5 minutes or until set.

Minted Almond Yogurt

Prep time: 5 minutes   •   Serves: 4

Each serving has: 96 calories   •   7 g protein   •   7 g animal protein   •   1 g vegetable protein   •   10 g carbohydrates   •   0 g dietary fiber   •   10 g net carbohydrates   •   4 g fat   •   1 g saturated fat   •   7 mg cholesterol   •   86 mg sodium   •   Exchanges: 1 skim milk, 1 fat

2 cups low-fat plain yogurt	½ tsp. pure almond extract
¼ cup Splenda	2 TB. slivered or sliced almonds
1 TB. minced fresh mint leaves	Mint sprigs as garnish (optional)
1 TB. lemon juice	

Mix yogurt, sweetener, mint, lemon juice, and almond extract in a bowl. If possible, mix yogurt ahead of time and chill to allow the mint flavor to spread. Distribute among serving bowls, sprinkling each bowl with slivered almonds and garnishing with a sprig of mint.

Lemon-Cranberry Fruit Dip

Prep time: 5 minutes   •   Serves: 4

Each serving has: 90 calories   •   4 g protein   •   3 g animal protein   •   0 g vegetable protein   •   18 g carbohydrates   •   2 g dietary fiber   •   16 g net carbohydrates   •   1 g fat   •   1 g saturated fat   •   4 mg cholesterol   •   43 mg sodium   •   Exchanges: 1 fruit, ¼ skim milk

1 cup plain low-fat yogurt	¼ tsp. ground cinnamon
¼ cup unsweetened cranberries, minced	Pinch ground cloves
2 TB. Splenda	3 apples or 3 crisp pears, sliced
1 TB. lemon zest	

Mix yogurt, cranberries, sweetener, lemon zest, cinnamon, and cloves in a serving bowl. If possible, mix yogurt ahead of time and chill to allow the flavors to spread. Serve yogurt dip surrounded by apple and pear slices.

The Least You Need to Know

◆ Yes, chocolate does have a place in the carb-conscious diet. Bypass the heavily sugared chocolates and use the pure ingredient for a variety of delicious chocolate desserts.

◆ Decadent desserts can be quickly prepared "out of the box," enabling a low-carb dessert in minutes.

◆ Creamy textures are an important part of the appeal of many desserts. Pick low-carb, relatively healthful sources for this texture, such as yogurt, light sour cream, and light cream cheese, and you're off to a fast dessert start.

◆ Baked desserts, such as low-carb cookies, are possible even in a short time.

17

Fruit for Dessert

In This Chapter

- ◆ Fruit treats
- ◆ Dream cream themes
- ◆ Quick-cooked fruit treats
- ◆ Low-carb pie crust? Yes, it's possible

Fruit and fruit desserts deserve special attention for the carb-conscious cook. On one hand, many fruits are natural sources of carbohydrates. On the other, fruits bring a number of benefits. For satisfying the sweet tooth, fructose (the predominant sugar in fruits) is a lower-glycemic sugar than regular table sugar. Fruits bring terrific flavor to the table with little effort and can be not only a healthy but also a convenient ingredient for many delicious dishes. Some fruits are also low in carbohydrates relative to others, so in this chapter we focus on those. (See Chapter 5 for a breakdown of the carbs in fruit.)

Carbohistory _____

I've found that my dessert tastes have changed as I've learned more about fruits. I have less of a sweet tooth *for sugar,* but I look forward to a dessert of dried apricots or a bowl of blueberries and cream. Knowing that what you eat is not only good but also *good for you* makes it all the more appealing. In my book, you can't get much better than that!

Fresh Fruit

Fruits were probably one of the first fast desserts. Naturally sweet and needing little or no preparation, fruit is a natural starting point for a good-carb recipe.

Fruit and Cream

Fruits are delicious by themselves, but add cream and you've got something irresistible. From sour cream to whipped cream, I give you several variations on the fruit-and-cream theme in this chapter.

With cream-based fruit desserts, carb-conscious gourmands have the option of sour cream, plain yogurt, and whipped cream. All are low carb and provide the creamy texture we love in a dessert. Where possible, however, I encourage you to try light sour cream: It is both low carb and relatively low in saturated fat. Whipped cream, although extremely low carb, is very high in saturated fat. Plain, low-fat yogurt brings a few more carbs.

Carb Alert _____

It's tempting to use cans of point-and-shoot whipped cream or tubs of whipped topping, but use these in moderation. This version of whipped cream has plenty of sugar. Note that to achieve the low, nominal amount of carbs in a serving, the serving size is 2 tablespoons. How many people do you know who use only 2 tablespoons? Whipped topping brings similar amounts of carbs in that 2 tablespoon serving, as well as hydrogenated oils.

I Found My Thrills ...

Because blueberries have always been one of my favorite fruits, I was quite happy to find out that these flavorful little treats are also relatively low carb and loaded with other nutritional benefits. Even if you don't want all-blueberry, all the time, you can substitute another fruit for the little blue one.

Cheesecake

While discussing this book with friends, several talked about how much they loved cheesecake. "Wouldn't it be nice," I heard, "if there was a low-carb cheesecake?" I aim to please!

Carb Smarts

There are as many kinds of fruit cheesecakes as there are days in the year (probably more). For the carb-conscious cook in a hurry, we'll stick to two types of fruity-cheesy delights. The first takes only a few minutes to set up but does require hang time in the fridge. The result is a rich, very cheesy dessert. The second cheats a little with instant pudding, resulting in a tasty result that can be served in 10 minutes flat.

Hot Fruit Fast

Cooked fruit desserts evoke the dinner table of yesteryear, from apple crisp to blueberry pies. The focus of these dreamy desserts is fruit, and we preserve that focus, while avoiding some of the more carb-laden ingredients on the outside. I wrap up this chapter with some low-carb, but still delicious, cooked fruit desserts.

Orchard Fruit Bowl

Prep time: 15 minutes • Serves: 8

Each serving has: 80 calories • 1 g protein • 0 g animal protein • 1 g vegetable protein • 20 g carbohydrates • 3 g dietary fiber • 17 g net carbohydrates • 0 g fat • 0 g saturated fat • 0 mg cholesterol • 1 mg sodium • Exchanges: 1⅓ fruit

3 cups (about 10 oz.) green grapes, rinsed and halved

2 crisp apples, rinsed, cored, and chopped into ¼-inch pieces

2 cups (about 8 oz.) fresh blueberries, rinsed

3 TB. lemon juice

Gourmand's Glossary

Amaretto is a popular almond liqueur. A drizzle on fresh fruit works flavor-enhancing magic. Don't use more than that (you don't need it for flavor, and you'll be adding unnecessary carbs).

Mix grapes, apples, and blueberries in a large bowl. Drizzle with lemon juice, toss to coat, and distribute to serving bowls.

Variations: You can, of course, peel your apples before using them. I like the texture of the peels, though, and the nutrition that comes with them. The time you save is an added bonus.

All kinds of fruit, such as raspberries, strawberries, and peaches, will work well in this dish. A splash of *amaretto* on fresh fruit does amazing things with all those fresh flavors. Give it a try, and you'll have a new dessert secret.

Tropical Fruit Bowl

Prep time: 15 minutes • Serves: 8

Each serving has: 50 calories • 1 g protein • 0 g animal protein • 1 g vegetable protein • 12½ g carbohydrates • 2½ g dietary fiber • 10 g net carbohydrates • 0 g fat • 0 g saturated fat • 0 mg cholesterol • 1 mg sodium • Exchanges: ¼ fruit

3 kiwi fruit, peeled and sliced into ¼-inch rounds

1 grapefruit, sectioned, sections cut in half, juice reserved

1 seedless orange, peeled and sectioned, sections cut in half

¼ medium (1½ cups) ripe cantaloupe, carved into balls with a melon-baller

Juice of ½ lemon

Mix kiwi, grapefruit, orange, and cantaloupe in a large bowl, drizzle with lemon juice and reserved grapefruit juice, and serve.

 Carb Alert _____

Just remember that fruits, especially tropical ones, are natural sources of carbohydrates. These are good carbs, but pay close attention to portion sizes. Some fruits, such as bananas and mangos, are such high-carb sources that they should be enjoyed in small amounts in the context of a carb-conscious diet.

Strawberries and Sour-Sweet Cream Dip

Prep time: 5 minutes • Serves: 4

Each serving has: 138 calories • 3 g protein • 2 g animal protein • 1 g vegetable protein • 16 g carbohydrates • 4 g dietary fiber • 12 g net carbohydrates • 7½ g fat • 4½ g saturated fat • 23 mg cholesterol • 27 mg sodium • Exchanges: 1 fruit, 1½ fat

1 qt. fresh strawberries, rinsed, caps removed	½ tsp. pure vanilla extract
1 cup sour cream or light sour cream	¼ cup Splenda

Place strawberries in a large serving bowl. In a smaller serving bowl, mix sour cream, vanilla, and sweetener. Dip strawberries in cream and enjoy.

Variations: Distribute strawberries and cream to individual serving plates and use a dipping bowl. Other large berries, such as blackberries, are delicious with this cream.

Carb Smarts

With fruit-based desserts, you'll get the best flavor from fresh, in-season produce. And whether it's time for strawberries, peaches, blueberries, apples, or something else, they'll always taste better when they're local. Check out your local farmers' market for fresh goods.

Grapes and Cream

Prep time: 5 minutes • Serves: 4

Each serving has: 80 calories • 1½ g protein • 0 g animal protein • 1½ g vegetable protein • 12 g carbohydrates • 1 g dietary fiber • 11 g net carbohydrates • 4 g fat • 2 g saturated fat • 12 mg cholesterol • 20 mg sodium • Exchanges: 1 fruit, 1 fat

½ lb. seedless grapes, rinsed and halved	⅛ cup Splenda
½ cup low-fat sour cream	

Mix grapes, sour cream, and sweetener, and distribute to serving bowls. Done.

Peach Yogurt Parfait

Prep time: 5 minutes • Serves: 4

Each serving has: 62 calories • 4 g protein • 3 g animal protein • 1 g vegetable protein • 11 g carbohydrates • 1 g dietary fiber • 10 g net carbohydrates • 0 g fat • 0 g saturated fat • 1 mg cholesterol • 48 mg sodium • Exchanges: ½ fruit, ¼ skim milk

1 cup low-fat plain yogurt	3 medium (4-oz.) ripe peaches, peeled, pitted, and chopped into ¼-inch pieces
3 TB. Splenda	

Mix yogurt and sweetener in a bowl. In 4 tall glasses, layer 1 inch chopped peaches, about ½ inch yogurt, and repeat to fill each glass equally.

Carb Smarts

Some grocery stores carry Greek-style yogurt, which even in its low-fat and nonfat forms offers a rich, creamy base for desserts and, at least in the versions I sampled, has lower carbs than other plain yogurts. If you find it, try it in place of regular low-fat plain yogurt.

Apricots and Almond Cream

Prep time: 3 minutes • Serves: 4

Each serving has: 89 calories • 3 g protein • 2 g animal protein • 1 g vegetable protein • 11 g carbohydrates • 1 g dietary fiber • 10 g net carbohydrates • 4 g fat • 2 g saturated fat • 10 mg cholesterol • 58 mg sodium • Exchanges: 1 fruit, 1 fat

¼ cup plus 1 TB. (about 3 oz.) light cream cheese, softened	¼ tsp. pure almond extract
	20 dried apricots (160 g, about 5 oz.)
Pinch ground cinnamon	1 TB. sliced almonds

Mix cream cheese, cinnamon, and almond extract in a small bowl. Scoop about ⅔ teaspoon cream cheese on top of each dried apricot, distribute 5 apricots to each of 4 serving plates, and top each apricot with a slivered almond.

Variation: Mix 1 or 2 tablespoons sweetener with cream cheese. As a fruity alternative in place of almond extract, crush a handful of ripe raspberries into cream cheese before topping apricots.

Blueberries and Cream

Prep time: 5 minutes • Serves: 4

Each serving has: 121 calories • 2 g protein • 1½ g animal protein • ½ g vegetable protein • 12 g carbohydrates • 2 g dietary fiber • 10 g net carbohydrates • 7½ g fat • 4½ g saturated fat • 23½ mg cholesterol • 26 mg sodium • Exchanges: 1 fruit, 1½ fat

1 cup light sour cream	3 TB. spoon-for-spoon sweetener
1 tsp. pure vanilla extract	2 cups (1 pt.) fresh blueberries, rinsed

Mix sour cream, vanilla, and sweetener in a bowl. Gently stir in berries, taking care not to break them too much. Distribute to serving bowls and enjoy on your patio as you look out over Blueberry Hill.

Variation: Frozen blueberries, thawed, will work in place of fresh blueberries. And raspberries will work. And blackberries. And strawberries, too.

Emergency Raspberry Cheesecake Mousse

Prep time: 10 minutes including cooling time • Serves: 6

Each serving has: 120 calories • 7 g protein • 7 g animal protein • < 1 g vegetable protein • 15 g carbohydrates • 2 g dietary fiber • 13 g net carbohydrates • 3 g fat • 2 g saturated fat • 13 mg cholesterol • 202 mg sodium • Exchanges: 1 medium-fat meat, ½ skim milk, ½ fruit

1½ cups skim milk	1 cup (8 oz.) part-skim ricotta cheese
1 (1.4-oz.) pkg. sugar-free, fat-free instant vanilla pudding mix	1 cup fresh raspberries (or your favorite good-carb fruit)

In a large bowl, mix milk and pudding mix. Thoroughly whisk in ricotta. Distribute cheese mixture among ramekins or small bowls, and chill for 5 minutes. Top with raspberries and serve, each in their individual serving bowls.

Variations: Chill this cheesecake in an Almond Pie Crust (recipe earlier in this chapter) for a delicious, pie-style cheesecake.

No-Bake Blueberry Ricotta Pie

Prep time: 15 minutes, plus chilling time • Serves: 8

Each serving has: 170 calories • 7 g protein • 7 g animal protein • < 1 g vegetable protein • 6 g carbohydrates • ½ g dietary fiber • 5½ g net carbohydrates • 13½ g fat • 8 g saturated fat • 50 mg cholesterol • 77 mg sodium • Exchanges: 1 medium-fat meat, ¼ fruit, 1½ fat

1 cup whipping cream	1 TB. lemon juice
1 (15-oz.) tub part-skim ricotta cheese	1 cup frozen blueberries
½ cup Splenda	Almond Pie Crust (recipe follows)
1 tsp. pure vanilla extract	½ cup sliced almonds

Whip cream. In a food processor or mixer, thoroughly blend ricotta, sweetener, vanilla, and lemon juice until smooth and creamy. Pour this mixture into a large bowl and carefully fold in whipped cream and blueberries. Scrape this mixture into piecrust, sprinkle sliced almonds on top, and chill, if possible, a couple hours or overnight. Serve in wedges.

Variation: Chill individual servings without the crust in small serving bowls.

Carb Smarts

Frozen blueberries help accelerate the chilling process in No-Bake Blueberry Ricotta Pie. Just be sure they are frozen separately, so you're not trying to mix in a block of frozen berries!

Almond Pie Crust

Prep time: 8 minutes • Cook time: 12 • Serves: 8 as part of a pie

Each serving has: 133 calories • 5 g protein • 1 g animal protein • 4 g vegetable protein • 3½ g carbohydrates • 2 g dietary fiber • 1½ g net carbohydrates • 9 g fat • 2 g saturated fat • 26 mg cholesterol • 169 mg sodium • Exchanges: ½ high-fat meat, 1 fat

1½ cups chopped unsalted almonds	½ tsp. salt
2 TB. Splenda	4 TB. (¼ cup) Smart Balance–type spread or butter
½ tsp. ground cinnamon	1 egg

Preheat the oven to 375°F. In a food processor fitted with a steel blade, process almonds, sweetener, cinnamon, and salt to a coarse powder. Melt spread in the microwave. Mix melted spread into almonds. Whisk egg in a cup and mix this into almond mixture. Coat a pie plate with cooking spray and spread almond crust mixture across the bottom and the sides, spreading to approximately even thickness throughout. Bake for 10 to 12 minutes or until pie crust is crisp.

Carb Smarts

Make two of these crusts at a time. Keep one, in its pie plate, in the freezer, ready to accelerate your next low-carb dessert masterpiece.

Use this crust for No-Bake Blueberry Ricotta Pie or any other pie, for a real low-carb taste treat.

Variation: If you can find almond flour at your grocery store, use that (1½ cups) in place of the almonds (this will save processing time).

Strawberry Cheesecake Cupcakes

Prep time: 5 minutes plus cooling time   •   Serves: 6

Each serving has: 168 calories   •   9 g protein   •   9 g animal protein   •   < 1 g vegetable protein   •   10 g carbohydrates   •   1 g dietary fiber   •   9 g net carbohydrates   •   10 g fat   •   6 g saturated fat   •   35 mg cholesterol   •   170 mg sodium   •   Exchanges: ½ high-fat meat, 1 medium-fat meat, ½ fruit

6 muffin cup liners	1 tsp. pure vanilla extract
1 (8-oz.) pkg. light cream cheese, at room temperature	¼ cup spoon-for-spoon sweetener
1 cup (8 oz.) part-skim ricotta cheese	½ qt. (2 cups) fresh strawberries, rinsed, caps removed, and cut into ¼-inch slices

Line 6 muffin cups. In a large bowl, mix cream cheese, ricotta, vanilla, and sweetener. Distribute cheese mixture among muffin cups, and chill, if possible, overnight (to ensure cheesecakes are firm).

When ready to serve, carefully remove the muffin liners and place cheesecake "muffins" on serving plates. Top with a big spoonful of sliced strawberries and serve.

Variations: Chill this cheesecake in an Almond Pie Crust (recipe earlier in this chapter) for a delicious, pie-style cheesecake. If you have small serving-size bowls, chill your cheesecake in those and serve topped with strawberries.

Mixed Fruit Betty

Prep time: 5 minutes • Cook time: 15 minutes • Serves: 8

Each serving has: 95 calories • 1 g protein • 0 g animal protein • 1 g vegetable protein • 10 g carbohydrates • 4 g dietary fiber • 6 g net carbohydrates • 12 g fat • 7½ g saturated fat • 30 mg cholesterol • 42 mg sodium • Exchanges: ½ fruit, ¼ starch, 3 fat

1 (1-lb.) pkg. frozen mixed berries, about 1 cup each blueberries, blackberries, and raspberries

3 TB. lemon juice

1 cup plus ¼ cup Splenda

4 TB. butter or Smart Balance–type spread, room temperature, sliced into tablespoon-size chunks

¼ cup old-fashioned oatmeal (not instant)

¼ cup unprocessed bran

½ tsp. apple pie spice, or ½ tsp. ground cinnamon

Preheat the broiler. Place berries in a large bowl and toss with lemon juice and then 1 cup sweetener. Pour mixture into a microwave- and oven-safe pie plate or 8×8 baking dish. Place pie plate in microwave and thaw berries for 5 minutes, stirring occasionally, then cook on high for 4 minutes or until fruit is beginning to bubble. Remove from microwave and stir fruit.

Gourmand's Glossary

A **Betty** is a dessert dish of sweet baked fruit topped with a crisp topping, usually breadcrumbs, but in this low-carb version we take some healthful liberty.

Meanwhile, in a separate bowl mix butter, remaining ¼ cup sweetener, oatmeal, bran, and apple pie spice to a crumbly texture by pinching together with your fingers. When fruit is done in the microwave, sprinkle oatmeal mixture over the top of fruit in an even layer. Broil on the next-to-highest rack for 5 minutes or until top begins to crisp.

Variation: This dish can also be cooked completely in a preheated 375°F oven for 30 to 40 minutes.

(How 'Bout Them) Warm Apples

Prep time: 5 minutes • Cook time: 10 minutes • Serves: 4

Each serving has: 175 calories • 1½ g protein • 0 g animal protein • 1½ g vegetable protein • 19 g carbohydrates • 3 g dietary fiber • 16 g net carbohydrates • 12 g fat • 7½ g saturated fat • 30 mg cholesterol • 324 mg sodium • Exchanges: 1 fruit, 3 fat

4 TB. butter or Smart Balance–type spread

8 dried apricots, chopped into ¼-inch pieces (about ¼ cup)

½ tsp. apple pie spice, or ½ tsp. ground cinnamon

2 crisp apples, such as Granny Smith, peeled, cored, and thinly sliced

2 TB. heavy cream (optional)

Additional cinnamon as garnish

Melt butter in a large skillet over medium-low heat. Cook apricots and apple pie spice for 3 minutes, stirring. Add apples and cook for another 5 minutes. Serve, drizzling each serving with cream (if using) and sprinkling each serving with a pinch of cinnamon.

Variations: If you've got a sweet tooth, sprinkle ¼ cup spoon-for-spoon sweetener over apples as you're stirring.

For added texture and flavor, top Warm Apples with oatmeal mixture used for the Mixed Fruit Betty (recipe earlier in this chapter) and broil for 5 minutes.

Carbohistory

Cooked fruits and spice evoke images of Grandma's kitchen and a Norman Rockwell world. These visions, swirling through the air on the scent of warm cinnamon, might just help bring you and the people you are serving to a frame of mind of security and family. That's not bad for a few minutes work!

Sherried Pears

Prep time: 5 minutes   •   Cook time: 10   •   Serves: 4

Each serving has: 143 calories   •   1 g protein   •   0 g animal protein   •   1 g vegetable protein   •   30 g carbohydrates   •   5 g dietary fiber   •   25 g net carbohydrates   •   0 g fat   •   0 g saturated fat   •   0 mg cholesterol   •   2 mg sodium   •   Exchanges: 2 fruit

1½ cups cooking sherry or red wine	1 tsp. lemon juice
½ cup water	4 pears, peeled, sliced in half lengthwise, and cored
½ cup Splenda	
1 tsp. apple pie spice, or 1 tsp. ground cinnamon	Confectioners' sugar as garnish

Heat sherry, water, sweetener, spice, and lemon juice in a saucepan over medium heat to a simmer. Turn the heat to medium-low, add pear halves, and cook for 10 minutes or until pears are tender. Turn off the heat and allow fruit to cool in its juices. Place two halves on each plate, spoon some sauce over, and garnish with a sprinkle of confectioners' sugar.

The Least You Need to Know

◆ Fresh fruits, a source of good-carb fruit sugar, offer delicious, ready-to-eat flavors with minimum prep time.

◆ Add cream (in its many forms) to fruit, and you've got an irresistible, quick dessert.

◆ Cooked fruit desserts are delicious and nostalgic—and possible in 20 minutes or less.

◆ Blueberries are a delicious, nutritious, and good-carb starting point for fruit desserts.

Glossary

accoutrement   An accoutrement is an accompaniment, trapping, or garnish.

al dente   Italian for "against the teeth." Refers to pasta (or other ingredient such as rice) that is neither soft nor hard, but just slightly firm against the teeth. This, according to many pasta aficionados, is the perfect way to cook pasta.

all-purpose flour   Flour that contains only the inner part of the wheat grain. Usable for all purposes from cakes to gravies.

allspice   Named for its flavor echoes of several spices (cinnamon, cloves, nutmeg), allspice is used in many desserts and in rich marinades and stews.

almonds   Mild, sweet, and crunchy nuts that combine nicely with creamy and sweet food items.

amaretto   A popular almond liqueur.

anchovies (also **sardines**)   Tiny, flavorful preserved fish that typically come in cans. The strong flavor from these salted fish is a critical element in many recipes. Anchovies are a traditional garnish for Caesar salad, the dressing of which contains anchovy paste.

artichoke hearts   The center part of the artichoke flower, often found canned in grocery stores and used as a stand-alone vegetable dish or as a flavorful base for appetizers or main courses.

arugula   A spicy-peppery garden plant with leaves that resemble a dandelion and have a distinctive—and very sharp—flavor.

au gratin   The quick broiling of a dish before serving to brown the top ingredients. The term is often used as part of a recipe name and implies cheese and a creamy sauce.

bake   To cook in a dry oven. Baking is one of the most popular methods of cooking and is used for everything from roasts, vegetables, and other main courses to desserts such as cakes and pies. Dry-heat cooking often results in a crisping of the exterior of the food being cooked. Moist-heat cooking, through methods such as steaming, poaching, etc., brings a much different, moist quality to the food.

balsamic vinegar   Vinegar produced primarily in Italy from a specific type of grape and aged in wood barrels. It is heavier, darker, and sweeter than most vinegars.

bamboo shoots   Crunchy, tasty white parts of the growing bamboo plant, often purchased canned.

barbecue   This is a loaded word, with different, zealous definitions in different parts of the country. In some cases it is synonymous with grilling (quick-cooking over high heat); in others, to barbecue is to cook something long and slow in a rich liquid (barbecue sauce).

basil   A flavorful, almost sweet, resinous herb delicious with tomatoes and used in all kinds of Italian or Mediterranean-style dishes.

beat   To quickly mix substances.

Belgian endive   A plant that resembles a small, elongated, tightly packed head of romaine lettuce. The thick, crunchy leaves can be broken off and used with dips and spreads.

bisque   A creamy, thick soup made with puréed vegetables, meats, and especially seafood.

blanch   To place a food in boiling water for about 1 minute (or less) to partially cook the exterior and then submerge in or rinse with cool water to halt the cooking. This is a common method for preparing some vegetables such as asparagus for serving and also for preparing foods for freezing.

blend   To completely mix something, usually with a blender or food processor, more slowly than beating.

boil   To heat a liquid to a point where water is forced to turn into steam, causing the liquid to bubble. To boil something is to insert it into boiling water. A rapid boil is when a lot of bubbles form on the surface of the liquid.

bok choy (also **Chinese cabbage**)   A member of the cabbage family with thick stems, crisp texture, and fresh flavor. It is perfect for stir-frying.

bouillon   Dried essence of stock from chicken, beef, vegetable, or other ingredients. This is a popular starting ingredient for soups as it adds flavor (and often a lot of salt).

bouquet   The aroma or fragrance of a wine.

braise   To cook with the introduction of some liquid, usually over an extended period of time.

bread flour   Wheat flour used for bread and other recipes.

brie   A creamy cow's milk cheese from France with a soft, edible rind and a mild flavor.

broil   To cook in a dry oven under the overhead high-heat element.

broth   *See* stock.

brown   To cook in a skillet, turning, until the surface is brown in color, to lock in the juices.

brown rice   Whole-grain rice with a characteristic brown color from the bran coating; more nutritious and flavorful than white rice.

bruschetta (or **crostini**)   Slices of toasted or grilled bread with garlic and olive oil, often with other toppings.

Cajun cooking   A style of cooking that combines French and Southern characteristics and includes many highly seasoned stews and meats.

canapés   Bite-size hors d'oeuvres made up of any number of ingredients but prepared individually and usually served on a small piece of bread or toast.

capers   Usually sold preserved in jars, capers are the flavorful buds of a Mediterranean plant. The most common size is *nonpareil* (about the size of a small pea); others are larger, including the grape-size caper berries produced in Spain.

caramelize   The term's original meaning is to cook sugar over low heat until it develops a sweet caramel flavor. However, the term is increasingly gaining use to describe cooking vegetables (especially onions) or meat in butter or oil over low heat until they soften, sweeten, and develop a caramel color. Caramelized onions are a popular addition to many recipes, especially as a pizza topping.

caraway   A distinctive spicy seed used for bread, pork, cheese, and cabbage dishes. It is known to reduce stomach upset, which is why it is often paired with, for example, sauerkraut.

cardamom   An intense, sweet-smelling spice, common to Indian cooking, used in baking and coffee.

casserole dishes   Primarily used in baking, these covered containers hold liquids and solids together and keep moisture around ingredients that might otherwise dry out.

cayenne   A fiery spice made from (hot) chili peppers, especially the cayenne chili, a slender, red, and very hot pepper.

cheddar   The ubiquitous hard cow's milk cheese with a rich, buttery flavor that ranges from mellow to sharp. Originally produced in England, cheddar is now produced worldwide.

cheese boards or **cheese trays**   A collection of three or four mixed-flavor cheeses arranged on a tray, platter, or even cutting board. One classic example would be at least one cheese made from cow's, sheep's, and goat's milk. Often restaurants will offer a selection of cheeses as a "cheese flight," or course.

chevre   Goat's milk cheese, a typically creamy-salty soft cheese delicious by itself or paired with fruits or chutney. Chevres vary in style from mild and creamy to aged, firm, and flavorful. *Artisanal* chevres are usually more expensive and sold in smaller quantities; these are often delicious by themselves. Other chevres produced in quantity are less expensive and often more appropriate for combining with fruit or herbs.

chickpeas (also **garbanzo beans**)   The base ingredient in hummus, chickpeas are high in fiber and low in fat, making this a delicious and healthful component of many appetizers and main dishes.

chili peppers (also **chile peppers**)   Any one of many different "hot" peppers, ranging in intensity from the relatively mild ancho pepper to the blisteringly hot habanero.

chili powder   A seasoning blend that includes chili pepper, cumin, garlic, and oregano. Proportions vary among different versions, but they all offer a warm, rich flavor.

chives   A member of the onion family, chives are sold as bunches of long leaves that resemble the green tops of onions. They provide an easy onion flavor to any dish. Chives are very easy to grow, and many people have them in their garden.

chop   To cut into pieces, usually qualified by an adverb, such as "*coarsely* chopped," or by a size measurement, such as "chopped into ½-inch pieces." "Finely chopped" is much closer to "minced."

choucroute garni   An Alsatian dish that comes in many forms, but commonly includes sauerkraut (*choucroute* is French for "sauerkraut"), caraway, white wine, potatoes, and cooked meats, such as sausage.

cider vinegar   Vinegar produced from apple cider, popular in North America.

cilantro   A member of the parsley family and used in Mexican cooking and some Asian dishes. Cilantro is what gives some salsas their unique flavor. Use in moderation, as the flavor can overwhelm.

cinnamon   A sweet, rich, aromatic spice commonly used in baking or desserts. Cinnamon can also be used for delicious and interesting entrées.

cloves   A sweet, strong, almost wintergreen-flavor spice used in baking and with meats such as ham.

coat   To cover all sides of a food with a liquid, sauce, or solid.

cookie sheet   A large, thin, flat tray used for baking cookies and other foods.

core   To remove the unappetizing middle membranes and seeds of fruits and vegetables.

coriander   A rich, warm spice used in all types of recipes, from African to South American, from entrées to desserts.

cottage cheese   A mild, creamy-texture cheese made from curds from fresh cow's milk cheese. Curds vary in size; containers will indicate, for example, "small curd" or "large curd." In its low-fat and nonfat forms, cottage cheese is a useful component of low-fat dips, spreads, and other recipes.

count   On packaging of seafood or other foods that come in small sizes, you'll often see a reference to the count, how many of that item compose 1 pound. For example, 31 to 40 count shrimp are large appetizer shrimp often served with cocktail sauce; 51 to 60 are much smaller.

couscous   Granular semolina (durum wheat) that is cooked and used in many Mediterranean and North African dishes.

cream   To blend an ingredient to get a soft, creamy liquid or substance.

crimini mushrooms   A relative of the white button mushroom but brown in color and with a richer flavor. *See also* portobello mushrooms.

croutons   Pieces of bread, usually between ¼ and ½ inch in size, that are sometimes seasoned and baked, broiled, or fried to a crisp texture.

crudités   Fresh vegetables served as an appetizer, often all together on one tray.

cuisine   A style of cooking, typically reflecting a country or region (such as "Spanish cuisine"), a blending of flavors and cuisines (called "fusion"), or an updated style (such as "New Latin").

cumin A fiery, smoky-tasting spice popular in Middle-Eastern and Indian dishes. Cumin is a seed; ground cumin seed is the most common form of the spice used in cooking.

curry A general term referring to rich, spicy, Indian-style sauces and the dishes prepared with them. Common ingredients include hot pepper, nutmeg, cumin, cinnamon, pepper, and turmeric.

dash A dash refers to a few drops, usually of a liquid, that is released by a quick shake of, for example, a bottle of hot sauce.

dice To cut into small cubes about ¼-inch square.

Dijon mustard Hearty, spicy mustard made in the style of the Dijon region of France.

dill A slightly sour, unique herb that is perfect for eggs, cheese dishes, and, of course, vegetables (pickles!).

dolce Italian for "sweet." Refers to desserts as well as styles of a food (*Gorgonzola dolce* is a style of Gorgonzola cheese).

dollop A spoonful of something creamy and thick, like sour cream or whipped cream.

double boiler A set of two pots designed to nest together, one inside the other, and provide consistent, moist heat for foods that need delicate treatment. The bottom pot holds water (not quite touching the bottom of the top pot); the top pot holds the ingredient you want to heat.

dough A soft, pliable mixture of liquid and flour that is the intermediate step, prior to cooking, for many bread or baked-goods recipes such as cookies or bread.

dredge To cover a piece of food with a dry substance such as flour or corn meal.

dressing A liquid mixture usually containing oil, vinegar, and herbs used for seasoning salads and other foods. Also, the solid dish commonly called "stuffing" used to stuff turkey and other foods.

drizzle To lightly sprinkle drops of a liquid over food. Drizzling is often the finishing touch to a dish.

dry In the context of wine, a wine that has been vinified to contain little or no residual sugar.

dust To sprinkle a dry substance, often a seasoning, over a food or dish.

entrée The main dish in a meal.

extra-virgin olive oil *See* olive oil.

fennel In seed form, a fragrant, licorice-tasting herb. The bulbs have a much milder flavor and a celerylike crunch and are used as a vegetable in salads or cooked recipes.

feta This white, crumbly, salty cheese is popular in Greek cooking, on salads, and on its own. Traditional feta is usually made with sheep's milk, but feta-style cheese can be made from sheep's, cow's, or goat's milk. Its sharp flavor is especially nice with bitter, cured black olives.

fiber Minimally processed foods, including whole grains, nuts, fruits, and vegetables, are sources of both complex carbohydrates and fiber (or "roughage"), a carb that is not digested. Because fiber is included in the total carbohydrate listing on nutrition labels, it is subtracted from the total carb count for the purpose of a low-carb diet. Fiber is considered important to general health and is specifically related to cholesterol reduction.

fillet A piece of meat or seafood with the bones removed.

fish basket A grill-top metal frame that holds a whole fish intact, making it easier to turn.

fish poacher A long, rectangular pan with a separate metal basket designed to hold a fish either above boiling water for steaming or in simmering liquid for poaching. Fish poachers come in varying sizes up to 24 inches, although an 18-inch version will cover all but the largest meals.

flake To break into thin sections, as with fish.

floret The flower or bud end of broccoli or cauliflower.

flour Grains ground into a meal. Wheat is perhaps the most common flour, an essential component in many breads. Flour is also made from oats, rye, buckwheat, soybeans, etc. Different types of flour serve different purposes. *See also* all-purpose flour; bread flour; whole-wheat flour.

foie gras A goose liver from specially grown geese, foie gras is considered quite a delicacy for many. Pâté de foie gras contains mostly goose liver with pork liver or other ingredients added.

fold To combine a dense and light mixture with a circular action from the middle of the bowl.

fritter A food such as apples or corn coated or mixed with batter and deep-fried for a crispy, crunchy exterior.

fry Pan-cooking over high heat with butter or oil.

fusion To blend two or more styles of cooking, such as Chinese and French.

garam masala   A famous Indian seasoning mix, rich with cinnamon, pepper, nutmeg, cardamom, and other spices.

garlic   A member of the onion family, a pungent and flavorful element in many savory dishes. A garlic bulb, the form in which garlic is often sold, contains multiple cloves. Each clove, when chopped, provides about 1 teaspoon garlic.

garnish   An embellishment not vital to the dish but added to enhance visual appeal.

ginger   Available in fresh root or ground form, ginger adds a pungent, sweet, and spicy quality to a dish. It is a very popular element of many Asian and Indian dishes, among others.

glycemic index   A way of describing how fast a given food raises blood sugar levels. The higher the number, the faster these levels spike after eating that food. Typically, refined flours and sugars (and foods made from them) have a high glycemic index. Whole grains and foods with complex carbohydrates that break down slowly have a low glycemic index.

glycemic load   The blood sugar spike one would experience after consuming a single serving of a particular food.

Gorgonzola   A creamy and rich Italian blue cheese. "Dolce" is sweet, and that's the kind you want.

goulash   A rich, Hungarian-style meat-and-vegetable stew seasoned with paprika, among other spices.

grate   To shave into tiny pieces using a sharp rasp or grater.

grill   To cook over high heat, usually over charcoal or gas.

grind   To reduce a large, hard substance, often a seasoning such as peppercorns, to the consistency of sand.

grits   Coarsely ground grains, usually corn.

Gruyère   A rich, sharp cow's milk cheese made in Switzerland. It has a nutty flavor.

gyoza (also **pot stickers**)   Small, usually 1½- to 2-inch-long, Chinese dumplings filled with chicken, seafood, or vegetables. They are traditionally served with soy sauce for dipping.

handful   An unscientific measurement term that refers to the amount of an ingredient you can hold in your hand.

Havarti   A creamy, Danish, mild cow's milk cheese perhaps most enjoyed in its herbed versions such as Havarti with dill.

hazelnuts (also **filberts**)   A sweet nut popular in desserts and, to a lesser degree, in savory dishes.

hearts of palm   Firm, elongated, off-white cylinders from the inside of a palm tree stem tip. They are delicious in many recipes.

herbes de Provence   A seasoning mix including basil, fennel, marjoram, rosemary, sage, and thyme.

herbs   The leaves of flavorful plants characterized by fresh, pungent aromas and flavors, such as parsley, sage, rosemary, and thyme.

hors d'oeuvre   French for "outside of work" (the "work" being the main meal). An hors d'oeuvre can be any dish served as a starter before the meal.

horseradish   A sharp, spicy root that forms the flavor base in many condiments from cocktail sauce to sharp mustards. It is a natural match with roast beef. The form generally found in grocery stores is prepared horseradish, which contains vinegar and oil, among other ingredients. If you come across pure horseradish, use it much more sparingly than the prepared version, or try cutting it with sour cream.

hummus   A thick, Middle Eastern spread made of puréed chickpeas (garbanzo beans), lemon juice, olive oil, garlic, and often tahini (sesame seed paste).

Italian seasoning (also **spaghetti sauce seasoning**)   The ubiquitous grocery store blend, which includes basil, oregano, rosemary, and thyme, is a useful seasoning for quick flavor that evokes the "old country" in sauces, meatballs, soups, and vegetable dishes.

jicama   A juicy, crunchy, sweet, Central American vegetable that is eaten both raw and cooked. It is available in many large grocery stores as well as from specialty vendors. If you can't find jicama, try substituting sliced water chestnuts.

julienne   To slice into very thin pieces.

kalamata olives   Traditionally from Greece, these medium-small long black olives have a smoky rich flavor, very different from run-of-the-mill canned black olives. Try them, and you'll be hooked.

kosher salt   A coarse-grained salt made without any additives or iodine, used by many cooks because it does not impart a chemical flavor.

marinate   To soak meat, seafood, or other food in a seasoned sauce, called a marinade, which is high in acid content. The acids break down the muscle of the meat, making it tender and adding flavor.

marjoram   A sweet herb, a cousin of and similar to oregano, popular in Greek, Spanish, and Italian dishes.

marmalade   A fruit-and-sugar preserve that contains whole pieces of fruit peel to achieve simultaneous sweetness (from the sugar) and tartness (from the fruit's natural acids). The most common marmalades are made with citrus fruits such as orange and lemon.

medallion   A small round cut, usually of meat or vegetables such as carrots or cucumbers.

meld   A combination of *melt* and *weld*, many cooks use this term to describe how flavors blend and spread over time throughout dips and spreads. Melding is often why recipes call for overnight refrigeration and is also why some dishes taste better as leftovers.

meringue   A baked mixture of sugar and beaten egg whites, often used as a dessert topping.

mesclun   Mixed salad greens, usually containing lettuce and assorted greens such as arugula, cress, endive, and others.

Mexican-style cheese blend   A grated combination of Monterey Jack, pepper Jack, and cheddar cheese used in Mexican and Southwestern cooking.

mince   To cut into very small pieces smaller than diced pieces, about ⅛ inch or smaller.

miso   A fermented, flavorful soybean paste. It is a key ingredient in many Japanese dishes.

mold   A decorative, shaped metal pan in which contents, such as mousse or gelatin, set up and take the shape of the pan.

mull (or **mulled**)   To heat a liquid with the addition of spices and sometimes sweeteners.

mushrooms   Any one of a huge variety of *edible* fungi (note emphasis on "edible"; there are also poisonous mushrooms). *See also* crimini mushrooms; porcini mushrooms; portobello mushrooms; shiitake mushrooms; white mushrooms.

nutmeg   A sweet, fragrant, musky spice used primarily in baking.

nuts   Shell-covered seeds (or fruits) whose meat is rich in flavor and nutrition. A critical component in many dishes, many nuts are tasty on their own as well. *See also* almonds; hazelnuts; pecans; walnuts.

olive oil   A fragrant liquid produced by crushing or pressing olives. Extra-virgin olive oil is the oil produced from the first pressing of a batch of olives; oil is also produced from other pressings after the first. Extra-virgin olive oil is generally considered the most flavorful and highest quality and is the type you want to use when your focus is on the oil itself. Be sure the bottle label reads "extra-virgin."

olives   The fruit of the olive tree commonly grown on all sides of the Mediterranean. There are many varieties of olives but two general types: green and black. Black olives are also called ripe olives. One popular flavorful variety of black olive, originally from Greece, is kalamata.

oregano   A fragrant, slightly astringent herb used in Greek, Spanish, and Italian dishes.

oxidation   The browning of fruit flesh that happens over time and with exposure to air. Although it's best to prepare fresh fruit dishes just before serving, sometimes that's not possible. If you need to cut apples in advance, minimize oxidation by rubbing the cut surfaces with a lemon half.

pan-broil   Quick-cooking over high heat in a skillet with a minimum of butter or oil. (Frying, on the other hand, uses more butter or oil.)

pancetta   Salted, seasoned bacon; an important element in many Italian-style dishes.

paprika   A rich, red, warm, earthy spice that also lends a rich red color to many dishes.

parboil   To partially cook in boiling water or broth. Parboiling is similar to blanching, although blanched foods are quickly cooled with cold water.

pare   To scrape away the skin of a food, usually a vegetable, as part of the preparation for serving or cooking.

Parmesan   A hard, dry, flavorful cheese primarily used grated or shredded as a seasoning for Italian-style dishes.

parsley   A fresh-tasting green leafy herb used to add color and interest to just about any savory dish. Often used as a garnish just before serving.

pâté   A savory loaf that contains meats, spices, and often a lot of fat, served cold, spread or sliced on crusty bread or crackers.

peanuts   The nutritious and high-fat seeds of the peanut plant (a relative of the pea) that are sold shelled or unshelled and in a variety of preparations, including peanut butter and peanut oil. Some people are allergic to peanuts, so care should be taken with their inclusion in recipes.

pecans   Rich, buttery nuts native to North America. Their flavor, a terrific addition to appetizers, is at least partially due to their high unsaturated fat content.

pepper   A biting and pungent seasoning, freshly ground black pepper is a must for many dishes and adds an extra level of flavor and taste.

peppercorns   Large, round, dried berries that are ground to produce pepper.

pesto   A thick spread or sauce made with fresh basil leaves, garlic, olive oil, pine nuts, and Parmesan cheese. Other new versions are made with other herbs. Rich and flavorful, pesto can be made at home or purchased in a grocery store and used on anything from appetizers to pasta and other main dishes.

pickle   A food, usually a vegetable, such as a cucumber, that has been pickled in brine.

pinch   An unscientific measurement term that refers to the amount of an ingredient—typically a dry, granular substance such as an herb or seasoning—you can hold between your finger and thumb.

pine nuts (also **pignoli** or **piñon**)   Nuts grown on pine trees, that are rich (read: high-fat), flavorful, and, yes, a bit pine-y. Pine nuts are a traditional component of pesto, and they add a wonderful hearty crunch to many other recipes.

pinzimonio   An Italian vegetable dish in which combinations of sliced vegetables are served with olive oil, vinegar, salt, and pepper.

pita bread   A flat, hollow wheat bread that can be used for sandwiches or sliced, pizza-style, into slices. Pita bread is terrific soft with dips or baked or broiled as a vehicle for other ingredients.

pizza stone   Preheated with the oven, a pizza stone cooks a crust to a delicious, crispy, pizza-parlor texture. It also holds heat well, so a pizza removed from the oven on the stone will stay hot for as long as a half-hour at the table. Can also be used for other baking needs, including bread.

poach   To cook a food in simmering liquid, such as water, wine, or broth.

porcini mushrooms   Rich and flavorful mushrooms used in rice and Italian-style dishes.

portobello mushrooms   A mature and larger form of the smaller crimini mushroom, portobellos are brownish, chewy, and flavorful. They are trendy served as whole caps, grilled, and as thin sautéed slices. *See also* crimini mushrooms.

pot stickers   *See* gyoza.

preheat   To turn on an oven, broiler, or other cooking appliance in advance of cooking so the temperature will be at the desired level when the assembled dish is ready for cooking.

presentation   The appealing arrangement of a dish or food on the plate.

prosciutto   Dry, salt-cured ham, rich and evocative of Italy. Prosciutto is popular in many simple dishes in which its unique flavor is allowed to shine.

purée   To reduce a food to a thick, creamy texture, usually using a blender or food processor.

quesadilla   At its most basic, two tortillas with something in between, sort of like a grilled cheese sandwich. The "in between" is what makes all the difference. Cheese is a natural (in this country, start with Monterey Jack or cheddar; Swiss might not be what you would use first in Mexico, but it's still delicious), meats, vegetables, and of course, Southwestern-style seasonings.

red pepper flakes   Hot yet rich, crushed red pepper, used in moderation, brings flavor and interest to many savory dishes.

reduce   To heat a broth or sauce to remove some of the water content, resulting in more concentrated flavor and color.

refried beans (also **refritos**)   Twice-cooked beans—most often pinto beans—softened into a thick paste and often seasoned with peppers and spices. Most refried beans include lard, but many fat-free, lard-free versions are available.

render   To cook a meat to the point where its fat melts and can be removed.

reserve   To hold a specified ingredient for another use later in the recipe.

rice vinegar   Vinegar produced from fermented rice or rice wine, popular in Asian-style dishes.

risotto   A popular Italian rice dish made by browning arborio rice in butter or oil, then slowly adding liquid to cook the rice, resulting in a creamy texture.

roast   To cook something uncovered in an oven.

Roquefort   A world-famous (French) creamy but sharp sheep's milk cheese containing blue lines of mold, making it a "blue cheese."

rosemary   A pungent, sweet herb used with chicken, pork, fish, and especially lamb. A little of it goes a long way.

roux   A mixture of butter or another fat and flour used to thicken liquids such as sauces.

saffron   A famous spice made from the stamens of crocus flowers. Saffron lends a dramatic yellow color and distinctive flavor to a dish. Only a tiny amount needs to be used, which is good because saffron is very expensive.

sage   An herb with a musty yet fruity, lemon-rind scent and "sunny" flavor. It is a terrific addition to many dishes.

salsa A style of mixing fresh vegetables and/or fresh fruit in a coarse chop. Salsa can be spicy or not, fruit-based or not, and served as a starter on its own (with chips, for example) or as a companion to a main course.

satay (also **sate**) A popular Southeast Asian dish of broiled skewers of fish or meat, often served with peanut sauce.

sauté To pan-cook over lower heat than used for frying.

savory A popular herb with a fresh, woody taste.

scant A measurement modification that specifies "include no extra," as in 1 scant teaspoon.

Scoville scale A scale used to measure the "hot" in hot peppers. The lower the Scoville units, the more mild the pepper. Ancho peppers, which are mildly hot, are about 3,000 Scovilles; Thai hot peppers are about 6,000; and some of the more daring peppers such as Tears of Fire and habanero are 30,000 Scovilles or more.

scrapple A sausagelike mixture of seasoned pork and cornmeal that is formed into loaves and sliced for cooking.

sear To quickly brown the exterior of a food over high heat to preserve interior moisture (that's why many meat recipes involve searing).

sesame oil An oil, made from pressing sesame seeds, that is tasteless if clear and aromatic and flavorful if brown.

shallot A member of the onion family that grows in a bulb somewhat like garlic and has a milder onion flavor. When a recipe calls for shallot, you use the entire bulb. (They might or might not have cloves.)

shellfish A broad range of seafood, including clams, mussels, oysters, crabs, shrimp, and lobster. Some people are allergic to shellfish, so care should be taken with its inclusion in recipes.

shiitake mushrooms Dark brown mushrooms originally from the Far East with a hearty, meaty flavor that can be grilled or used as a component in other recipes and as a flavoring source for broth. They can be used either fresh or dried.

shred To cut into many long, thin slices.

simmer To boil gently so the liquid barely bubbles.

skewers Thin wooden or metal sticks, usually about eight inches long, that are perfect for assembling kebabs, dipping food pieces into hot sauces, or serving single-bite food items with a bit of panache.

skillet (also **frying pan**)   A generally heavy, flat metal pan with a handle designed to cook food over heat on a stovetop or campfire.

slice   To cut into thin pieces.

slow cooker   An electric countertop device with a lidded container that maintains a low temperature and slowly cooks its contents, often over several hours or a full day.

steam   To suspend a food over boiling water and allow the heat of the steam (water vapor) to cook the food. Steaming is a very quick cooking method that preserves the flavor and texture of a food.

stew   To slowly cook pieces of food submerged in a liquid. Also, a dish that has been prepared by this method.

Stilton   The famous English blue cheese, delicious with toasted nuts and renowned for its pairing with Port wine.

stir-fry   To cook food in a wok or skillet over high heat, moving and turning the food quickly to cook all sides.

stock   A flavorful broth made by cooking meats and/or vegetables with seasonings until the liquid absorbs these flavors. This liquid is then strained and the solids discarded. Stock can be eaten by itself or used as a base for soups, stews, sauces, risotto, or many other recipes.

stripe   To scrape off a fruit's or vegetable's skin in lengthwise strokes, leaving a "stripe" of the skin between each scrape.

succotash   A cooked vegetable dish usually made of corn and peppers.

sweetbreads   The thymus gland from common food animals, most popularly from veal. They are prized for their creamy, delicate texture.

Tabasco sauce   A popular brand of Louisiana hot pepper sauce used in usually small portions to season savory food. The name also refers to a type of hot pepper from Tabasco, a state in Mexico, that is used to make this sauce.

tahini   A paste made from sesame seeds that is used to flavor many Middle Eastern recipes, especially baba ghanoush and hummus.

tapenade   A thick, chunky spread made from savory ingredients such as olives, lemon juice, and anchovies. Adventuresome grocery and gourmet stores are likely to have different versions focusing on specific ingredients, from olives to peppers and mushrooms.

tarragon   A sour-sweet, rich-smelling herb perfect with seafood, vegetables (especially asparagus), chicken, and pork.

tender-crisp   To cook something, usually a vegetable, just to the point of holding some appetizing crisp texture.

teriyaki   A delicious Asian-style sauce composed of soy sauce, rice wine, ginger, and sugar. It works beautifully with seafood as well as most meats.

terroir   All the elements that affect a grape vine in the vineyard, including the sun, wind, soil, and climate. All the external factors that affect how that vine grows are respected for the role they play in the grapes used to make a wine.

thyme   A minty, zesty herb whose leaves are used in a wide range of recipes.

toast   To heat something, usually bread, so it is browned and crisp.

toast points (also **toast triangles**)   Pieces of toast with the crusts removed that are then cut on the diagonal from each corner, resulting in four triangle-shape pieces.

tofu   A cheeselike substance made from soybeans and soy milk. Flavorful and nutritious, tofu is an important component of foods across the globe, especially from the Far East.

tripe   The stomach of a cow.

turmeric   A spicy, pungent yellow root used in many dishes, especially Indian cuisine, for color and flavor. Turmeric is the source of the brilliant yellow color in many prepared mustards.

twist   A twist (as in lemon or other citrus fruit twist) is simply an attractive way to garnish an appetizer or other dish. Cut a thin, about $\frac{1}{8}$-inch–thick cross-section slice of a lemon, for example. Then take that slice and cut from the center out to the edge of the slice on one side. Pick up the piece of lemon and pull apart the two cut ends in opposite directions.

varietal   The type of grape used to make a wine, such as Cabernet Sauvignon, Merlot, or Chardonnay.

veal   Meat from a calf, generally characterized by mild flavor and tenderness. Certain cuts of veal, such as cutlets and scaloppini, are well suited to quick-cooking.

vegetable steamer   An insert for a large saucepan. Also a special pot with tiny holes in the bottom designed to fit on another pot to hold food to be steamed above boiling water. The insert is generally less expensive and resembles a metal poppy flower that expands to touch the sides of the pot and has small legs. *See also* steam.

vehicle   A food that is used to scoop or dip another ingredient, such as vegetables or pitas with dip.

vinegar   An acidic liquid widely used as dressing and seasoning. Many cuisines use vinegars made from different source materials. *See also* balsamic vinegar; cider vinegar; rice vinegar; white vinegar; wine vinegar.

vintage   The year in which the grapes were harvested and, usually, in which the wine was produced. A 2002 Sauvignon Blanc means that the grapes were harvested in 2002.

walnuts   Grown worldwide, walnuts bring a rich, slightly woody flavor to all types of food. For the quick cook, walnuts are available chopped and ready to go at your grocery store. They are delicious toasted and make fine accompaniments to cheeses.

wasabi   Japanese horseradish, a fiery, pungent condiment used with many Japanese-style dishes, including sushi. Most often sold as a powder; add water to create a paste.

water chestnuts   Actually a tuber, water chestnuts are a popular element in many types of Asian-style cooking. The flesh is white, crunchy, and juicy, and the vegetable holds its texture whether cool or hot.

whisk   To rapidly mix, introducing air to the mixture.

white mushrooms   Ubiquitous button mushrooms. When fresh, they will have an earthy smell and an appealing "soft crunch." White mushrooms are delicious raw in salads, marinated, sautéed, and as component ingredients in many recipes.

white vinegar   The most common type of vinegar found on grocery store shelves. It is produced from grain.

whole-wheat flour   Wheat flour that contains the entire grain.

wild rice   Actually a grain with a rich, nutty flavor, popular as an unusual and nutritious side dish.

wine vinegar   Vinegar produced from red or white wine.

wok   A wonderful tool for quick-cooking.

Worcestershire sauce   Originally developed in India and containing tamarind, this spicy sauce is used as a seasoning for many meats and other dishes.

zest   Small slivers of peel, usually from a citrus fruit such as lemon, lime, or orange.

zester   A small kitchen tool used to scrape zest off a fruit. A small grater also works fine.

Resources

These books, magazines, and web resources provide a wealth of information and guidance on carb-conscious cooking.

Books

These books contain information useful to the carb-conscious cook.

Agatston, Arthur, M.D. *The South Beach Diet: Good Fats, Good Carbs Guide.* Emmaus, PA: Rodale, 2004.

Atkins, Robert, M.D. *Dr. Atkins' New Diet Revolution.* New York: M. Evans and Company, Inc, 1999.

Barkie, Karen E. *Sweet and Sugarfree.* New York: St. Martin's Press, 1982.

Barrett, Judith. *From an Italian Garden.* New York: Macmillan, 1992.

Beale, Lucy, and Sandy G. Couvillon, M.S., L.D.N., R.D. *The Complete Idiot's Guide to Low-Carb Meals.* Indianapolis: Alpha Books, 2004.

Chalmers, Irena. *Good Old Food.* Hauppauge, NY: Barron's, 1993.

Child, Julia. *The French Chef Cookbook, 30th Anniversary Edition.* New York: Ballantine, 1998.

Creasy, Rosalind. *The Edible Flower Garden.* Boston: Periplus, 1999.

Culinary Institute of America, The, with Jennifer S. Armentrout, ed. *Techniques of Healthy Cooking.* Indianapolis: John Wiley and Sons, Inc., 2000.

Cunningham, Marion. *The Fanny Farmer Cookbook.* New York: Alfred A. Knopf, 1990.

Dimmick, Tod. *The Complete Idiot's Guide to 5-Minute Appetizers.* Indianapolis: Alpha Books, 2003.

———. *The Complete Idiot's Guide to 20-Minute Meals.* Indianapolis: Alpha Books, 2002.

———. *The Complete Idiot's Guide to Cooking—for Guys.* Indianapolis: Alpha Books, 2004.

Gardiner, Anne, and Sue Wilson. *The Inquisitive Cook.* New York: Henry Holt, 1998.

Gassenheimer, Linda. *Low-Carb Meals in Minutes.* San Francisco: Bay Books, 2000.

Gorman, Donna, and Elizabeth Heyert. *The Artful Table.* New York: William Morrow and Company, 1998.

Green, Henrietta. *Farmer's Market Cookbook.* London: Kyle Cathie, 2001.

Harlow, Joan S. *The Loaf and Ladle Cookbook.* Camden, ME: Down East Books, 1983.

Hay, Donna. *New Food Fast.* Ontario: Whitecap, 2001.

Heller, Richard F., and Rachel F. Heller. *Carbohydrate Addict's Lifespan Program.* New York: Dutton, 1997.

Herbst, Sharon Tyler. *Food Lover's Companion.* Hauppauge, NY: Barron's Educational Series, 2001.

Jenkins, Steven. *Cheese Primer.* New York: Workman Publishing, 1996.

Joyes, Claire. *Monet's Table.* New York: Simon & Schuster, 1989.

Katzen, Mollie. *Moosewood Cookbook.* Berkeley: Ten Speed Press, 1977.

Loomis, Susan Herrmann. *Farmhouse Cookbook.* New York: Workman Publishing, 1991.

MacMillan, Diane D. *The Portable Feast.* San Francisco: 101 Productions, 1984.

Moosewood Collective, The. *Moosewood Restaurant Cooks at Home.* New York: Simon & Schuster/Fireside, 1994.

Murphy, Margaret Deeds. *The Boston Globe Cookbook, Third Edition.*, Chester, CT: Globe Pequot Press, 1990.

Oliver, Jamie. *The Naked Chef.* London: Michael Joseph, 1999.

Ostmann, Barbara Gibbs, and Jane L. Baker. *The Recipe Writer's Handbook.* New York: John Wiley and Sons, 2001.

Rosso, Julee, and Sheila Lukins. *The New Basics Cookbook.* New York: Workman Publishing, 1989.

———. *The Silver Palate Cookbook.* New York: Workman Publishing, 1982.

———. *The Silver Palate Good Times Cookbook.* New York: Workman Publishing, 1985.

Scicolone, Michele. *The Antipasto Table*. New York: William Morrow and Company, 1991.

Sears, Barry. *Mastering the Zone*. New York: ReganBooks, 1997.

Sears, Barry, and Bill Lawren. *The Zone*. New York: ReganBooks, 1995.

Seranne, Ann, ed. *The Western Junior League Cookbook*. New York: McKay, 1979.

Stone, Sally, and Martin Stone. *The Instant Bean*. New York: Bantam Books, 1996.

Vegetarian Times editors. *Vegetarian Times Cooks Mediterranean*. New York: William Morrow and Company, Inc., 1999.

Weil, Andrew, M.D. *Eating Well for Optimum Health*. New York: Alfred A. Knopf, 2000.

Weil, Andrew, M.D., and Rosie Daley. *The Healthy Kitchen*. New York: Alfred A. Knopf, 2002.

Magazines

Saveur
www.saveur.com/

Cooking Light
www.cookinglight.com

Bon Appétit
www.bonappetit.com/

Cook's Illustrated
www.cooksillustrated.com/

Wine Spectator
www.winespectator.com

Food & Wine
www.foodandwine.com/

Fine Cooking
www.taunton.com/finecooking/index.asp

Favorite Food Websites

Selected cooking-related web pages reviewed by Tod Dimmick in his e-mail newsletter for WZ.com. (© Copyright WZ.com Inc., reprinted with permission.)

General Recipe Sites (with Information on Low-Carb Cooking)

Allrecipes

www.allrecipes.com

Allrecipes draws on a massive database of recipes and provides advice on techniques, meal planning, and more. The "ingredient search" enables mix-and-match creativity; think shrimp and garlic or apples and cream. Type them in, the inspiration flows, and you can save your favorites to your personal recipe box.

Sam Cooks

www.samcooks.com

Longtime gourmet columnist for *Wine Spectator*, Sam Gugino has constructed a clean, information-packed site for the intelligent cook. Check out "Cooking to Beat the Clock."

Epicurious

www.epicurious.com

Epicurious claims more than 13,000 recipes, drawing from years of *Gourmet* and *Bon Appétit*, among other sources. Try visiting the search engine with random ingredients you have on hand that need a "common destiny." You'll be surprised what you come up with: ground turkey and sun-dried tomato meatloaf is a surprising delight I make every winter. Assemble your favorites and create your own personal recipe file.

Cooking Light

www.cookinglight.com

Find tips, recipes, and themes (French, Italian, celebration menus, etc.) for those of us who want taste and quality, but are concerned with what we eat.

Eat Smart

www.usaweekend.com/food/carper_archive/index.html

A collection of articles from Jean Carper, the well-known columnist for *USA Weekend*, covers everything from vitamins and whole grains to avoiding carcinogens when grilling. I need those tips.

Vegetarian Times

www.vegetariantimes.com

Vegetarian never looked so good as the collection of mouthwatering recipes here.

Vegetarian Across the Globe

www.ivu.org/recipes/regions.html

The International Vegetarian Union offers a multitude of recipes divided by region of the world and by type of cuisine. From tofu to curry, chili to portobello bruschetta, it's here, along with everything you ever wanted to know about the vegetarian movement.

Fatfree

www.fatfree.com/recipes/sauces

The antidote for some of the richer sauces we eat. Fat-free Alfredo?

Reluctant Gourmet

www.reluctantgourmet.com

Reluctant Gourmet is refreshing for its modesty. The site covers tasks simply and completely, from cooking techniques (how to braise) to a glossary of gourmet terms. I grin as soon as I see the photo on the home page. You'll see what I mean.

Southern Living

www.southernliving.com

Comfort food with a regional slant comes from *Southern Living.* Click on the "Foods" link. Tantalizing recipes throughout make it tough to decide where to start. Well, I guess it will be Apple Pancakes for me—as long as they're low-carb, of course.

The Cook's Thesaurus

www.foodsubs.com

The Cook's Thesaurus contains a truly massive gourmet glossary. Ever wonder where that cut of beef is from? Voilà! There it is, with diagrams. Each section provides guidance on substitutions—very useful if you cook with what's on hand.

Global Gourmet

www.globalgourmet.com

Global Gourmet will draw you in to articles on everything from "Holiday Helpers" to "I Love Chocolate (Let's Get to the Point Already)."

Quick-Cooking Sites

My Meals

www.my-meals.com

This site includes a section devoted to recipes requiring 30 minutes or less. Some are very basic; others decidedly less so. Hot Carameled Apples with Pie Crust Dippers?

Simple Pleasures

www.allfood.com/mmeal.cfm

Minutemeals challenges the assertion that cooking quickly requires sacrifice of quality and taste. The listing of complete holiday menus is especially soothing.

Theme Cuisine

All Fins, All the Time

www.seafoodrecipe.com

This subset of the Allrecipes site has it all, organized by cooking method, ethnic origin, or specific undersea creature.

White Meat

www.eatchicken.com

This is a chicken-lover's paradise, with information from technique to recipes and poultry statistics. Follow the "show a little leg" link to Peruvian Grilled Chicken Thighs with Tomato Cilantro Sauce.

Penzey's Spices

www.penzeys.com

Each recipe makes use of one or more assertive, characteristic spices. Check out Grilled Asparagus, using bold cracked pepper. I'm a big fan of these guys.

Food and Wine Sites

Start Simple

www.adwfoodandwine.com/index.asp

Here's a basic chart, courtesy of Clos du Bois, explaining matches that work and why.

EatDrinkDine

www.eatdrinkdine.com

What a great site! Sommelier Evan Goldstein offers a wonderfully complete yet easy-to-use page that you can approach from "Start with Food" or "Start with Wine." Chicken cacciatore goes with …

Carb Smarts

TastingTimes (www.tastingtimes.com), the author's own site, offers a growing section on food and wine pairing, wine menus, and recipes. It also features a free e-mail newsletter, the *Wine Minute*, with recommendations under $15.

Mondavi

www.robertmondavi.com/FoodWine/index.asp

Here is a friendly database of neatly organized menus with suggested wines. Butternut Squash Risotto with a friendly Merlot—it's a winner.

Wine and the Good Life

www.winespectator.com

Winespectator.com, one of the largest wine-related sites on the web, offers a mountain of information on wine, travel, restaurants, and more.

Wine Sauce

www.corkcuisine.com

A fun site for lovers of food and wine, you'll find history, recipes, and a wealth of wine and food tips.

Favorite Vendors

Here are a few of my favorite vendors.

Trader Joe's

www.traderjoes.com

This national chain offers an eclectic yet tempting array of ingredients helpful to the cook in a hurry.

King Arthur Flour

www.kingarthurflour.com

This mail- and Internet-order company provides a huge range of specialty flours and baking ingredients. Add a little buckwheat flour to quick pancakes, and you'll never go back to white.

Penzey's Spices

www.penzeys.com

Another mail- and Internet-order company with a huge selection of top-quality herbs and spices and a recipe-filled catalog to salivate over.

Your Local Farmers' Market

www.ams.usda.gov/farmersmarkets/map.htm

A farm stand is the place to go for the freshest, tastiest farm produce, key ingredients of healthful cuisine. This link takes you to a U.S. map where you can find the market nearest you.

Glycemic Index and Carbohydrate List

The following table lists the glycemic index ranking and the carbohydrate content of base ingredients frequently used in this book.

(Adapted with permission from *The Complete Idiot's Guide to Low-Carb Meals.*)

Foods	Glycemic Index Value	Amount	Carbs (g)	Fiber (g)	Nutritive Carbs
Almonds	0	1 cup	28	15	13
Apple juice	40	1 cup	25	0	25
Apples	38	1 medium	22	5	17
Applesauce, unsweetened	40	½ cup	13	3	10
Apricots, dried	30	¼ cup	25	2	23
Artichoke hearts	0	½ cup	5	3	2
Asparagus, chopped	0	1 cup	6	3	3
Avocado, California	0	1 medium	12	9	3
Beef	0	any amount	0	0	0

continues

continued

Foods	Glycemic Index Value	Amount	Carbs (g)	Fiber (g)	Nutritive Carbs
Black beans, boiled	30	½ cup	20	8	12
Blueberries	n/a	½ cup	9	2	7
Brazil nuts	0	6 large	4	2	2
Broccoli, raw, chopped	0	½ cup	2	1	1
Broth, beef	0	½ cup	1	0	1
Broth, chicken	0	½ cup	1	0	1
Broth, vegetable	0	½ cup	1	0	1
Brown rice, cooked	55	½ cup	22	2	20
Cabbage, raw, shredded	0	½ cup	2	1	1
Canola oil	0	1 TB.	0	0	0
Cantaloupe, cubed	65	1 cup	13	2	11
Capers	0	1 TB.	1	0	1
Carrots, raw, shredded	47	½ cup	6	2	4
Cashews	22	¼ cup	8	3	5
Cauliflower, 1-inch pieces	0	½ cup	3	2	1
Celery, diced	0	½ cup	2	1	1
Cheddar cheese Parmesan	0	¼ cup	0	0	0
Cherries, sweet with pits	22	½ cup	12	2	10
Chicken, skinless	0	4 oz.	0	0	0
Chickpeas, canned	42	½ cup	18	7	11
Cocoa powder	55	1 TB.	3	1	2
Cottage cheese	32	½ cup	4	0	4
Cream, heavy	0	½ cup	3	0	3
Cream cheese	0	1 TB.	0	0	0
Cream cheese, light	27	1 TB.	1	0	1
Cucumber, sliced	0	½ cup	1.4	0.4	1
Eggplant, diced	0	1 cup	5	3	2

Foods	Glycemic Index Value	Amount	Carbs (g)	Fiber (g)	Nutritive Carbs
Eggs, large	0	1	0.6	0	0.6
Feta cheese	27	½ cup	3	0	3
Garlic	0	1 clove	1	0.1	0.9
Garlic, chopped	0	1 TB.	1	0	1
Goat's milk cheese (hard)	0	1 TB.	0	0	0
Grapefruit	25	½ medium	16	6	10
Grapes, green	46	1 ½ cups	24	1	23
Green beans, cooked	0	½ cup	5	2	3
Green onions	0	¼ cup	2	1	1
Hazelnuts, diced	0	1 cup	18	7	11
Jicama	0	½ cup	5	3	2
Kidney beans, boiled	46	½ cup	20	7	13
Lamb	0	any amount	0	0	0
Leafy vegetables, raw	0	1 cup	2	1	1
Lemon juice	0	1 TB.	0	0	0
Lentils, cooked	29	½ cup	20	8	12
Lima beans, frozen	32	½ cup	22	5	17
Lime juice	0	1 TB.	0	0	0
Macadamia nuts	0	¼ cup	5	3	2
Mayonnaise	0	1 TB.	0	0	0
Milk, full fat	27	½ cup	6	0	6
Milk, skim	32	½ cup	6	0	6
Mushrooms, portobello	0	½ cup	3	1	2
Mushrooms, white	0	½ cup	2	1	1
Oat bran	n/a	½ cup	25	6	19
Oat flour	n/a	⅓ cup	21	3	18
Oatmeal, cooked	42	½ cup	13	2	11
Olive oil	0	1 TB.	0	0	0
Olives, black	0	4 oz.	6	3	3

continues

continued

Foods	Glycemic Index Value	Amount	Carbs (g)	Fiber (g)	Nutritive Carbs
Onions, chopped	0	½ cup	7	1	6
Oranges, sections	42	1 cup	19	4	15
Orange juice	53	1 cup	27	0	27
Parmesan cheese	0	¼ cup	0	0	0
Peaches, sliced	42	1 cup	19	3	16
Peanuts, roasted	14	¼ cup	12	2	10
Pear	38	1 medium	25	4	21
Pecan flour	0	1 cup	15	15	0
Pecans, half	0	¼ cup	5	5	0
Pepper, red or green, diced	0	¾ cup	4	2	2
Pineapple, diced	66	½ cup	10	1	9
Pine nuts	0	¼ cup	5	2	3
Pinto beans, canned	45	½ cup	18	6	12
Plums, sliced	39	½ cup	11	1	10
Pork	0	any amount	0	0	0
Rice, brown, uncooked	50	¼ cup	37	3	34
Ricotta, part skim	32	½ cup	6	0	6
Scallions, chopped	0	¼ cup	3	1	2
Shellfish, seafood	0	any amount	0	0	0
Sour cream	27	¼ cup	2	0	2
Sour cream, light	27	¼ cup	3	0	3
Snow peas	0	1 cup	6	2	4
Soy flour	n/a	½ cup	16	8	8
Split peas, uncooked	32	¼ cup	27	11	16
Squash, cooked, cubed	0	1 cup	15	2	13
Strawberries, sliced	40	½ cup	6	2	4
Sweet potato, mashed	44	½ cup	24	3	21
Tofu	20	3 oz.	6	0	6

Foods	Glycemic Index Value	Amount	Carbs (g)	Fiber (g)	Nutritive Carbs
Tomato, chopped	0	1 cup	8	2	6
Tuna and fish	0	any amount	0	0	0
Turkey, sliced	0	4 oz.	0	0	0
Veal	0	any amount	0	0	0
Vital wheat gluten	n/a	1 TB.	3	0	3
Walnuts	0	¼ cup	3	3	0
Wheat bran	30	1 TB.	2	1	1
Wheat germ	n/a	2 TB.	7	4	3
White beans	31	½ cup	23	9	14
Whole-wheat flour	71	¼ cup	21	3	18
Yogurt, plain	14	½ cup	8	0	8
Zucchini, diced	0	½ cup	3	1	2

Each ingredient has a glycemic index ranking (GI). This tells how much your blood sugar level increases when you eat this food. The ranking is based on 100—being that the blood sugar rises from eating glucose. The lower the number, the less likely the food will trigger a quick rise in blood sugar.

A quick rise in blood sugar stimulates the pancreas to secrete the hormone insulin. Insulin lowers the blood sugar level to a safe range. When the body has a high increase in blood sugar as when eating a high-glycemic food, the pancreas, in a sense, produces more insulin than needed. Excess insulin results in …

- A person getting hungry again soon after eating.
- Increased body-fat storage.

Because you don't want those two things to happen in your body, it's best to get low to moderate GI foods.

High	> 70
Medium	56 to 69
Low	< 55

Listed with the GI of each ingredient is the carbohydrate count based on the amount of food. Use this information to figure the carbohydrate count of other recipes and foods you might eat.

Index

The Complete Low-Carb Collection

The Complete Idiot's Guide® to Low-Carb Meals
ISBN: 1-59257-180-8
$18.95
The original, best-selling The *Complete Idiot's Guide®* low-carb cookbook with more than 300 delicious recipes.

The Complete Idiot's Guide® to Quick and Easy Low-Carb Meals
ISBN: 1-59257-313-4
$18.95
More than 200 great tasting recipes for the busy low-carb dieter.

ALPHA